P9-APM-017

ILLUSION
in nature and art

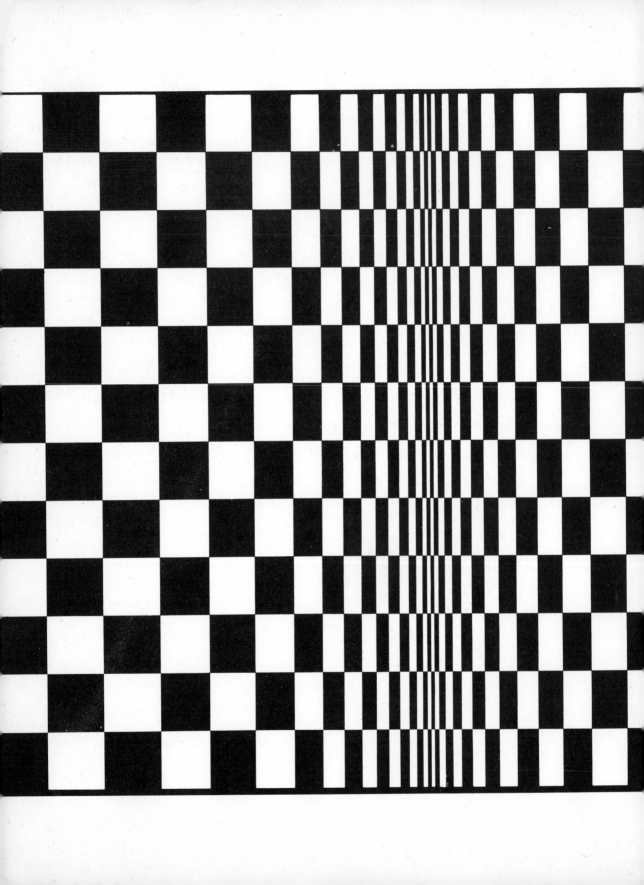

ILLUSION
in nature and art

Edited by R.L. Gregory
and E.H. Gombrich

with contributions by
Colin Blakemore
Jan B. Deregowski
E.H. Gombrich
R.L. Gregory
H.E. Hinton
Roland Penrose

CHARLES SCRIBNER'S SONS
NEW YORK

Copyright © 1973 Colin Blakemore, Jan B. Deregowski,
E.H. Gombrich, R.L. Gregory, H.E. Hinton,
Roland Penrose

This book published simultaneously in the
United States of America and in Canada —
Copyright under the Berne Convention

All rights reserved. No part of this book
may be reproduced in any form without the
permission of Charles Scribner's Sons.

1 3 5 7 9 11 13 15 17 19 I/P 20 18 16 14 12 10 8 6 4 2

Printed in Great Britain
Library of Congress Catalog Card Number 73-21146
ISBN 0-684-13800-X (cloth)
ISBN 0-684-14185-X (paper)

Contents

Contributors

Colin Blakemore is Lecturer in Physiology in the University of Cambridge, and Fellow of Downing College, Cambridge

Jan B. Deregowski is Lecturer in Psychology in the University of Aberdeen

Sir Ernst Gombrich, FBA, is, Director of the Warburg Institute, University of London

R.L. Gregory is Professor of Neuropsychology and Director of the Brain and Perception Laboratory, University of Bristol

H.E. Hinton, FRS, is Professor of Zoology in the University of Bristol

Sir Roland Penrose is President of the Institute of Contemporary Arts in London

List of colour plates

Foreword

This book brings students of art and science together in trying to solve the problems posed by illusion. Since early times illusion has been considered the stuff of art. For science, illusion may seem to be no more than error, usually to be avoided easily or corrected by instruments. It is, however, a genuine scientific question why the senses of man, and other animals, should be misleading in certain situations. Illusions are not mere random variations of the nervous system: many are systematic large errors, which can be measured, and demonstrated with dramatic effect. It is this dramatic quality of some illusions which gives power to art. Indeed, artists were the first to experiment with the mechanisms of illusion on the stage, in sculpture and in painting.

Illusions are also tools for discovering processes of perception. In medicine, in engineering, and very frequently in biology, the abnormal and the surprising lead to key ideas and facts for understanding the normal. So here we may expect abnormal perceptions (deviations from truth) to give insights and data for understanding normal (correct) perception.

The issues are difficult, and the available ideas and facts are widely scattered. There is not even general agreement as to what kinds of question should be asked – or whether art or science would benefit by close mutual scrutiny. Nevertheless, this is just what we have attempted here. It will be a curious paradox if art sees science and science art, through the strangely twisting glass of illusion. But bent and twisted light has revealed the heavens and the structures of life in incredible detail through curved glasses – which at the time of the invention of the telescope and the microscope were distrusted as distorting reality seen through them. If we are right here, perceptual distortions – the complex facts of illusions as they are understood – reveal new aspects of the world and of ourselves.

The book has its origins in the setting up of an exhibition initiated by Sir Roland Penrose, CBE, at the Institute of Contemporary Arts, London, and intended for international circulation. The exhibition is designed by Mr Keith Albarn. The Editors of this book, and its other authors, are consultants to the exhibition, which, it is hoped, will be set up in a permanent form.

R.L. GREGORY and E.H. GOMBRICH

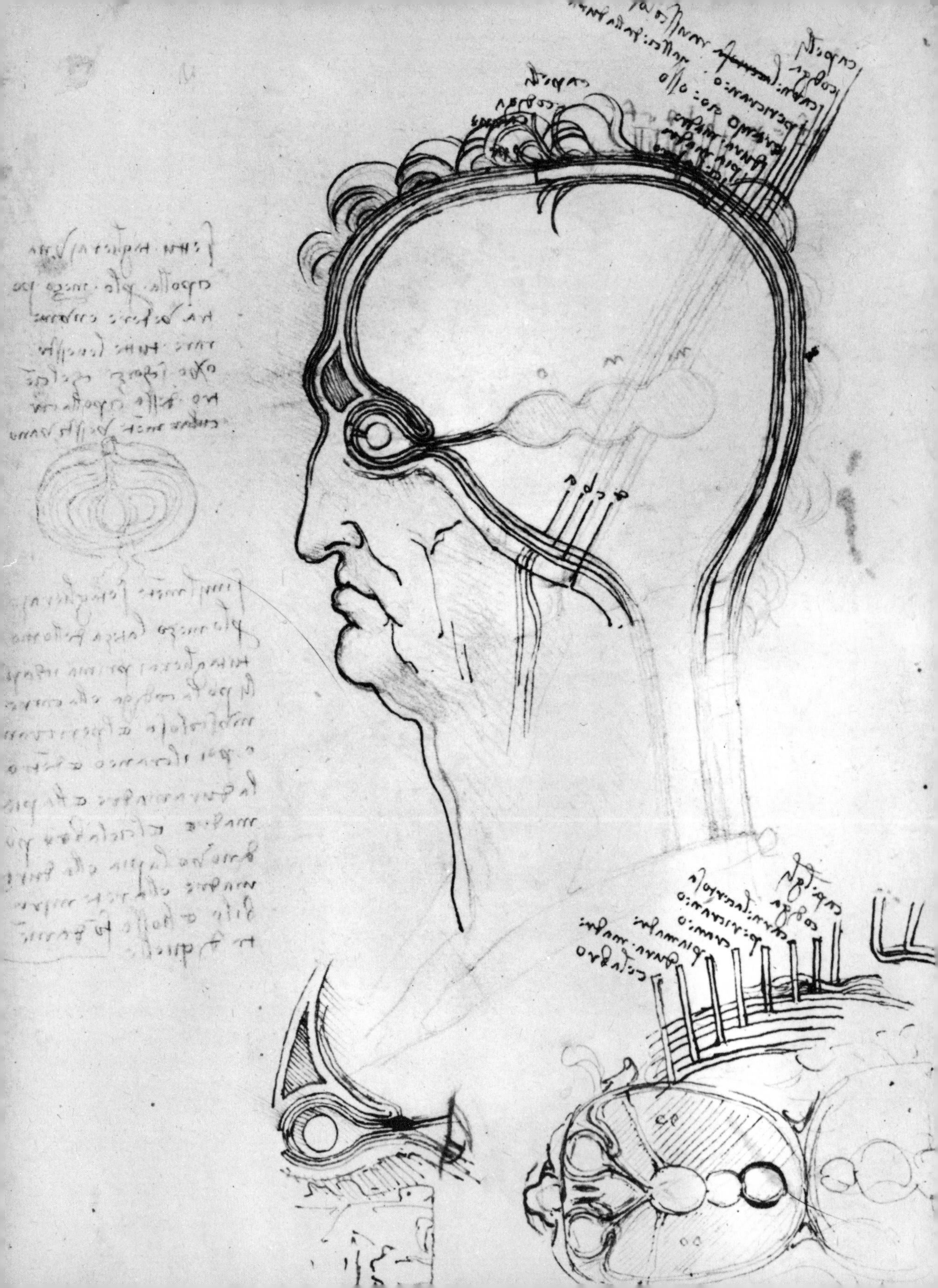

1 *The Baffled Brain*

Colin Blakemore

Fig. 1 *Leonardo, about 1500, accepted the eye as an outgrowth of the brain. In these cross sections he misrepresents the lens, but correctly shows the optic nerves converging.*

The brain, a strange grey substance that fills the skull, is a biological instrument more complex, more compact, more sophisticated than any machine made by man. Within this enigmatic kilogram-and-a-half of jelly resides a power of computation that embarrasses the weightiest computer, a power of communication that outperforms all the telephone systems in the world and a power of creation that has generated the *Mona Lisa* on the one hand and nuclear weapons on the other.

Just consider the way that we can see. Undoubtedly vision is man's primary sense, and our familiarity with normal sight makes us forget how incredible is our capacity to collect and store visual information. Shut your eyes for a moment and try to think of all the people that you know, or have known, personally: there must be hundreds, maybe thousands of them, yet you could presumably recognize every one. Now consider all the politicians, the entertainers and other public figures that you could also name if you saw their photographs. At the end of this exercise you should be duly impressed with the storage capacity of visual memory; but it also tells you about the incredible *processing* power of the sensory system that gathers and collates visual information, before it is stored away. How is the visual system able to discriminate and recognize the featural differences, for example, that distinguish one face from another?

The recognition of patterns is a question of interest not only to psychologists and artists, but also to engineers and computer technologists. All communication systems involve the detection and encoding of patterns of information. Surely designers of artificial communication networks can learn something from biological communication systems, which have stood the test of two thousand million years of evolution.

Unfortunately we cannot turn the tables and gain insight into the workings of the eye and the brain by comparing them with cameras,

9

photographs, movie films or even television systems. The aim of any kind of camera is simply to *reproduce* an image that is a minified or magnified projection of a scene. There is no interpretation, no subtle symbolic representation, no extraction of information. The truly remarkable thing about photographs, and all other forms of graphic representation, is that they provoke perceptions whose content far exceeds the patterns of light and dark on the paper, canvas or projection screen.

Until very recently the only scientists who could make any real contribution to our understanding of vision were psychologists (though they might have called themselves philosophers). But particularly in the last twenty years, physiologists, who study the actual stuff and substance of the brain, have made enormous advances in the analysis of the processes underlying visual perception.

Visual illusions and distortions of perception have been crucially important tools for the psychologist, but the physiologist is generally more interested in how the brain handles simple but more natural visual stimuli. So in this short review of the physiology of vision I shall cover the present knowledge of some of the functions of the visual system, and only towards the end will there be anything to say about illusions.

The brain and its code

The whole nervous system is constructed from special cells called nerve cells or *neurons*, together with certain supporting cells that are not directly involved in transmitting nervous signals. A neuron

fig. 2

usually has three parts: a cell body, a long fibre or *axon* attached to the cell body and many short fibres called *dendrites*. At its end the axon usually breaks up into fine branches with *terminal buttons* that are closely attached to the dendrites or cell body of the next neuron in the chain. These contacts between one neuron and another are called *synapses*.

The special feature of nerve cells is their ability to transmit nerve impulses from the cell body all the way along the axon, which can be up to 2 metres long. The nerve impulse (also called an *action potential*) is a brief local change in the electrical potential of the interior of the cell, caused by rapid changes in the permeability of the cell's membrane.[13] At any one point in an axon this depolarization lasts only about one millisecond but it spreads along the fibre quite slowly, at between 1 and 100 metres/second.

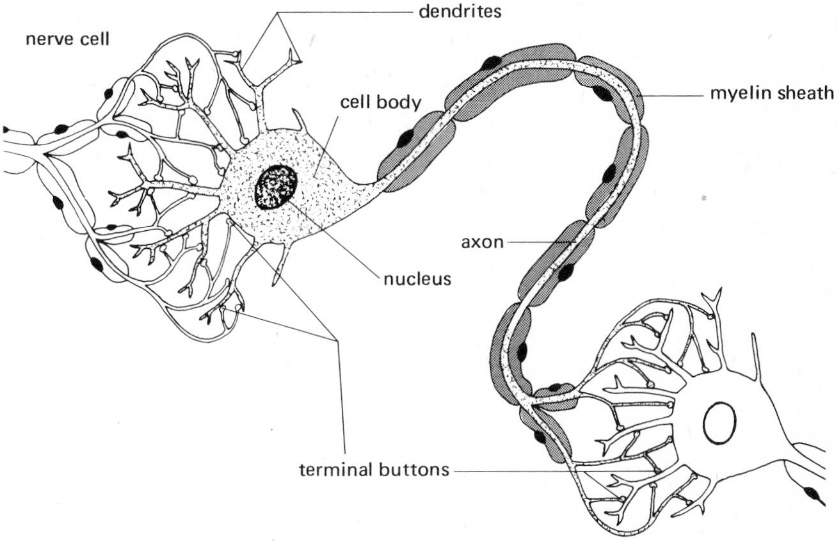

nerve cell

dendrites

cell body

myelin sheath

axon

nucleus

terminal buttons

Fig. 2 *A typical neuron has a cell body, dendrites and axon. The axon, often covered with an insulating sheath of a fatty material called myelin, ends as a cluster of terminal buttons on the dendrites and cell body of another neuron in the chain.*

Every action potential produced by a neuron is virtually identical in amplitude and duration. So impulses only come in one size: either they are present or they are not. This basic rule of nerve conduction is known as the *all-or-none law*. At the end of the axon the arrival of each impulse causes the release of a tiny quantity of a chemical transmitter substance which acts on the membrane of the next nerve cell. The transmitter substance may either make the cell depolarize and tend to produce an impulse of its own (in an *excitatory synapse*) or make it increase its potential and thus reduce the chance of it firing (in an *inhibitory synapse*).

This way of communicating along nerve fibres is totally different from the usual method of transmitting signals in a telephone cable, where information is conveyed by the *amplitude* of potential changes conducted along a metal wire, almost at the speed of light. Deprived of this means of signalling information by the amplitude of a voltage, nerve cells use a system in which the *frequency* of impulses in each burst tells the next cell about the strength of the signal. Neurons are constantly chattering away, in their own Morse code that has only dots and no dashes.

There are more than one hundred thousand million neurons in the human brain and each cell can have up to tens of thousands of terminal buttons ending on it. A computer with so many components and connections could administer the world. (Perhaps it is not surprising that a few famous and infamous brains in history have tried to do the same.)

11

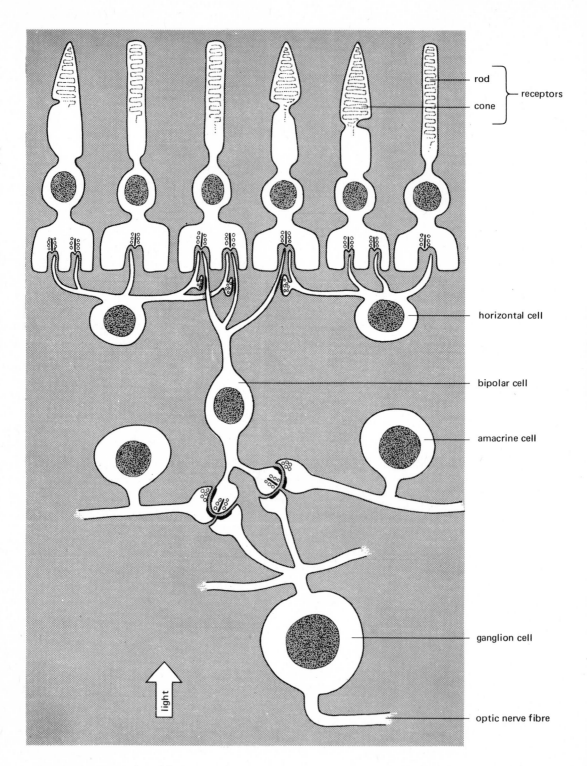

rod

cone

receptors

horizontal cell

bipolar cell

amacrine cell

ganglion cell

optic nerve fibre

light

12

The final output signals leaving this great 'ravelled knot' pass along the peripheral nerves to the muscles and other effector organs of the body. The input comes from the sense organs and supreme amongst these are the eyes, each of which sends more than a million nerve fibres to the brain.

The structure of the eye

The retina itself, the photo-sensitive layer at the back of the eye, is actually part of the brain, which pushes out in the developing embryo to meet the specialized skin tissues that eventually form the eyeball and lens. In fact the retina is a mini-brain: there are five different kinds of neuron in the retina, and recent examination with the electron microscope[10] has revealed their complex inter-connections.

fig. 3

Oddly, the very first cells in the chain, the photosensitive *rods* and *cones*, are at the back of the retina. Light focused by the eye must pass through the transparent layers of nerve cells, and the blood vessels that cover them before it forms an inverted image on these photoreceptors. The messages from the rods and cones pass through synapses to the *bipolar cells* and from them to the large *ganglion cells* whose axons make up the optic nerve. The other two kinds of cells (*horizontal* and *amacrine*) have fibres that run horizontally across the retina, linking the neurons that are handling nearby parts of the image. These horizontally running cells are thought to exercise an inhibitory influence and, as we shall see, they have a profound influence on visual perception.

In most mammals, and in many other species, one or more regions of the retina are specially adapted for more detailed vision. In man the central region, called the *fovea*, has tiny, closely packed receptors and there are no overlying cells or blood vessels to distort the image. This is the region of the retina that we direct towards objects of interest when we look at them. If any part of the body could be legitimately called the seat of the self it is surely the fovea. Probably the main task for the rest of the retina is to try to detect those parts of the image that might entertain the special powers of the fovea and to command the eye muscles to move the eyeball appropriately. All mammals with forward-pointing, very mobile eyes have some sort of central specialized region of the retina, but in a cat, for instance, it is not quite so distinct as in monkey or man.

Many animals such as rabbits have eyes on the sides of their heads, to give them panoramic vision, so that they can literally see in almost every direction. They usually do not move their eyes very actively

Fig. 3 *This simplified diagram of the monkey's retina shows the inter-connections discovered by electron microscopy.[10] The rods and cones (photoreceptors) lie at the back of the eye, so light must pass through the layers of other neurons before it reaches them.*

13

Colin Blakemore

and their specialized retinal region is a long horizontal *visual streak* aimed at the horizon. Not surprisingly animals with lateral, panoramic eyes are usually herbivorous and hunted, while those with mobile, frontal eyes are usually predatory.

The visual pathways

Because of the great difficulty of following nerve bundles through the brain, almost nothing was known about the projections of the optic nerves within the brain until the last century. Descartes'[9] fanciful picture is based more on his own expectations than on serious anatomical study. The great Spanish anatomist Ramón y Cajal[23] gave us our present-day view of the basic connections in the visual pathway. It is now clear that fibres in the optic nerves project to two main centres in the brain: some go directly to an area called the *superior colliculus* in the brain stem (the lower part of the brain); others travel up to the *visual cortex* at the back of the great cerebral hemispheres, which enfold the whole brain.

The pathway to the superior colliculus seems to be evolutionarily more primitive and it is particularly important in lower vertebrates like amphibians and birds. The route up to the cortex claims more and more optic nerve fibres higher up the evolutionary tree. These axons do not run directly to the cortex but have a synapse on the way in a structure called the *lateral geniculate nucleus*. It is the axons of geniculate cells that finally enter the fantastically complicated nerve networks in the cortex. Beyond the primary visual cortex, where the fibres arrive, the ramifications of the visual pathway are almost unfathomable. Certainly there are many other visual areas in the cortex, close to the primary visual area, which receive fibres from it. From these regions there are projections into other cortical areas on the sides of the brain. But the visual cortex also sends signals to the superior colliculus, down to the brain stem centres that control the eye muscles, and even back to the lateral geniculate nucleus.

In both the colliculus and the cortex there is quite an orderly arrangement of incoming visual axons. Different parts of the retina project to different parts of the cortex and colliculus, producing two *maps* of the visual world. When this mapping of visual space on to the substance of the brain was first discovered it caused great excitement, not least amongst psychologists.[25] Could it be that the whole function of the visual pathway was simply to recreate a faithful electrical picture on the surface of the brain? Of course, this is far too simple an idea. On logical grounds alone, a picture in the

fig. 4

Fig. 4 *Descartes*[9] *thought that each eye was connected separately to the brain, and that they both communicated with the pineal gland, a tiny structure in the brain that Descartes thought of as an interface between the senses and the soul. This illustration is from his* Traité de l'homme, *1686.*

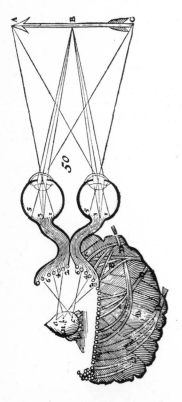

14

The baffled brain

Fig. 5 below *Ramón y Cajal's brilliant anatomical experiments*[23] *led him to discover the true nature of the connections from eye to brain. This illustration of 1899 shows the way that the nerve fibres from the retina to the visual cortex split into two groups, one set projecting to the opposite side of the brain, the other to the same side. So each half of the visual cortex has messages from both eyes, and Cajal predicted in this diagram that signals from the two eyes converge on to individual nerve cells in the cortex.*

Fig. 6 *Nerve fibres from the retina reach two main brain areas: the superior colliculus in the brain stem and the visual cortex in the cerebral hemispheres.*

head is no explanation for perception. Seeing is an *interpretive* process, not merely a *representational* one. And in any case, the harder the map is studied the less accurate it is seen to be. For one thing the scale of the map is peculiarly stretched with a disproportionate area devoted to the fovea,[8] particularly in the cortex. For another thing the map is only a two-dimensional one, spread across the surface of the brain, whereas perceptual space is not only three-dimensional, in spatial terms, but has such extra dimensions as the colour of objects, that have no simple place in the brain's maps.

Physiological strategies in the study of perception

Evidence from brain damage

What techniques can the physiologist bring to bear in experiments on the brain? First, the easiest procedure to use, but the hardest to interpret, is the analysis of damage to some part of the system. In experimental animals the surgeon can literally remove or destroy selected regions, very large or quite tiny. Anatomists use this method to unravel the frustrating complexity of connections in the brain, because all the nerve fibres leaving a damaged region soon degenerate

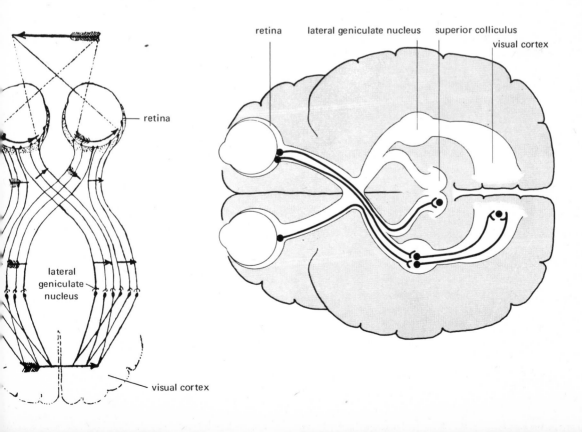

retina — lateral geniculate nucleus — superior colliculus — visual cortex

— retina

lateral geniculate nucleus

— visual cortex

Colin Blakemore

and they can be stained selectively when the brain is later examined microscopically. Other experimenters go further in their interpretation. They try to infer the *function* of the damaged part from the behaviour of the animal after the operation. This method can be used in humans too, because wars and accidents unfortunately provide a continuous supply of patients with all sorts of brain damage. But the interpretation of the results is often hopelessly complicated. Imagine that when some part of the brain is injured the only consequence is total paralysis of all the voluntary muscles. Even if the animal could still see perfectly, the physiologist could not know that it was *not* blind. Would he be right in concluding that he had damaged the seat of all perception? An experimental brain injury may be just a spanner in the works of the most complicated computer known.

However, an experiment involving damage has provided the strongest evidence for a basic functional difference between the visual pathway to the cortex and that to the superior colliculus. Gerald Schneider[24] studies hamsters, in which about half the optic nerve fibres go to the colliculus and half to the cortex. Normally hamsters can easily spot small objects moved across the visual field, look at them, and gobble them up if they happen to be sunflower seeds or some other favourite food. But if the colliculus alone is removed, hamsters seem almost blind. They will not react to any peripheral visual stimulus and they stare blankly into space. But if an object is literally held right in front of them they can still discriminate food from non-food with great ease. In short, they can still see but they do not know what to look at.

A hamster with no visual cortex is totally different. The animal still turns to any interesting new stimulus in the visual field but is totally incapable of distinguishing objects by sight when it looks at them. This led Schneider to postulate that there are really *two* visual systems: the 'where' system (in the colliculus), telling the animal what direction to look in, and the 'what' system (in the cortex), telling it the nature of the object under observation.

Unfortunately Schneider's conclusions may not be applicable to anything but hamsters, at least not in quite such simple terms. A bird without a cortex can easily fly around and seems quite normal. But a man with massive damage to his visual cortex usually can never see anything at all.[6] So it seems that if we want to know about the physiology of our perception we must turn to the visual cortex.

Stimulation of the brain

Another method available to the physiologist is electrical *stimulation*. He can apply a minute electric current through an electrode on, or in, the brain, and observe the behaviour that occurs. This can be done in humans, for the brain is sometimes exposed under local anaesthesia during neurosurgery. Wilder Penfield, a Canadian neurosurgeon, made a complete study of the effects of stimulating the human cerebral cortex.[20] When he stimulated the visual cortex his patients saw flashing, swirling coloured shapes moving in front of them, in a part of the visual field related to the known map in the cortex. Stimulation further along in the pathway, particularly in the cortex on the sides of the brain, made the patient imagine whole complicated visual scenes. Never did a patient report that the sensations were inside his head. They were always *externalized* as bizarre, but compelling perceptual experiences.

This raises an interesting point, recognized by Johannes Müller, about 1840, in his Law of Specific Nerve Energies.[19] He realised that different sorts of sense organ are specialized for detecting different sorts of energy and that the brain always assumes that a message from a particular sense organ is the result of the *expected* form of stimulation. This law is too simple to cover every type of sensory system, but it is particularly true of the visual pathway. Although the retina is uniquely situated and designed for detecting light, it can also be stimulated by passing a weak electric current through the eye or even just by pressing lightly on the white of the eyeball. Both of these unnatural retinal stimulations produce *visual* sensations that look like moving coloured shapes. In the same way mechanical stimulation of the visual cortex by a blow to the skull makes the victim see stars. The cause of these stars is in the brain but the stars themselves are just as much part of the perceptual world as real stars are. So, how much of our everyday perception is really created entirely within our brains, without any equivalent external stimulus? And how much of the real world are we simply incapable of perceiving because we have no neural apparatus to do so?

Recording from the brain

There are relatively simple methods literally to listen in on the messages of the brain. The electronic eavesdroppers that make this possible are microelectrodes — tiny probes (usually metal wires, insulated except at the tip) that can be implanted painlessly into the brain of an anaesthetized or even a conscious animal. These devices pick up the external potential change around a nerve cell or axon as an action potential passes. The tiny signals are amplified and displayed as vertical deflections on an oscilloscope and played as pulses through a loudspeaker. In this manner the physiologist can listen to the impulses being transmitted by a single nerve cell. This technique has been used with mixed success to study many parts of the brain but has been particularly useful in analysing the visual pathway.

The usual procedure is to insert a microelectrode into some part of the visual pathway (such as the optic nerve coming from the eye, or the visual cortex), pick up impulses from a single neuron, and then project flashing or moving patterns on a screen in front of the animal's stationary eyes. In this way one can discover which region of retinal receptors is connected to that neuron, because patterns projected on one part of the screen will make the cell respond with a stream of impulses. The area of the screen that causes the neuron to *fig. 7* respond is called its *receptive field*. The properties of the neuron's receptive field — the kinds of patterns that make the cell respond — tell the physiologist something about the detailed connections between the photoreceptors and the cell itself.

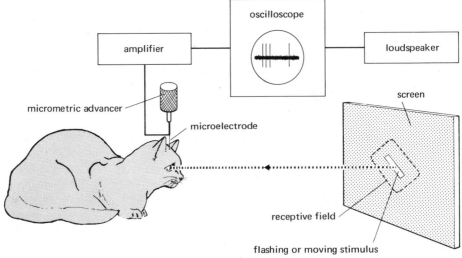

Fig. 7 *If a microelectrode is inserted into the brain and picks up impulses from a single nerve cell, the neuron's responses can be studied by projecting patterns of light in front of the stationary eyes.*

Human perception depends ultimately on activity within the nerve cells of the brain. The physiological properties of neurons quite peripheral in the visual pathway can explain some of the remarkable properties of normal perception and even some of the bizarre abnormalities called illusions.

The retina

fig. 3

Modern electron microscopy has made it much easier to interpret physiological experiments on the retina.[10] Many physiologists have recorded activity from the ganglion cells (whose axons run in the optic nerve to the brain), in all sorts of animals, from frogs to monkeys. In the higher mammals, like cats and monkeys, nearly all the ganglion cells have so-called *concentric receptive fields*.[17] If part of a neuron's receptive field on the screen is illuminated, the cell gives a burst of impulses either when the light turns *on*, or when it turns *off* (or sometimes at both on and off). For about 50 per cent of ganglion cells, light falling in the very centre of the receptive field gives *on-responses* while a spot of light limited to a surrounding area actually suppresses the activity of the cell while it is turned on and causes an *off-response* when it is extinguished. So, not surprisingly,

fig. 8

Fig. 8 *left The receptive field of an on-centre retinal ganglion cell in a cat, plotted on a screen in front of the eyes. Plus signs show areas of on-responses.* Right *Demonstrations of these responses when a spot or edge of light is flashed on the receptive field and then turned off 5 seconds later. Every vertical deflection in the oscilloscope recordings is an impulse from the ganglion cell. First, a small spot is centred in the on area, then the same spot falls on the off area. A large spot then covers the whole receptive field, causing very little response, and lastly, a correctly positioned edge leaves much of the inhibitory surround unstimulated and so produces a vigorous response.*

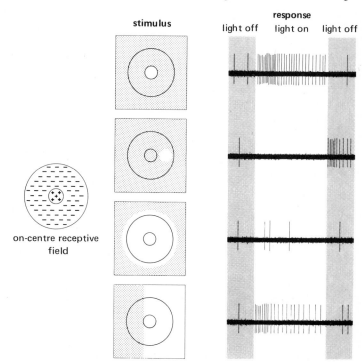

on-centre receptive field

stimulus

response

light off   light on   light off

19

Colin Blakemore

illumination of both the central and surrounding regions of the receptive field by a large spot of light causes a much weaker response than light on the centre alone. These cells are said to have *on-centre* receptive fields.

The other 50 per cent of ganglion cells have just the opposite arrangement: *off-centre* receptive fields. Light in the central region causes inhibition and an off-response, while light in the surround causes an on-response. Again, a large spot, covering the whole receptive field, gives a weaker response (when it is turned off) than a small spot on the centre alone. So this means that ganglion cells are detectors of localized contrast: on-centre cells respond best to white objects on a dark background, while dark objects on a light background are best for off-centre cells.

Two American physiologists, Frank Werblin and John Dowling,[26] have managed to sort out how the structure of the retina makes up the ganglion cells' receptive fields. They studied the mud-puppy, an odd fish that lives in the muddy bottoms of dark rivers, and can almost certainly see very little! The unusual attribute that puts this peculiar creature into physiological history is the fact that it has enormous nerve cells in its retina. In the mud-puppy even the rods and cones are large enough to permit a special glass microelectrode to be pushed through the membrane of the cell to record electrical activity inside the neuron itself. Werblin and Dowling were able to record intracellularly from all the different kinds of cell in the retina and so work out how each ganglion cell's receptive field is built up. They came up with the scheme shown in fig. 9.

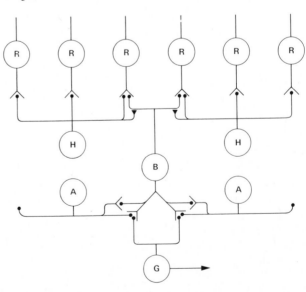

Fig. 9 *In the mud-puppy's retina each ganglion cell (G) picks up the centre of its receptive field from a group of photoreceptors (R) via one or more bipolar cells (B). The nearby horizontal cells (H) antagonize the bipolars and hence produce the inhibitory surround.*

The baffled brain

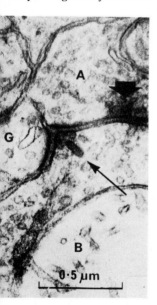

Fig. 10 *This electron micrograph shows a complex synapse between a bipolar cell (B), a ganglion cell (G) and an amacrine cell (A) in the monkey retina. The clusters of round spots in the region of the synapse are thought to be tiny vesicles containing the chemical substance responsible for transmitting signals. One synapse (thin arrow) signals from the bipolar to the amacrine cell and the ganglion cell. Nearby is a reverse synapse (thick arrow) back from the amacrine to the bipolar: this signal may be an inhibitory one providing a simple negative feedback.*

A

G

B

0·5 μm

Each ganglion cell picks up from one, or a few bipolar cells, each of which contacts a few receptors. This whole group of receptors forms the centre of the ganglion cell's receptive field. Some ganglion cells are excited by light falling on this area (the on-centre cells) while others are inhibited (the off-centre cells). The horizontal cells, which pick up from the surrounding receptors feed on to the bipolar cells to *reduce* their activity. So light falling on these surrounding receptors reduces the response caused by light in the centre. This is how the concentric receptive field of the ganglion cell is constructed and the whole process is known as *lateral inhibition*. The exact role of the other kind of horizontally-spreading cell, the amacrine cell, is not really clear. These cells pick up activity from bipolar cells and they seem to feed back on to the same, and neighbouring, bipolar cells. If the feedback were a negative one, which would switch off the active bipolar cell, then amacrine cells would be responsible for the fact that ganglion cells respond best at the beginning or the end of a flash of light, not so well for steady light or darkness.

Two important facts emerge from these studies of the retina. First, the retina is telling the brain mainly about the beginning and end of each retinal illumination. Secondly, localized illumination is much better than diffuse light. So the ganglion cell is detecting *changes* in the level of light – differences of illumination in time or space.

What does this tell us about perception? It must mean that the brain is virtually totally unaware of any large, uniform light or dark object, except at the edges of the area. And even the borders of objects must be invisible to the brain unless the image is moving across the retina, from the receptive field of one ganglion cell to the overlapping receptive fields of its neighbours. Of course, this is not to say that we can only perceive moving objects, for our eyes are continuously and involuntarily in motion, moving the retina under the image of the outside world. There are experimental, optical methods of stabilizing the retinal image and keeping it fixed despite the movements of the eye, and in these conditions the visual image rapidly seems to fade away completely.[22,28] Likewise, the blood vessels that run across the surface of the retina, between the incoming light and the receptors below, cast distinct shadows on the rods and cones. But we normally never see these shadows because they are always fixed on the same part of the retina.

If it is difficult to believe that nothing stationary is visible, it is even harder to admit that we simply cannot see uniform areas of light and dark except by virtue of their edges. And yet this is certainly true. It is even possible to fool the brain into thinking that two identical

21

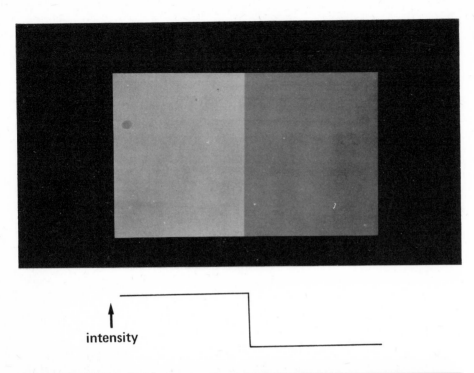

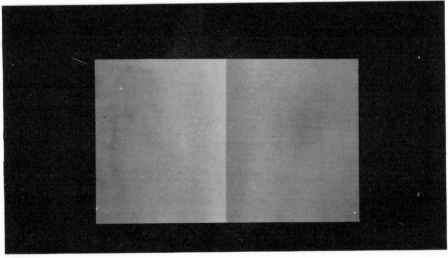

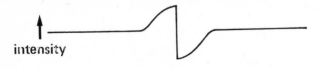

Fig. 11 *These two patterns look much the same. But the distributions of light, plotted below each one, show that the lower one is an illusory edge created by a sudden local change in intensity in the middle of an area of equal intensity. Cover up this apparent edge with a pencil and see how the two sides become equal in brightness.*

22

areas differ in brightness simply by creating an *apparent edge* between them. The two patterns in fig. 11 look similar but the two distributions of light are certainly not the same. In the top pattern the two grey areas actually differ in intensity, and the graph below them shows the distribution of light. But in the bottom pattern the two sides are really identical except that there is a gradual and imperceptible change in intensity close to the sudden transition zone between them. Again the graph shows the distribution of light. Only the transition edge can be detected by our ganglion cells, but we perceive the pattern as if the intensity on each side continued uniformly away from the edge. Try covering the pseudo-edge in fig. 11 with a pencil and compare the brightness of the two sides.

fig. 8

Many of the tricks that our ganglion cells play on us in the perception of brightness were noticed by the eminent physicist Ernst Mach,[18] and they conjured in him a strong interest in visual perception. Mach actually postulated (several decades before the microelectrode) that there must be lateral inhibition in the retina.

One of the best known illusions that probably depends on retinal inhibition is the so-called Hermann grid. At the junction of each white cross there seems to be a slightly darker patch. (This is more effective if you look at the black background rather than directly at

fig. 12

Fig. 12 *The Hermann grid. Hold the page at arm's length and small grey dots will appear at the intersections of the white lines.*

23

fig. 14

fig. 13

fig. 5

a white cross.) The Hermann grid phenomenon is one of the visual effects that make Vasarely's *Supernovae* so disturbing. There is a very simple and plausible explanation for this odd illusion, which puts its cause fairly and squarely in the retina. Imagine the image of a grid falling on the receptive fields of retinal ganglion cells. A cell with its on-centre receptive field directly underneath the image of a straight white bar will be quite strongly stimulated because rather little light falls on its inhibitory surround. But a receptive field lying directly under a white cross will have twice as much light on its inhibitory surround and so the neuron's activity will be much reduced. If these ganglion cells tell the brain about the brightness of the stimulus, the crosses should look darker than the bars, and they do.

So even the processing in the retina contributes to, and puts restrictions on visual perception. In lowly animals, such as frogs, pigeons and even rabbits, many retinal ganglion cells are much more complicated in their properties than the concentric receptive fields already described. But in cats, monkeys and probably in humans, it is the visual cortex that has the main job of processing visual information.

The visual cortex

Rather little seems to happen to the details of the visual message at the synapse in the lateral geniculate nucleus. Geniculate cells, just like the ganglion cells that feed them, also have concentric on-centre or off-centre receptive fields.[14] It seems as if each cell in the nucleus is being excited by a very small number of incoming fibres from a cluster of neighbouring ganglion cells. It is worth noting that the lateral geniculate nucleus also receives information from the other

Fig. 13. *Here are the receptive fields of two on-centre ganglion cells superimposed on a Hermann grid pattern. The one on the left has much of its inhibitory surround in darkness, so it should produce a large response; but the receptive field under the intersection has light on most of its inhibitory surround, and so would give a weaker signal.*

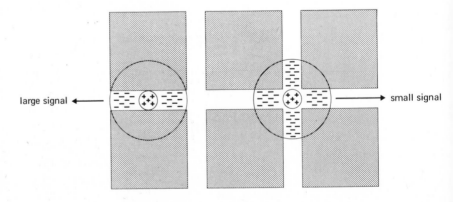

large signal ←   → small signal

The baffled brain

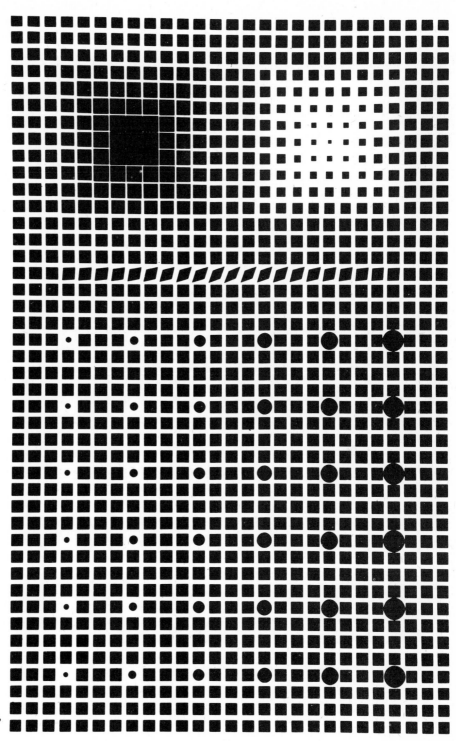

Fig. 14 *Victor Vasarely, Supernovae, 1959-61.*

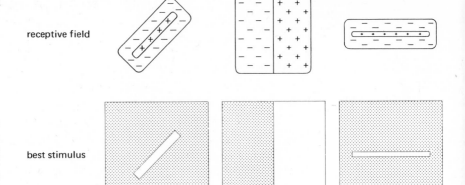

receptive field

best stimulus

Fig. 15 *Some typical receptive fields for simple cells in the visual cortex (+ = on-response, — = off-response). Below each is a picture of the pattern that would excite the cell most.*

sense organs, even the organ of balance in the inner ear. Perhaps the main function of the nucleus is not to process visual information by transforming the messages from the eyes but to filter the signals, depending on the activity of the other sense organs. Certainly we are able to attend specifically to one sense or another. Perhaps selective attention has its physiological explanation in the lateral geniculate nucleus.

There is a quite remarkable transformation between the cells of the lateral geniculate nucleus and the cells of the visual cortex that they contact. David Hubel and Torsten Wiesel, working on cats and monkeys at Harvard, discovered that the receptive fields of cortical cells (given to them by the incoming geniculate fibres) are quite unlike the concentric receptive fields of ganglion cells.[15] Even the simplest types of cell that they found (they called them *simple cells*) are much more specific in their properties. They generally have no spontaneous activity at all and never respond to diffuse illumination of the whole screen. Sometimes they respond grudgingly to small spots of light; however the *on* and *off* regions are not concentric but are elongated into rectangular areas. The best stimulus is therefore a white bar, or black bar, or a black-white border, flashed in the correct position on the receptive field. In every case the edge between the light and dark areas must be at a particular *orientation*. If a bar is flashed on the receptive field at different angles, only a limited range of orientation causes any response. The same is true for moving lines and edges. For this reason these cortical cells have been called *orientation detectors*.

There are other kinds of orientation-detecting neurons in the visual cortex, which are even more complicated in their properties. They probably receive connections from simpler cortical cells as well

fig. 15

fig. 16

as from the incoming geniculate fibres. One class are called *complex cells*. They generally have larger receptive fields than simple cells (although all classes of receptive field vary tremendously in size) and they rarely respond to any flashing patterns. What they prefer is a *moving* bar or edge anywhere within the receptive field. Once again they only respond for one particular orientation or very similar angles.

One step more sophisticated are *hypercomplex cells*, which will only respond if the edge or bar is not too long at one end or both.

fig. 18

The best stimulus for them is a short bar or sometimes a 90° corner.

Different cells in the visual cortex prefer different orientations, some horizontal, some vertical, others in between; but they are not arranged randomly within the cortex. If the microelectrode

Fig. 16 *Responses from a simple cortical cell that responds best to a vertical white bar. The bar is flashed on the receptive field at different orientations. The graph below shows that this cell, like most in the visual cortex, is very selective for the orientation of the stimulus.*

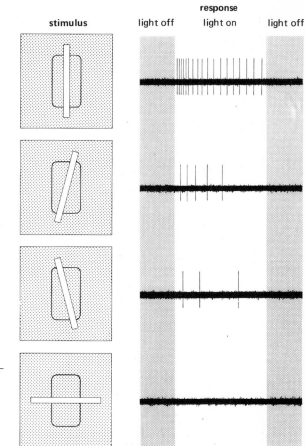

27

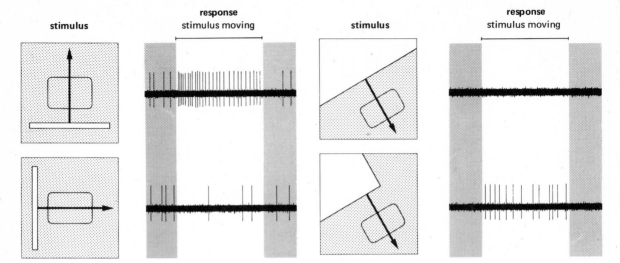

Fig. 17 *In each diagram the large rectangle on the left shows the receptive field of a complex cortical cell. This neuron prefers a horizontal white bar moving across the receptive field.*

Fig. 18 *This hypercomplex cell will not respond when an unlimited white edge moves across the screen (upper record), but it responds vigorously when one end is covered to make a 90° corner.*

fig. 19

penetrates exactly perpendicular to the surface of the cortex it finds cell after cell (simple, complex and hypercomplex) all responding to exactly the same orientation. If it is inserted about half a millimetre away, then all the cells there are found to respond to a different orientation. Even further away the cells respond to yet another, more different angle. So there is a kind of map of orientation in the cortex, as well as the map of the visual world. If the electrode penetrates diagonally through the cortex it reveals that this map is discontinuous. There are sudden changes in preferred orientation between one group and the next. Each block of like-minded orientation detectors is called a *column*.

Each column is a tiny neuronal computer that analyses every contour, of the appropriate orientation, that happens to fall in its territory on the retina. Within one column, different neurons prefer different sizes of target, different velocities of movement and occasionally (in the monkey) even different colours.

There are almost certainly orientation detectors in the human visual cortex too. Giles Brindley[7] has repeated Penfield's experiments, stimulating the human visual cortex with permanently implanted, tiny electrodes. (Brindley's patients are in fact blind, because he is trying to develop a device to provide them with some sort of visual perception by stimulation of the brain.) Each stimulating electrode evoked the sensation of a bright spot, external-

28

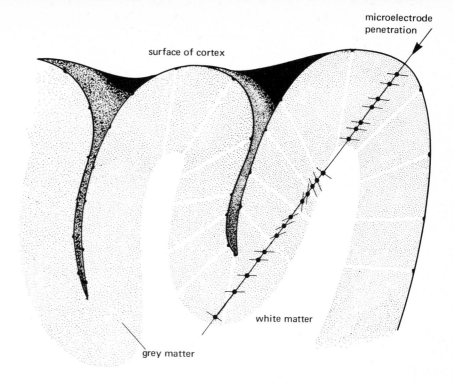

Fig. 19 *Penetration of a microelectrode through the visual cortex. At each position that a single neuron was recorded a line shows the best orientation for that cell. Within each cortical segment, or column, every neuron seems to prefer the same orientation.*

Fig. 20 Top *Altamira cave engraving, approx. 15,000 years old.* Centre *Picasso, Woman in an Armchair.* Bottom *Feiffer, cartoon.*

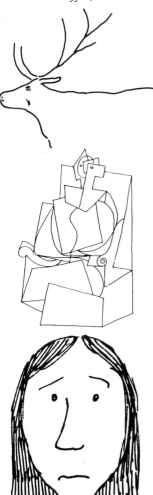

ized in the visual field. It is quite likely that some of the electrodes stimulated single cortical columns of neurons and for some of them the bright spot did indeed seem to be elongated into a bar of a particular orientation. One patient described the sensation as like 'a grain of sago at arms' length'. Presumably she was perceiving the activity of her orientation detectors without any message from her eyes – another example of Müller's law.

Towards a physiological explanation of perception

What does all this mean for perception? Is our apparently unified view of the outside world really dependent on the fragmented abstraction of a set of orientation detectors? Incredible though it seems, all our rich perceptual experience might rely on a simply analysis of the orientation and length of the borders of objects and of the angles between them. The power of simple line drawings to evoke very strong perceptions could rely on orientation detectors in the human cortex. From prehistoric cave painters to modern cartoonists, every graphic artist has known the power of a pattern of lines. But there is more rigorous evidence that human perception involves analysis of orientation and it comes from experiments on certain kinds of illusory perception.

29

Colin Blakemore   *Adaptation and after-effects*

It is a physiological fact that neurons in virtually every sensory system undergo a process called *adaptation*. If they are repetitively shown a strong stimulus most neurons rapidly fatigue and are less sensitive to further stimulation. This certainly happens to the orientation detectors of the cat's visual cortex and in humans there is a fascinating perceptual phenomenon which correlates with this process of adaptation. A pattern of high-contrast, black and white stripes, called a *grating*, is a very startling visual stimulus (used to great effect in the painting by Spencer Moseley in fig. 21). If a human observer looks at such a grating it gradually seems to fade, even though the image is not stabilized on the retina.[4] A grating can be generated on a television screen and its contrast can easily be altered, so the apparent reduction in contrast that occurs as one stares constantly at the grating can be measured. The observer looks fixedly

Fig. 21 *Spencer Moseley, Little Portuguese Bend, 1966.*

30

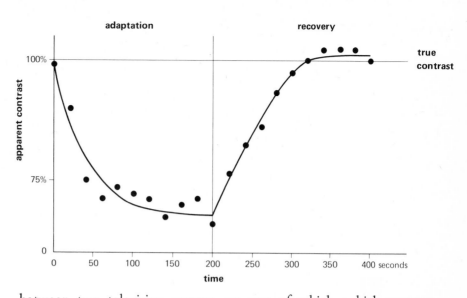

Fig. 22 *This graph shows the change in the apparent contrast of a grating while an observer stares at it constantly (adaptation). When it is switched off and only shown briefly every 10 seconds its apparent contrast is soon normal (recovery). Contrast = Imax-Imin/Imax + Imin, where Imax, Imin are the maximum and minimum intensities in the pattern.*

fig. 22

between two television screens, on one of which a high-contrast *adapting grating* is constantly visible. Every twenty seconds a similar *comparison grating* appears briefly on the other screen and the observer adjusts its contrast until they seem the same. During the recovery phase both gratings are turned off between these settings. Clearly the apparent contrast of the adapting grating decreases gradually and the visual system remains relatively insensitive to the grating for many seconds after this period of *visual adaptation*. Perhaps this perceptual phenomenon is due to the selective adaptation or fatigue of one population of orientation detectors in the human cortex.

Here is the clue to a valuable way of discovering the properties of human visual neurons. After a period of intense sensory stimulation the visual system only gradually recovers its sensitivity for the kind of pattern to which it has been exposed. An extreme demonstration of this same *after-effect* of adaptation is shown in fig. 23. The central square contains a low-contrast vertical grating; place the book about 3 metres away and these stripes should only just be visible. Now, from the same distance, adapt to the high-contrast vertical grating on the upper left. Let your eye drift around the central circle to avoid the formation of a conventional after-image of the pattern and after about a minute look back quickly at the dot in the middle of the low-contrast stripes. They should seem momentarily to disappear, due to the loss of sensitivity for vertical contours.[2]

Now after a minute or so to recover, repeat the experiment for the other adapting patterns in fig. 23 which have a horizontal grating, or vertical stripes of completely different width. After adapting to

31

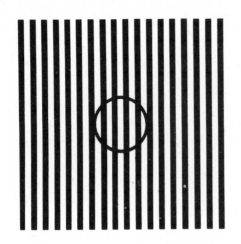 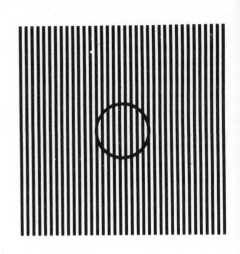

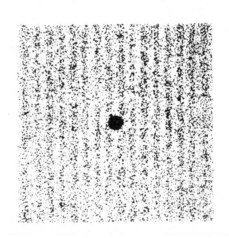

32

Fig. 23 left *A demonstration of an after-effect that depends on the orientation of the adapting stripes. The instructions for viewing appear in the text.*

Fig. 24 below *To produce this graph an observer adapted to gratings of various orientations and afterwards measured how much more contrast than normal he required just to be able to see a vertical grating.*

Fig. 25 below right *As in the graph of Fig. 24, but the observer adapted to various vertical gratings with bars of different widths and measured the increase in contrast necessary to detect a vertical grating with bars of a particular width. The width of the adapting bars is shown in relation to the width of the test bars.*

these, the central stripes do *not* disappear. The actual change in sensitivity can be measured by adjusting the contrast of a vertical grating on a television screen until it can only just be seen, after adapting to various patterns. Figs. 24 and 25 show the results of such experiments: the after-effect is indeed limited to patterns of similar orientation and bar-width to that of the adapting pattern. Naturally it is very tempting to compare the results of these perceptual experiments with the fact that cortical cells are specifically sensitive to the orientation and width of flashed or moving stripes.

If adaptation to stripes fatigues one particular population of cells that help to tell the brain about the orientations and sizes of visual stimuli, we should expect another kind of after-effect to occur. Stripes of a somewhat *different* orientation or size to those of the adapting grating ought to appear *changed* in orientation or size. The argument behind this prediction is illustrated in fig. 26. Each curve on the upper graphs represents the orientation selectivity of a single cortical neuron like that in fig. 16. Below the left-hand graph is a plot of the distribution of activity set up among these detectors by a test grating of one angle. One cell is excited much more than any other; presumably the brain could recognize the grating's orientation by identifying which cell is most active. Now imagine that the cells have been exposed to a different adapting orientation, indicated by a white arrow at a different position in the middle graph. It de-sensitizes a group of detectors, including the cell that should respond best to the test grating. Now when the test pattern is shown again (right-hand graph) it sets up a different distribution. A different neuron is now the most active, so presumably the grating should seem changed in orientation.

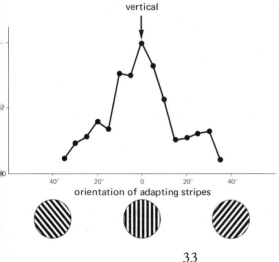

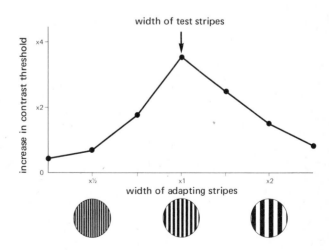

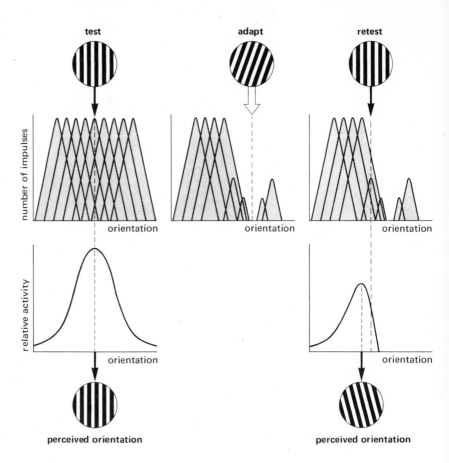

Fig. 26 *On the upper graphs every curve is the sensitivity of a single cortical cell for different stimulus orientations (as in Fig. 16). When a test grating of a particular orientation is shown to these cells (first graph) it produces a distribution of activity, shown below, where one cell is much more active than its neighbours. After adaptation at a slightly different orientation, which fatigues a group of orientation detectors (middle graph), the same test grating produces a different pattern of activity (third graph). Now the wrong detector cell is most active and therefore the orientation is misperceived.*

Fig. 27 demonstrates this predicted after-effect.[11] After adapting for a minute to the tilted gratings on the left, by fixating the bar between them, the vertical stripes in the middle seem tilted in the opposite directions. Exactly the same argument applies to the perception of the width of stripes, and fig. 27 also shows this expected after-effect.[5] Adapt to the pair of gratings on the right that have stripes of different width and then look back at the dot between the central pair of test gratings. They should seem changed in bar-width. Experiments like these may be the psychologist's answer to the microelectrode.

Physiology and illusions

It would be foolish ambition to attempt a universal explanation of every illusory perception, for the word illusion has been used to describe every quirk of the senses from after-images to ghosts. But it

34

Fig. 27 *Two distortion after-effects. View from 3 metres. See text.*

Fig. 28 *Poggendorff illusion.*

is certainly worth seeking some generalizations about the physiological basis of misperceptions.

First we must realize that a sensation can only be known to be illusory if there is a scale against which to judge the sensation and discover that it is false. Take the well-known Poggendorff illusion. The vertical ruler behind the rectangle is really straight and continuous, but the two sections seem misaligned. The sensation is only illusory because of our assumptions about the physical properties of rulers. The whole of our perception is really false, for it does not copy reality but symbolizes it. Only when the falsehood is manifest do we call it an illusion.

Many of the familiar illusions *are* familiar because we have an inbuilt scale by which to measure the misperceptions. The Zöllner illusion is a good example. The long diagonal lines are really parallel; yet they seem altered in orientation by the transverse lines. However, though none of the long lines appears parallel to its neighbours, yet

35

Fig. 29 *Zöllner illusion*

Fig. 30 *The round areas contain stripes that are really vertical and parallel to each other. They seem tilted by the surrounding patterns.*

at every point along the lines they seem the same distance apart. It is this conflict between one attribute of the stimulus and another (parallelism and separation in this case) that characterizes many geometric illusions.

Perhaps the uneasy feeling that often accompanies illusory perception arises from a discrepancy between two independent detector systems in the brain, which report on separate aspects of the stimulus. It is quite conceivable, for instance, that the simple cells of the visual cortex (with their very specific small receptive fields) are used to localize objects and judge their relative positions. Complex cells, on the other hand, being sensitive to the orientations of edges but having larger receptive fields, may be used to signal the orientations and shapes of objects, regardless of relative position. Possibly the contradictory perception of orientation and position that occurs in many geometric illusions implies that the generalized signal about orientation in the complex cells is being distorted, while the positional information in simple cells is undisturbed.

There is another strong piece of evidence that illusions arise when different detector neurons contradict each other. There is a vivid after-effect that follows the prolonged observation of a continuously moving pattern. It is called the Waterfall phenomenon because it is particularly powerfully produced by staring for some time at a waterfall and then looking at the stationary rocks beside it. Any object viewed after looking at movement seems to be drifting in the opposite direction. And yet the apparently *moving* object does not appear to change its *position* relative to its surroundings. Here again is a conflict between the uninfluenced position-detecting system and a movement-detecting system that has been fatigued by viewing continuous movement. It is very significant that many neurons in the visual cortex respond selectively for movement of an edge in one direction, and not in the reverse direction. Perhaps the normal judgment of movement depends on a comparison of the outputs from all these *direction-selective* cells. When one class of cell has been fatigued by constant stimulation, the cells sensitive to the opposite direction of movement are relatively more active, and a spontaneous sensation of movement might occur. Perceptual conflict could arise because the position-detecting cells are not disturbed.

It may be relatively simple to explain perceptual after-effects (such as the Waterfall phenomenon and those shown in fig. 27) in terms of fatigue of specific detector neurons, which analyse orientation, size and movement. But it is more tricky to try to account for the instantaneous distortions of orientation or size that

36

fig. 27

fig. 30
fig. 31

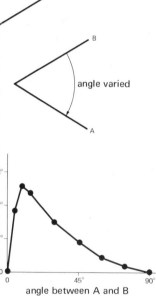

C

B

angle varied

A

angle between A and B

45°   90°

Fig. 31 *In the pattern above, at certain angles between lines A and B, line B appears more anti-clockwise than it really is, because of the presence of line A. This illusion can be measured by setting C until it seems parallel to B for different orientations of A. The graph shows the result.*[3]

make up the usual geometric illusions (e.g. figs. 28 and 29). However, there are so many similarities between the *successive* after-effects and the *simultaneous* illusions that one must suspect a common origin.

Consider the apparent change in orientation that happens after adapting to a slightly different orientation. An exactly analogous misperception can be induced by showing both the adapting and test patterns at the same time. In fact only two lines are needed to produce the change in orientation. Any two lines that are slightly different in orientation appear to be more different in angle than they really are. This apparent expansion of the acute angle between two lines can easily be measured[3] by adjusting a third distant line (C) until it seems to be parallel to one of the distorted lines (B) for various orientations of the other line (A).

Can we find any property of cortical neurons that might explain simultaneous orientational distortions, in the same way that fatigue of orientation detectors could account for orientation after-effects? One possibility is that neighbouring neurons in the cortex, handling similar orientations, are always *inhibiting* each other. Such mutual inhibition would reduce the noisy spontaneous activity in the system (cortical cells are indeed much less spontaneously active than retinal ganglion cells). It would also improve the selectivity of each detector neuron, because it would limit the cell's response to a narrow range of orientation for which its own excitatory input exceeds the inhibition from its neighbours. Mutual inhibition of this sort, however, should produce detection errors for two lines, because each line would cause a reduction in sensitivity for similar orientations, rather like that due to adaptation. So perhaps simple inhibition between nerve cells in the visual cortex might explain the illusory misperception of orientation just as lateral inhibition in the retina can account for our faulty sensations of brightness.

These simple distortions of orientation seem to be the prototype of many familiar geometric illusions, including the Poggendorff and Zöllner patterns. But it would be dangerous to think that all the geometric illusions can be explained in these simplistic physiological terms. Physiological explanations there must be, but probably not in the visual cortex alone.

Much more important is the question of why the brain permits itself to be fooled in these ways. We know that the retina signals almost exclusively about brightness changes at the edges of patterns and transmits very little information about uniform light or dark areas. Yet we usually perceive brightness quite appropriately. Somehow the brain knows about the properties of its retina and fills

37

in the missing information. The apparent brightness difference on each side of the pseudo-edge is caused by a sensible corrective procedure in the brain, inappropriately applied. Then why does the brain not also know about the physiological processes in the visual cortex, which lead to changes in signals about orientation when more than one line is present? Surely it should be possible for the brain to re-interpret information from the cortex and compensate for illusory distortion. The fact that illusions are *allowed* to manifest themselves in perception suggests that the misinterpretation of orientation might actually be of some positive benefit in the analysis of the visual world.

The perception of distance: a challenge for physiology

So far I have discussed entirely the physiological mechanisms for interpreting only two dimensions of visual space; but the third dimension of distance is a vital component in visual perception and is most important for the control of bodily movement. The recognition of distance is an intriguing problem, for the retinal image itself is merely a two-dimensional projection of the world. So any awareness that we have of the third dimension must depend on our interpretation of two-dimensional projections. This is perhaps the supreme accomplishment of visual perception.

left eye   right eye

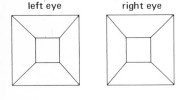

Stereopsis

There is one clue to the relative distances of objects that exists, not in one retinal image, but in a comparison of the two. Although, in an animal with forward-pointing eyes, the two retinae look at much the same region of the visual world, they do so from slightly different directions, because the eyes are horizontally separated in the head. Hold up a finger in front of your eyes and look at a window or a wall some distance away. If you close first one eye, then the other, you will discover that the finger appears at a different position against the background, through the two eyes. This geometric fact, that images of objects at different distances are in different relative positions on the two retinae, can be used by the brain to discriminate the distances of those objects. Imagine the views that your two eyes would actually have if you looked down on top of a solid four-sided pyramid with the top cut off. Charles Wheatstone[27] discovered about 1835 that if two such flat pictures are shown, one to each eye, then the observer actually perceives a solid object as if it were three-dimensional. The instrument for showing the eyes separate pictures is a *stereoscope*.

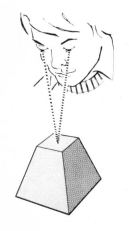

Fig. 32 *A stereoscopic picture of a top view of a pyramid with the top cut off. If these two images are shown, one to each eye, in a stereoscope a solid image of the pyramid appears.*

38

fig. 5

This ability to interpret minute disparities in the two retinal images is called steroscopic vision, or simply *stereopsis*. It is probably innate, since very young babies seem to be able to recognise depth even in stereoscopic patterns more abstract than those of fig. 32. Quite recently physiologists have discovered the probable way that the brain achieves stereopsis.[1,16,21]

It turns out that the orientation-detecting neurons of the visual cortex almost all receive similar messages from *both* eyes. The cells respond to the same orientation of edge shown to roughly the same part of the retina of either eye. Presumably these binocular cells are detecting the two retinal images of single objects in space. Indeed each neuron responds best of all if an appropriate image is shown *simultaneously* to the receptive fields on both retinae. This means of course that each binocular cortical cell responds best for an object at a particular *distance* from the eyes, whose images happen to fall in just the right place on both retinae.

In neurophysiological experiments, lines at different stereoscopic distances can be presented to the experimental animal through an optical device rather like Wheatstone's stereoscope. From these experiments we know that different cells have their receptive fields on slightly different relative positions in the two retina. So different cells prefer objects at different distances from the eyes. Surely this is the brain mechanism that accounts for stereopsis.

But the whole world does not appear to shrivel to a mere two-dimensional backdrop if you close one eye. Indeed, remarkably little seems to happen. So although we certainly *can* use binocular

Fig. 33 *In the cat's visual cortex most neurons pick up signals from a particular point on both retinae. If an object appears at the right distance from the cat its image will fall on the correct position in both eyes to excite a particular cortical cell. This diagram shows the two cells that respond best to objects A and B.*

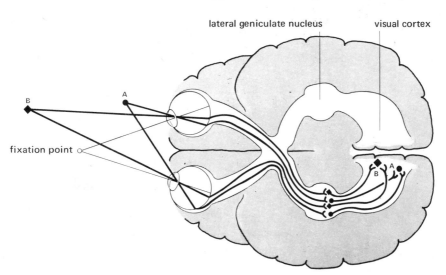

lateral geniculate nucleus   visual cortex

fixation point

Colin Blakemore   information to perceive distance, we do not necessarily *need* it. Somehow we must be able to interpret the single retinal image in order to make perceptual speculations about the third dimension.

Monocular distance perception

There are many aspects of the monocular retinal image that can be used by the brain to judge distance. They have been classified by psychologists, who use very simplified situations to study these clues to distance. But what better way to consider them than to see how they have been used by the great artists, since these are the only conventional devices by which a painter can create a sense of distance on a flat canvas.

Plate 1

1. *Position in the field*. One of the first methods employed by artists to convey an impression of distance was the positioning of objects in the visual field. It is an elementary rule of perspective, of course, that since we view the ground plane from above, the further away an object is on the ground plane the higher it is in the visual field.

Plate 2

Plate 3

2. *Linear perspective*. The detailed rules of perspective were worked out in the Renaissance, but there were informal attempts at perspective drawing long before the fifteenth century. The *Annunciation* of Bernado Daddi painted in Florence in the first half of the fourteenth century, contains some crude perspective projections. The corners of the room are drawn with fair accuracy but the tiles of the floor and the ceiling are shown as parallel rows on the surface of the painting. Compare this with the sheer revelry in the perfected technique shown by Crivelli in his *Annunciation*, painted in 1486.

Plate 4

3. *Texture gradient*. Any regular, or even irregular texture, lying on a surface that recedes into the distance, will appear to become coarser in grain the closer it is to the observer.[12] Monet uses this technique to great effect in the field of poppies in his *Les Coquelicots*.

Plate 5

4. *Size of familiar objects*. If we know the true relative sizes of objects then we can use the actual dimensions of their retinal images to tell us about their relative distances. The great sense of depth in Jan Brueghel's *Paradise* is created by a knowledge of the actual sizes of elephants and people, leopards and sheep.

40

Plate 1 *Distance conveyed by the placing of figures in a visual field. Illumination from a fifteenth-century Table of Christian Faith.*

Plate 2, below *An early attempt by Bernardo Daddi at visual perspective in the Annunciation, about 1340.*

OPVS CARO
LI CRIVELLI
VENETI

1486.

LIBERTAS · ECCLESIASTICA ·

Plate 3, left *Geometrical perspective in Crivelli's Annunciation.*

Plate 4 *Claude Monet, Les Coquelicots.*

Plate 5 *Jan Brueghel the Elder, Le Paradis Terrestre.*

Fig. 34 *Emil Nolde, Head of a Prophet.*

Plate 6 *Braque, Guitar and Jug.*

Plate 7 *Turner, Norham Castle, Sunrise.*

5. *Shadow.* Light and shade can conjure up a powerful perception of solidity. Emile Nolde's *Prophet* is a simple woodcut that relies on shadow alone to represent the man's craggy, solid features.

Plate 6

6. *Overlay.* Unless it is transparent, any object obscures anything further from the viewer and directly in line with the object. This clue to distance, the simplest and strongest of all, is virtually the only one that survives in the disruption of Braque's *Guitar and Jug.*

7. *Aerial perspective.* Minute particles in the atmosphere scatter light, and so reduce the contrast of distant objects. Blue light, of shorter wavelength, is best at penetrating atmospheric disturbances, so distant landscapes appear tinged with blue. England has more than its fair share of atmospheric disturbance and Turner captures the

Plate 7

aerial perspective of England magnificently in his *Norham Castle.*

Conclusions

In less than a century physiology has made considerable advance in the understanding of perception. We now have a good idea how one

45

Colin Blakemore

sees shape and movement, position and size, and even how stereo-scopic vision works. On the other hand it is impossible to comprehend how the monocular perception of distance is achieved. Perhaps the interpretation of linear perspective depends on signals from orientation-detecting neurons. Perhaps the recognition of texture gradients relies on messages from size-detecting cells. But no one could hazard a guess at how all the information is put together. So much of perception is still a total mystery to the physiologist.

   New methods are expanding the experimental assault on the brain. Extraordinarily sensitive anatomical methods, following the passage of radioactive materials through individual neurons, are telling us more about the connections between cells. New physiological techniques allow the injection of substances on to or into single neurons to try to discover their properties.

   Some people despair when they realize how little is really known about the workings of the brain, but most believe that the effort to understand it is worthwhile. The prizes for such comprehension would be rich indeed. Not only would computer technicians dearly love to know the secrets of human memory, but the value to humanity of an understanding of the brain would be incalculable. All in all, there seems much more to learn and every reason to attempt to learn it.

References

1 Barlow, H.B., Blakemore, C. & Pettigrew, J.D. (1967), 'The neural mechanism of binocular depth discrimination', *J. Physiol. 193*, 327-342.
2 Blakemore, C. & Campbell, F.W. (1969), 'Adaptation to spatial stimuli', *J. Physiol, 200*, 11-13 P.
3 Blakemore, C., Carpenter, R.H.S. & Georgeson, M.A. (1970), 'Lateral inhibition between orientation detectors in the human visual system', *Nature, Lond. 228*, 37-39.
4 Blakemore, C., Muncey, J.P.J. & Ridley, R.M. (1971), 'Perceptual fading of a stabilized cortical image', *Nature, Lond. 233*, 204-205.
5 Blakemore, C. & Sutton, P. (1969), 'Size adaptation: a new after-effect', *Science 166*, 245-247.
6 Brindley, G.S. (1970), *Physiology of the Retina and Visual Pathway*, 2nd ed., London.
7 Brindley, G.S. & Lewin, W.S. (1968), 'The visual sensations produced by electrical stimulation of the medial occipital cortex', *J. Physiol. 194*, 54-55 P.
8 Daniel, P.M. & Whitteridge, D. (1961), 'The representation of the visual field on the cerebral cortex in monkeys', *J. Physiol. 159*, 203-221.

9 Descartes, R. (1686), *Traité de l'homme.*

10 Dowling, J.E. (1970), 'Organization of vertebrate retinas', *Investigative Ophthalmol. 9*, 655-680.

11 Gibson, J.J. (1933), 'Adaptation, after-effect and contrast in the perception of curved lines', *J. exp Psychol. 16*, 1-31.

12 Gibson, J.J. *The Perception of the Visual World*, Boston.

13 Hodgkin, A.L. (1964), *The Conduction of the Nerve Impulse*, Liverpool.

14 Hubel, D.H. & Wiesel, T.N. (1961), 'Integrative action in the cat's lateral geniculate body', *J. Physiol. 155*, 385-398.

15 Hubel, D.H. & Wiesel, T.N. (1962), 'Receptive fields, binocular interaction and functional architecture in the cat's visual cortex', *J. Physiol. 160*, 106-154.

Hubel, D.H. & Wiesel, T.N. (1965), 'Receptive fields and functional architecture in two non-striate visual areas (18 and 19) of the cat', *J. Physiol. 28*, 229-289.

16 Joshua, D.E. & Bishop, P.O. (1970), 'Binocular single vision and depth discrimination. Receptive field disparities for central and peripheral vision and binocular interaction on peripheral single units in cat striate cortex', *Expl. Brain. Res. 10*, 389-416.

17 Kuffler, S.W. (1953), 'Discharge patterns and functional organization of mammalian retina', *J. Neurophysiol. 16*, 37-68.

18 Mach, E. (1897), *Contributions to the Analysis of Sensations* tr. by C.M. Williams, Chicago.

19 Müller, J. (1842), *Elements of Physiology*, vol. 2, tr. by W. Baly, London.

20 Penfield, W. & Rasmussen, T. (1955), *The Cerebral Cortex of Man: a Clinical Study of Localization of Function*, New York.

21 Pettigrew, J.D. (1972), 'The neurophysiology of binocular vision', *Sci. Amer. 227*, 2, 84-95.

22 Pritchard, R.M. (1961), 'Stabilized images on the retina', *Sci. Amer.* (June 1961).

23 Ramón y Cajal, S. (1911), *Histologie du système nerveux de l'homme et des vertébrés*, tome 2, Paris.

24 Schneider, G.E. (1967), 'Contrasting visuomotor functions of tectum and cortex in the golden hamster', *Psychol. Forsch. 31*, 52-62.

25 Talbot, S.A. & Marshall, W.H. (1941), 'Physiological studies on neural mechanisms of visual localisation and discrimination', *Amer. J. Ophthal. 24*, 1255-1264.

26 Werblin, F.W. & Dowling, J.E. (1969), 'Organization of the retina of the mudpuppy, *Necturus maculosus*. II: Intracellular recording', *J. Neurophysiol. 32*, 339-355.

27 Wheatstone, C. (1838), 'Contributions to the physiology of vision. Part the first: on some remarkable and hitherto unobserved phenomena of binocular vision', *Phil. Trans. Roy. Soc. 2*, 371-394. (Abstract in *Proc. Roy. Soc. Lond.* (1843) *4*, 76-77.)

28 Yarbus, A.L. (1967), *Eye Movements and Vision*, New York.

2 The Confounded Eye

R. L. Gregory

As the tortoise said: 'I can't make progress without sticking my neck out.'

Scientists fight error, while artists court illusion. This may tempt us into thinking that science is the White Knight seeking truth, while art is the Black Knight sunk in error – but this would be unfair. Many illusions of perception are more than mere errors: they may be experiences in their own right. They can illuminate reality. It is this power of illusion to illuminate which the artist somehow commands. To the scientist illusions present a curious challenge: for though phenomena, they are not phenomena of his physical world – they are phenomena just because they are deviations from what he takes to be reality.

In certain situations the eye and brain are confounded, to generate illusions. Illusions may be mere errors; or they may be frightening or fascinating unearthly experiences, which may stimulate the imagination to seduce us from reality. Some illusions are irritating or dangerous; but others are at least as interesting and as much fun as reality.

Illusion as a problem for science

Much of science has progressed by examining trivial-looking but puzzling phenomena, and perhaps the nature of perception may be revealed by puzzling over illusions. Illusions are essentially *phenomena of perception*. They cannot be phenomena of the physical object world for they are systematic deviations from physical fact. This makes the study of illusion a curious and perhaps unique case in science: for here we are not concerned with the universe – but rather with departures from the object of study of the whole of the rest of science. Does this mean that science is powerless to explain illusion? Certainly many 'illusory' phenomena, such as mirages, are given explanation in physics textbooks: in this case, as due to the bending of light by refraction in air having steep temperature gradients.

Again, seeing one's own face *through* a mirror – though one

Fig. 1 *Personal Values by René Magritte. The weird effect is given by unusual combinations of familiar objects having surprising relative scale.*

49

knows it to be *in front* of the mirror, where one feels it to be — can be described in terms of optics. Or can it? Why doesn't one's knowledge that one's own face is not through, but in front of the mirror serve to correct the error? Again, in a mirror we see ourselves the right way up but left-right reversed — why should this be? Is it due entirely to the optics of mirrors? Do mirrors distinguish between vertical and horizontal? Surely not. It is curious that we look into mirrors throughout our lives and yet may never question why we appear *through* them, *left-right* reversed but the right way up! Is the answer to the puzzle — the source of mirror-illusions — in the mirror or is it in ourselves? If it is in ourselves what kind of explanation would be appropriate?

When one starts to ask questions about illusions, it is surprisingly difficult to know just what questions to ask and how to think about them. Should we be thinking in terms of optics, of physiology, of psychology, or even of the nature of consciousness? Do we need to know how normal perception functions to understand how it can go wrong?

Eye and brain combine to give detailed knowledge of objects beyond the range of probing touch. Just how this is achieved remains in many ways mysterious; but we know now that specific features of objects are selected and combined to give an internal account of the object world. This must surely require processes of the utmost complexity. The ease with which we see, apparently by merely opening our eyes, hides the fact that this is probably the most sophisticated of all the brain's activities: calling upon its stores of memory data; requiring subtle classifications, comparisons and logical decisions for sensory data to become perception. This general notion of perception has not, however, always been held. A traditional, and still not wholly abandoned, philosophical position is that perception is an immediate (and God-like) knowledge of external reality. This was developed by the philosopher Immanuel Kant[16] (1724-1804), who used the German word 'Anschauung', usually translated as 'intuition'. To Kant this immediate knowledge given by perception is linked with seeing truth intuitively as in mathematical propositions. The notion that we see the world through the eyes and the other senses directly, or 'intuitively', much as we seem to 'see' the truth of a mathematical or geometrical proposition with a gasp of understanding — an 'Aha! experience', as A. J. Ayer puts it — is by no means dead. There are several distinguished people working on perception who hold this passive, or intuitive view of it. They have however, little or nothing to say about

Figs 2-8 *This is a wooden cube. When seen in silhouette it appears flat; with increasing frontal illumination its true three-dimensional form becomes gradually apparent — and then its outline shape is subtly changed. Evidently constancy, initiated by the information of its three-dimensional form, modifies the silhouette. This is a situation which has not been fully investigated.*

50

illusions. What could they say? That some perceptions are not so direct after all? That some intuitive knowledge is false? But then if some perception is not direct awareness of reality, and if some intuitions can turn out to be false, why should we hold that any perception is direct knowledge of reality? The fact of illusions makes us doubt this philosophy.

The alternative view of perception is that perceptions of objects are given by inference, from data given by the senses and stored in memory. On this view, any perception may be false, just as any argument may be false. It may be false because its assumptions are incorrect, or because the form of the argument is fallacious. On this view of perception, illusions take on the same importance that paradoxes and ambiguities have for philosophers concerned with the nature of argument; or how data can be used to discover a truth, or a fact. Illusions then become symptoms of fallacies and unwarranted assumptions about the world of objects.

Illusions are sometimes regarded merely as deviations from fact; but this is not a sufficient description. In the first place it is not helpful to call *any* deviation from fact illusion. All observations — whether by senses or instruments — suffer random disturbances, so that they fluctuate around some average reading or report. It is not helpful to call each fluctuation an 'illusion'. Illusions should, rather, be regarded as *systematic* deviations from fact. But then, we may ask, 'What is fact?' We may either take facts to be the objects of statements, or of perceptions, which are generally accepted as true; or we may take facts to be what are actually — in some God's eye view of things — true. Fortunately we do not (at least for the moment) have to decide between these views of truth, to discuss perception and illusion. The great proponent of perception as requiring inferences was the German physicist and physiologist Hermann von Helmholtz (1821-1894). Helmholtz[12] introduced the term 'unconscious inference'; regarding perceptions as 'conclusions', more or less likely to be true, depending on the sensory data available and the difficulty of the perceptual problem to be solved. Until recently the notion of unconscious inference seemed to many psychologists to be self-contradictory — as it used to be assumed that consciousness is necessary for inference to be possible. Perhaps again through the influence of computers (for no one regards them as conscious though they are capable of at least some kinds of inference) this objection no longer has force. To hold that 'unconscious inference' is a self-contradictory notion now appears as mere semantic inertia.

R.L. Gregory

For one reason or another, Helmholtz's lead was not followed for a century or more. Instead attention was concentrated on the physiological mechanisms subserving perception – and this has continued as an exciting and fruitful enquiry – together with philosophical or psychological theories of what these mechanisms are supposed to be doing, which has been a far less happy story. The main theory (in what I personally regard as the Dark Age) since Helmholtz is the Gestalt Theory.[19],[17] This is a curious kind of 'intuitionism', which tried to marry the notion of direct knowledge through perception with a physiological account. The Gestalt theorists did make interesting discoveries – including some new illusions – but their physiological notions were misconceived. They not only lacked the knowledge of brain physiology that we have now: their views had severe logical problems, which should have been recognised.

The essential idea behind the Gestalt theory of perception was the notion of electrical 'brain traces' supposed to adopt the shape of objects being perceived.[18] (This was called 'isomorphism'.) Thus, when viewing a circle, there was supposed to be a circular brain trace; for a sphere, a spherical brain trace, and presumably for a house a corresponding house-shaped trace. We now know that this is not the case (though admittedly there is a preliminary stage of mapping of the retinal pattern of stimulation upon the 'projection area' of the striate visual cortex).

The Gestalt brain traces were supposed to have dynamic properties, and so to generate perceptual phenomena. They were seen as electrical fields, which would tend to form certain shapes and thus produce visual effects, including some distortions. The brain traces were supposed to adopt stable forms which again were supposed to correspond to stable perceptions. Gaps in the perceptual field were supposed to be filled by the tendency of the brain fields to flow across gaps. This was extended to their discovery of the 'phi phenomenon' – apparent movement across a gap between two alternately flashing lights. Distortion illusions were attributed to the tendency of the brain fields to become as circular, or as 'closed', as possible. Thus ellipses were supposed to look nearly circular, for this reason. A further feature of the theory was an almost complete denial of learning as important for perception: this also goes for any 'intuitionist' theory. Learning is generally limited by them to discovering strategies for extracting direct knowledge; such as where to direct the eyes, or which features are useful.

Much of what the Gestalt school held may seem attractive. It

maintained the comforting thought that we know reality directly – without guessing or betting – while giving the brain something to do. It is quite surprising how the brain gets totally left out of some psychological theories of perception. It perhaps also appealed to some artists, as apparently providing a reason for some shapes being superior to others. Why, then, is it largely (though not completely) abandoned as a theory of perception – and so as a way of thinking about illusion? There are many reasons and we can only touch upon them here.

In the first place, there is far more to perception than the recognition of shape. How does the 'isomorphism' idea cope with other perceptual features? Consider colour: are we supposed to believe that when we see a green traffic light, part of our brain turns green? It certainly does not – and if it did would it help us to see green? Only if there were some kind of 'internal eye' to 'see' the green trace – but this would generate an endless regress of traces and eyes and traces and eyes ... leading to an infinite distance, with nothing different from the start of the regress. This indeed is a logical problem of the whole trace notion: what do the traces do? If they are electrical toy models of reality how are they seen without the inner eye which generates a useless regress? This question was never answered. Considering illusions, it has been suggested that – like springs or bubbles – the traces tend toward certain shapes: but this is a weak kind of explanation. It is weak partly because the supposed Gestalt tendencies to 'closure', gap-filling and so on only occur in special cases; but they should always occur if they are due to basic physical properties of the traces. Then again, why should the stable states of the traces correspond to stable perceptions for such a variety of shapes? For example, face shapes are extremely stable; but why should there be a physical reason, of this kind, for face-shaped brain traces being stable forms? We should not expect this of electrical fields. This question of perceptual stability is a deep objection to the Gestalt trace theory. The simple fact that perceptions tend towards, and are stable for, *familiar objects* is very strong evidence for the important of experience and learning for perception.

Once learning is accepted as important for perception, any direct 'intuitionist' account fails: for no one holds that we have immediate knowledge of the past. The past cannot be perceived directly; but if stored information, from past experience, is vital for present perception – if the present is read in terms of the past – then we are driven away from an Intuitional or Gestalt position, towards a theory

53

R.L. Gregory

much closer to Helmholtz's notion of perceptions given by inference from sensory and stored data.

What can physiology tell us? The major lesson from physiology is that a limited number of features of objects are available to the brain, at any one time. This is indeed obviously true – if I look at my table from a distance I cannot feel that it is solid; but I must be assuming that it is solid and strong or I would not trust my possessions to its support, or myself to my chair. This holds even for unfamiliar objects, for we do not have available direct sensory data for signalling properties which have to be known, or assumed, for behaviour to be appropriate. This much was realised by seventeenth- and eighteenth-century philosophers (though it has been forgotten by many psychologists since); but current physiological knowledge is far more specific on this point. It is providing evidence of what features are accepted by the brain from the sense organs; especially what features of retinal images are accepted for vision[13] – which was discussed in more detail by Blakemore in the last chapter. Briefly, the orientation of lines, movement and certain shapes, such as corners or angles, are represented by the firing of single cells in the 'visual' striate cortex. These features are selected by specific neural 'circuits' which are 'tuned' to accept them. There is recent evidence, largely from Blakemore, that this 'tuning' for specific features is a result of early experience of features such as orientation of lines. This is vitally important information, but it leaves the question: how are these selected features as neurally represented, combined to give perception of objects? One suggestion is that no combination of features is required – that there are single cells 'tuned' to any object, however complicated, which we can recognise. These have been described as 'grandmother cells'. The joke brings out the difficulty: how could a single cell be tuned to one's grandmother, though she has turned her head to change her profile, or hides part of her face behind a paper she is reading? The difficulty of seeing how this could work is so great, that it is generally assumed that many signalled features are somehow pieced together, to build up perceptions of objects from available data.

Here we return to Helmholtz's notion of perception as unconscious inference. Do we *infer* the presence of our grandmother, from various sensed features typical of her? Do we infer tables and chairs, from combinations of available features, as represented by activity and silence of brain cells signalling each feature's presence or absence?

If perceptions are inferences, based on signalled data from the

54

senses and stored in memory, then we should ask: what are these inferences like? Are they like other kinds of inferences? Do they depend upon assumptions? What happens if the assumptions are wrong? We may not as yet know the physiology behind all this; but at least we can ask, and hope to answer, this kind of question.

It now seems most unfortunate that there has been a gap of virtually a whole century between Helmholtz and us during which these questions have not been asked. If we go on to enquire 'What is illusion?' we might well expect some illusions to be fallacies of unconscious inference. Helmholtz was creeping up on this when he wrote (his italics): 'The simple rule for all illusions is this: *we always believe that we see such objects as would, under conditions of normal vision, produce the retinal image of which we are actually conscious.*' Our aim is to try to develop this idea, which seems to be the key to many illusions. It also allows illusions to be data for discovering some of the assumptions behind perception.

Once we make the conceptual move to thinking of perception as *inferences from data* we can look at the physiological mechanisms as carrying out functions necessary for collecting and storing data, and drawing inferences from available sensory and stored data. Also, when we see the physiological mechanisms as carrying out logical functions, by following more or less appropriate strategies, we at once see rich possibilities for the generation of illusions. It becomes clear that illusions might be generated in two basic ways: (i) by the physiology functioning in some abnormal way – *malfunction of the mechanisms*; (ii) by the inference, or other strategy carried out by the mechanisms, not being suitable to the current problem – *inappropriateness of the strategies*. These kinds of error seem to be basically different – which implies that we should expect to find two corresponding basic kinds of perceptual illusions. In biological terms, these might be called, respectively, 'physiological' and 'cognitive'. In engineering terms they might be called 'mechanism' or 'strategy' errors: more precisely, as due to failure of mechanisms, or of strategy being carried out by the mechanism. It is important to extend our concepts, and our terminology, beyond biology if we are to understand illusion – especially strategy illusions. The reason for this is basic: if a strategy is misleading, we do not need to know the way in which it is being carried out to understand the reason for the error, or the illusion. (Thus, if I write nonsense at this point, it does not matter to you, gentle reader, whether I am writing it with a quill, a pencil, a ball-point or a typewriter. If I become convinced that I have written in error, I shall not blame my pen or my typewriter –

and I should not necessarily blame my brain or any part of my neural system or physiology: they may not be responsible for the error although all my actions are controlled by them.)

Here we may take an analogy. Suppose you are finding your way by car, with the aid of a map. Then you find you are lost. Some error has occurred — why has the error occurred? The car has not broken down, and you managed to control it without difficulty. The trouble could be: (a) you followed an incorrect route on the map; (b) the map was incorrect. Now there could be many reasons for missing your way on the map; but suppose the map is wrong. Suppose that *the road system has changed since the map was printed.* You are now dealing with the present according to a true record of the past, but the world has in the meantime changed. Now this kind of error is bound to occur when the world changes, if the present has to be dealt with in terms of stored information from the past. This is not a mechanical error, and it is inevitable whatever the mechanism employed to carry out the strategy, be it map, computer or brain. To understand the error, or illusion, we must know the strategy and discover why it was inappropriate in this situation. This approach, I believe, justifies the view that we can proceed to investigate perceptual illusions without waiting upon physiological knowledge of the mechanisms by which cognitive strategies are being carried out, by the brain and nervous system.

Having made this point, which will occupy most of our attention, let us now return briefly to mechanism errors due to malfunction of physiological systems.

Illusions due to 'mechanism' and 'calibration' errors

A 'mechanism' concept having immediate application to the sense organs is the notion of *transducers.* Transducers convert signals, represented with one kind of physical energy, into equivalent signals of a different physical kind. Thus a microphone is a transducer, converting air pressure changes into related voltage changes; photo-electric cells convert electromagnetic radiation (light or infra red) into electrical changes which may serve as signals. The neural system has many kinds of transducers apart from the ears and the retina's light-sensitive *rods* and *cones.* The skin, muscles and joints have many specialised transducers: for example, for *touch,* Merkel's corpuscles and Meissner's corpuscles; for *warmth,* Ruffini's endings; for *cold,* Krause's end bulbs; for *pressure,* Ruffini's endings; for *pain,* Free nerve endings. All of these, except for pain, readily adapt to

56

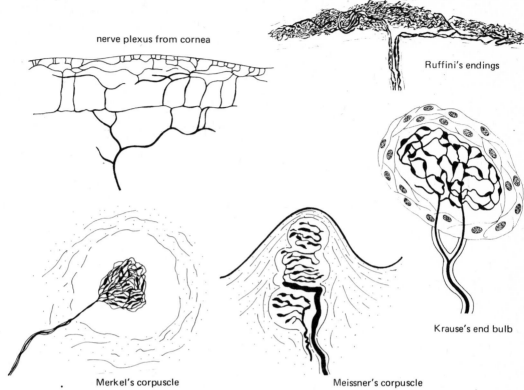

nerve plexus from cornea

Ruffini's endings

Krause's end bulb

Merkel's corpuscle

Meissner's corpuscle

Fig. 9 *Some of the receptors signalling touch, warmth and cold to the nervous system. These are 'transducers' – interfaces between the world and us.*

maintained stimuli. If changes of sensitivity are not corrected (by some higher level 'calibration correction') then adaptation, or other sensory changes, must produce related errors, or illusions. A familiar example is the dazzling brightness of sunlight after one has been in a darkened room: the eye's enhanced sensitivity, given by dark adaptation, gives an illusion of great brilliance. Conversely, the room will look too dark when the eye is light-adapted to the bright sunlight. In biology, or physiology, we would describe this as 'adaptation'. In engineering, or physics, it would be called 'loss of calibration'.

Consider for example a photographic exposure meter. If this is left open, with the sun shining on it, it may gradually lose its sensitivity so that a given reading on its scale will correspond to a brighter light than before. This would produce corresponding errors – so films would be over exposed if its readings were followed.

As is well known, all the senses become more-or-less *adapted* with continuous stimulation. Their calibration is upset, and if this goes uncorrected it will produce systematic errors – illusions. Where

Figs 10 and 11 opposite
These letters in fact lie on vertical and horizontal lines but look tilted. It is perhaps most likely that the orientation detectors are activated not by the individual tilted lines, and that their signals are not correctly summed to give the larger scale orientation of the figures. (In our terminology, this would be a 'mechanism' error.)

human judgment is especially important special means must be taken to avoid adaptive errors. In cheese making, where the consistency of the cheese is judged by hand, a 'standard rubber cheese' has been designed, to be kneaded every so often, to keep the hands in calibration.[3] Perhaps most sensitive to adaptive changes is colour vision; this is a very real problem in the paint and dye industries, and no doubt also for artists mixing pigments on their palettes.

Physicists and engineers apply corrections to compensate for calibration errors of their instruments. These may be called *calibration corrections*. (There is no comparable term in biology, so we are forced to use engineering terminology: but the concept exactly transfers.) In physics and in engineering, Master Instruments are kept isolated insofar as possible from environmental changes likely to affect them. They can then be used to check the day-to-day working instruments. There is considerable evidence that the various senses of organisms check each other, to give information for 'recalibration'. In general, the most reliable senses check and correct less reliable senses. Also, in situations where one sense is more reliable than another and they give incompatible data, the less reliable sensory data may be rejected. All this implies that the various mechanisms are operated according to strategies, by which data are selected, checked, compared and given weight according to circumstances.

A calibration (or scaling) correction may be applied not to an instrument, or a transducer, but to its readings. For example, if its readings are 10 per cent too high, then it is a simple matter to correct the calibration errors — providing the strategy is appropriate. If it is not appropriate, then the strategy will itself generate exactly comparable errors. So we see the two kinds of error — or sources of illusion. In practice they can very easily be confused.

In science calibration of instruments may take place by comparison with other 'standard' instruments; by comparison of readings with expected readings in a familiar situation, or from an hypothesis of what should be. Thus calibration can be 'upwards', from sensed inputs; 'sideways' by comparison with other instruments; or 'downwards' from hypotheses. Mistakes in any of these procedures will generate errors — and we shall find all three kinds of calibration errors generating associated illusions in perception.

We now have two concepts, which though easily confused are logically distinct. We have: (1) *State of sensory calibration* of sensory systems. This is readily affected by adaptation, and many illusions which follow intense sensory stimulation, (such as retinal after-images) fall into this class. The second, related but different concept

58

is: (2) *Perceptual calibration corrections*. There are many kinds of illusions which we could regard in this second way. For example, if distorting spectacles are worn, then after minutes or hours (or for some experiments several days or even months) the optical distortions given by the distorting prisms or lenses become gradually less apparent; and behaviour becomes normal, in spite of the continuing sensory-input distortions. So the perceptual system has developed fresh calibration constants, to correct for the distortion of the input. Now what happens when the optical distortion is removed? There are now *perceptual distortions, opposite to the former optical distortions*. So the *perceptual 'calibration corrections' now generate illusions* – because they are made inappropriate by the removal of the optical distortions they were correcting.

So we see the vital importance of strategies for deriving data from instruments – and from the sense organs. Whatever instruments or sense organs indicate, they cannot provide data until their readings, or signals, are calibrated against some standard; and interpreted in terms of likely hypotheses of what may be the case.

Illusions due to misplaced assumptions

All this, we shall go on to suggest, is important for understanding the classical visual distortion illusions. This kind of illusion, which perhaps can be understood only from strategy, and not from mechanism considerations, has its counterpart in the learning of all skills. Suppose we learn to play a game, such as tennis: and then take up another, in some ways similar, game, such as table tennis. The skill at tennis may in some ways help; but in other, and often quite specific ways, it can be a handicap. For example, the straight-arm manner of hitting a tennis ball is inappropriate for table tennis, where a bent arm and wrist-work give better results. So, if the straight arm of the tennis skill is transferred to table tennis, it is a handicap, described as 'negative transfer'.[10] It is equivalent to the generation of perceptual illusions by inappropriate strategies. These strategies may involve calibration corrections, or re-scalings of various kinds; but there are many other kinds of strategies which when inappropriate may generate illusions.

Consider a pair of objects which can be lifted by a single hand, one object being considerably *larger* than the other, though both objects have the *same scale weight*. When one is picked up after the other (or simultaneously, one with each hand) the *smaller* object will feel, and be judged to be, *heavier* than the *larger* object.[24,2] The illusion is up

Fig. 12 *The large and small tins are the same scale weight – but the large tin feels lighter. Further, if an empty tin is placed on top of the small one the two together feel lighter than the small tin alone. Evidently weight is not merely signalled by physiological transducers, but is also a matter of assumptions – that large objects are generally heavier than small ones. The assumption affects the experience – and can produce an illusion.*

59

to nearly 30 per cent increase (or decrease) in apparent weight. This illusion occurs provided there is any information of the sizes of the weights, generally given by looking at them. It is most simply explained by supposing that the muscles are set to lift the *probable* weight of the object, and of course large objects are generally heavier than small objects. So here a normally appropriate expectation has generated a powerful illusion — when the densities of the weights are unusual. This illusion is probably the clearest and simplest case of a *purely cognitive illusion*. The change in apparent weight is a function of the assumed mass of the object — and this is based on stored knowledge of previously sensed weights of objects. The illusion can be traced directly to the assumption that a large object will be heavier than a small one — which in this case happens to be wrong. The details of the physiology mediating weight judgment is irrelevant for understanding the basis of this illusion. There is an implication to this illusion which is seldom mentioned, namely: there must be more to the perception of even such 'elementary' sensations as weight than signals from passive transducers. Since expectation affects the felt weight (just as much, and as convincingly as adaptation) we must suppose that *prior knowledge of objects affects apparently primary sensations and perceptions*. It implies that perhaps all sensory inputs, or channels, are affected by the kind of object assumed to be sensed. So, to understand perception and illusion, we must know what assumptions are being held and whether they are appropriate. This is a far cry from a stimulus-response account — but it is necessary if we are to make progress, though the situation is complicated.

We may discover that someone suffers an illusion (say of size, shape or distance) by asking him to select (or adjust) a test object of the same size, shape or distance as that which may appear to him distorted. We then discover by measurement whether his judged-as-equal objects (or lines) are indeed the same. But of course we must ensure that these *test* objects are not themselves perceptually distorted — or our measurements will show nothing, or at any rate be misleading. It could be objected that all we can show is some kind of *behavioural* distortion. How do we know it is also *perceptual*? This is a tricky point and one often glossed over. The answer is, surely, that we can never be certain. When we regard perception as internal experience, we have to assume that the errors of performance, at matching or other tasks we set up to measure the illusion, correspond to the internal perceptual errors of illusion. We may receive word of mouth confirmation of his experience, of seeing or touching; but strictly we cannot be certain that it is his disturbed experiences which we are measuring; for our measures may be but indirectly related to his private perception.

It might be useful here to imagine a science fiction robot (with glass and metal eyes) being presented with illusion figures, and directed to estimate their lengths and so on, by pointing with its finger of steel. Do we have to believe that the robot *perceives* the figures or objects before it? Has it, hidden somewhere inside, an *experience* of the situation, which may be accurate or suffer illusion? This emphasises the problem that, strictly, we never know for each other, let alone for a robot . . . a primate . . . a dog . . . a butterfly . . . an amoeba . . . what they experience. Howard Hinton, in his chapter, discusses how animals, especially insects, can be misled; and how their susceptibility to illusion, and power to create illusion, is part of their biological armoury for survival. But just as for the imaginary robot we do not know what, if anything, they experience. Their experiences are for us hypothetical – and we may be wrong.

All we can do in this situation, I believe, is to regard perception in other people (or in animals) as a more-or-less reasonable postulate. We do not know how to prove it, and perhaps we each argue by a kind of analogy from ourselves. However, perhaps this postulation of other minds is not so different from postulating many other things not 'seen directly' in science: such as atoms, electrons, and forces alien to those we experience. The study of perception shows that nothing is seen as 'directly' as supposed in common sense. But it is not useful to say that 'all is illusion' – if only because perception (again like science) is predictive. 'All is illusion' destroys not the world, but the word 'illusion', which ceases to have meaning.

Perceptions regarded as hypotheses

It is possible that I am wrong that the wet-looking blue patch, apparently over there, is the sea; or even that this which I see and touch is indeed my desk. I might possibly be dreaming or drugged. This may be unlikely but it is possible; so my perceptions are not *certain*. Further, if the light is dim, or if there are confusing shadows, then I am quite likely to mistake even my own desk for another object or a shadow. This decrease in reliability of recognition proceeds gradually and continuously as sensory data are removed, or become unavailable. There seems to be no sudden break between *perceiving* an object and *guessing* an object. If all perceiving of objects requires some guessing, we may think of sensory stimulation as providing *data* for *hypotheses* concerning the state of the external

61

Fig. 13 *The tiles on this cafe wall are laid in straight lines, but they appear curved, and changing in curvature as the fixation of the eyes changes. The illusion is just as strong if one sees the cafe itself as it is when one looks at the photograph.*

world. The selected hypotheses, following this view, are perceptions.

By calling perceptions 'perceptual hypotheses' we are drawing an analogy between how the organism makes decisions, based on sensory data, and how science makes decisions and legislates about reality on its data. Thus, on this view, perception is no longer the unique case, closed to science — perception is similar to science itself. So we might use our knowledge of the methods of science to illuminate how we see. It may be that susceptibility to illusion is necessary for being creative, for if we were controlled directly by sensed events (and saw reality by direct intuition) we would surely be tyrannized by the here and now — imprisoned by what is. Artists, with their skill, somehow play upon our potentials for illusion, allowing us to see and invent new possibilities. Perhaps they are extending in us what we do routinely to see objects in the external world.

We can now investigate just how misplaced hypothesis-building and hypothesis-selecting strategies can generate errors in science: and — if our argument is correct — corresponding perceptual illusory phenomena. We shall proceed by taking literally the notion that perceptions are hypotheses. This allows us to compare the power to generate truth and error in science, with the power of perception to give appropriate behaviour and to generate illusions. Science, with all its dramatic successes has, from its beginning also generated wildly incorrect accounts: stars as pin-pricks in a crystal globe; electricity and heat as fluids; the brain as an organ to cool the blood; behaviour as controlled by stimulus-response arcs. These are dramatic deviations from what we now see as truth; and when invented they were deviations from what then appeared true. Science and perception, we may say, are both creative attempts to use current and stored data to account for the present and to predict at least the immediate future. This requires, in both cases, the power to escape reality: but it is ridiculous to suppose that leaps from what is, or what seems to be, can always be aimed at firmer ground. A leap into the dark may land upon a new world — or upon illusion.

Hypotheses in science, compared with the power and the illusions of perception

To start our enquiry, we shall summarize ways in which 'good' scientific hypotheses can give data power. Then we shall look at how inappropriate, or inadequate hypotheses can generate errors in science. This will lead us to compare scientific errors generated by 'bad' hypotheses with the phenomena of perceptual illusions. If it should turn out that there are clear parallels (as we suspect) between errors of science and illusions, then perhaps we shall already have made a step towards a useful philosophy of perception and illusion.

A. Scientific hypotheses when appropriate may:

1. Derive data, from signals and pointer readings of instruments.
Data are never given *directly* by instruments. Instruments must be used according to appropriate procedures. They must be checked and calibrated for their signals to have significance – to be data.

2. Derive facts from data.
Facts are never given *directly* by instrumental data. Assumptions and inference-procedures are required. Changes of 'paradigm' can change what is accepted as fact.

3. Generalize from data.
This makes prediction possible. The current view is that pre-classifications, or at least simple hypotheses, are necessary for data to be generalised into Laws. It is generalizations which give science power.

Prediction gives: (i) anticipation of (some) future states, events and objects; (ii) interpolation through gaps in data – so that events need only be samples; (iii) the power to control systems ballistically – to give control in 'real time' in spite of system delays; (iv) warning of new kinds of states, events and objects.

4. Link data and facts.
Neither data nor facts of the world can be said to have logical structure, until they are described by a theoretical account, such as a scientific hypothesis. At best, logical or mathematical relations may parallel facts – and then inference following logical relations may apply to the world, and be useful for prediction and control.

Without hypotheses we cannot assign causal relations from observed regularities. It is the logical structures of hypotheses which allow us to recognize the functions of parts of machines or organisms, and measure their efficiency.

5. Settle ambiguities.
Any set of data can be interpreted in many ways – can suggest many different hypotheses. There is always, potentially, ambiguity. To settle ambiguities science adopts criteria such as simplicity and elegance, as well as balancing probabilities based on data.

6. Resolve paradoxes.
Paradoxes (and also ambiguities) are characteristics of hypotheses, not of the world – which cannot be paradoxical or ambiguous. Paradoxes are seized upon as signs of logical error.

7. Create novelty.
Scientific novelty may be discovery or invention.

Now we may summarize some of the kinds of *error* which can be generated by inadequate, or inappropriate, scientific hypotheses:

B. Scientific hypotheses when inappropriate may:

1. Fail to derive — or distort — data, from signals and pointer readings of instruments.

False hypotheses (or inappropriate 'paradigms') suggest misleading assumptions, so that data are distorted or ignored. For example, incorrect calibration or scaling constants may be adopted.

2. Fail to derive — or distort — facts from data.

False hypothese (or inappropriate 'paradigms') suggest misleading assumptions so that facts are distorted or ignored: for example, clinical symptoms according to a current medical theory.

3. Derive misleading generalizations from data.

This must occur when situations change drastically — then the past cannot be a true guide to the present or the future. False hypotheses suggest inappropriate categories for generalizing data and fail to provide tests for Laws.

4. Mis-link data and facts.

Just because good hypotheses may give limited data great power, to predict and control, so bad hypotheses may generate serious errors with wide-ranging consequences. Without hypotheses, however, data have no power to predict or control through logical relations.

5. Generate ambiguities.

Data can never do more than *suggest* hypotheses. They restrict the range of acceptable alternatives, but a finite set of data can never rule out all possibilities. When remaining alternatives have roughly equal probability they may become rivals with no victor.

6. Generate paradoxes.

Paradoxes are characteristic of descriptions, or hypotheses — not of facts. They are violations of logical structure, not of the world.

7. Generate inappropriate novelty.

This may be (unintentional) science fiction. It may be dangerous, or it may be interesting and suggestive. Recognizing novelty as inappropriate is vitally important for testing the truth of hypotheses.

No doubt not every philosopher of science would agree with these in detail; but I hope that they will, at least, not be grossly misleading. We may now summarize in a similar way the most powerful features of perception — to be compared with 'good' scientific hypotheses. Then we may consider types of perceptual error — illusions — and compare these with errors generated by 'bad' hypotheses in science.

65

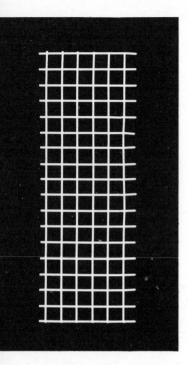

Figs 14 and 15 *Failure to see an object. This object is masked by a random 'noise' background opposite. The separation of objects from other objects and their backgrounds is a continual problem: it is the problem of establishing a valid hypothesis from data, some of which are irrelevant or confusing. This is a principal problem for science, as it is for perception.*

C. Perception when appropriate may:

1. *Process sensory signals as data.*
This must require 'calibration' and scaling procedures, of many kinds, before sensory signals can be used as data for perception.

2. *Infer objects from sensory data.*
We may see a gradual development through evolution from reflex behaviour (almost directly controlled by signals) to 'perceptual behaviour' from hypotheses indirectly related to sensory signals.

3. *Generalize from data.*
This is, essentially, learning. It makes prediction possible. Prediction starts with conditioned reflexes, (e.g. that food follows bell) leading to skills depending upon the *future* behaviour of objects. Perceptual prediction gives: (i) continuous behaviour through gaps in available data; (ii) anticipation of events, allowing skilled behaviour to have strictly zero reaction-time – in spite of the conduction delays of the nervous system; (iii) anticipation of unsensed properties of objects, such as the hardness of a table from a retinal image.

4. *Link data and facts.*
Although the centre of our argument is that perception is essentially inference from data – it must be confessed that we know hardly anything of the logical processes. How are these processes carried out by the brain's physiology? Are they related to linguistic structure? Are they formal, in a logical sense? Are they 'analogue' or 'digital'? Here we have few answers, but recent work in Machine Intelligence is suggestive. A large accessible 'data base' with linking rules of inference are vital for computer simulation of object recognition and behaviour.

5. *Use sensory data to settle ambiguities.*
Since any set of data is open to alternative interpretations there must be perceptual restraints on what is acceptable. These must be related to object characteristics.

6. *Use sensory data to resolve paradoxes.*
Although the world cannot be paradoxical (or ambiguous) perception can be – showing that it is a kind of description. Since paradoxes are violations of logical structure, perceptions must have logical structures.

7. *Generate appropriate novelty.*
Perception is continually faced with novel situations – so appropriate perception is a kind of creative novelty. This is perhaps the essence of intelligence, as well as perception.

Lastly, we shall consider perceptual phenomena – especially illusions of several kinds – as generated by inappropriate strategies.

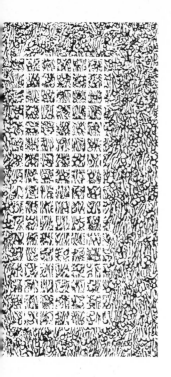

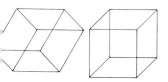

Fig. 16 *The perceptual hypothesis that it is a cube remains unchallenged — but there is ambiguity as to which way the cube is oriented. Viewed without a background, this figure shows shape changes with each reversal: whichever is the further face appears larger than the nearer — showing that scale can be set by the prevailing (orientation) hypothesis, and not only by depth-data.*

D. Perception when inappropriate may:

1. *Fail to process sensory signals as data.*

Errors of scaling (e.g. relating the size of retinal images to the size of objects) must generally give corresponding distortions of scale. Assumptions are always involved for scaling, and they may be inappropriate. Scaling may be by routine rule-following (a) 'upwards' from signals to data to hypotheses or (b) 'downwards' from the selected hypothesis to data and signals. Either of these should produce systematic perceptual distortions when inappropriate.

2. *Fail to infer objects from (sensory and stored) data.*

We see the ability to infer objects from data as developing gradually through evolution: data originally giving only reflex control of behaviour. The development of perception is seen essentially as the development of mechanisms and strategies for going beyond available data — by building and selecting perceptual hypotheses.

3. *Give misleading generalizations.*

This might happen through chance 'sampling errors', especially if small samples are accepted as adequate; through generalizations based on irrelevant features; or through systematic changes in the world. Generalizations can also be *applied* inappropriately, especially when they are inadequate guiding hypotheses, or 'paradigms'.

4. *Mis-link data and facts.*

This should be the fullest and most interesting of our categories of 'misplaced strategy' illusions; but alas — we know so little. Only when we know in detail the chains of perceptual inference, from data to object-hypotheses, can we state the mis-links in detail. We do however suggest that many distortions can be due to using assumptions about features usually related to distance, for setting apparent size (p. 74); while other misplaced assumptions can generate other paradoxes. We still have a great deal to learn.

5. *Fail to settle ambiguities.*

Selected hypotheses may be rivals on given data when their probabilities are nearly equal. This could happen even for optimal strategy hypothesis-selections (as for Necker cubes.) The more hypotheses which are put up for testing, the greater the potential ambiguity — so we may expect more illusions of ambiguity with advanced perception.

6. *Fail to resolve paradoxes.*

The presence of a paradox implies that there is some kind of description — for it must be a description, not reality, which is paradoxical. (This also applies to ambiguities.)

7. *Create inappropriate novelty.*

This might be described as fiction, or fantasy; but it may be suggestive — and may be art!

Fig. 17 *The Ames 'distorted' room. This is queer-shaped rather than distorted. It gives the same pattern to the eye as a normal rectangular room — and objects in it are scaled on the assumption that it is rectangular.*

Fig. 18 *The faces-in-the-fire effect. An unfamiliar shape can be almost infinitely ambiguous. Perception is unstable when no one hypothesis is selected. This may suggest a theory for the 'ink blot' personality test.*

Fig. 19 *Figure-ground reversal. Perception of 'figures' or 'objects' we regard as the selection of a hypothesis. There may be rivalry between hypotheses and there may be uncertainty as to what is a figure, or object, and what is background or 'noise'.*

Fig. 20 *A paradoxical figure. As a set of lines there is no problem. We try to construct a hypothetical object from the picture but here there is a selection of conflicting data.*

We find close parallels between the power of 'good' hypotheses in science and the power of perceptions to make effective use of limited data. Considering errors generated by 'bad', or inappropriate hypotheses — these, we find, parallel many perceptual illusions.

So we may summarize our position, by saying: *Perceptions are hypotheses: illusions are misplaced hypotheses*. Further, perceptual hypotheses may be misplaced, either because the (physiological) *mechanisms mediating the hypothesis-generating strategies are malfunctioning*; or because the (cognitive) *hypothesis-generating strategies are inappropriate*.

Before considering in more detail illusions as inappropriate hypotheses, we shall take a further look at the distinction between mechanism and strategy — physiology and cognition.

How deep is the distinction between mechanism and strategy?

Physiological mechanisms include the sense organs (transducers for converting stimuli from the object world into neural signals), the feature detectors (which we now know select specific features of sensory patterns such as line orientation, corners, intensity changes, movement and so on), and on to the vast elaboration of mechanisms which must store, generalise and classify data and perform the other logical operations evidently required for perception. We wish to describe these inference procedures in a language different from physiology, not for any metaphysical reason but because there is a deep distinction between *mechanism* and *strategy*. Possibly this distinction can sometimes be safely ignored, but in considering the origins of illusion it seems vitally important. To understand after-images, for example, the physiology is all-important; but to understand the size-weight illusion, what matters is the *assumption* that large objects are generally heavier than small ones. It is unimportant for our understanding of this illusion just how weight is signalled, or what mechanisms are involved in storing the assumption: it is the assumption itself, and the sometimes (false) inference drawn from it which gives us the clue and the explanation of the illusion.

We may distinguish between *mechanism illusions* and *strategy illusions* by considering whether or not illusion depends upon assumptions. If an illusion does not, we may classify it as an error of physiological mechanisms: if it does, as an error of cognitive assumptions.

It might be useful to distinguish between assumptions of the state

69

of the organism and assumptions of the state of the external world. The size-weight illusion demonstrates the power of object-assumptions. Are there corresponding illusions generated by false assumptions of the state of oneself? An example is Aristotle's illusion. Try crossing the first and second fingers of one hand. If the nose is rubbed gently with the now inner surfaces of the crossed fingers — which are normally their outer edges — one may experience, by touch, two noses! This is clearly due to an incorrect assumption about the positions of the fingers, and so the regions in contact with the nose. Phenomena of referred pain (where pains are located in places distance from the source of the trouble) may be related to this illusion.

fig. 21

We are arguing for a distinction between 'mechanism' illusions and hypothesis-generated 'strategy' illusions, in terms of a supposedly fundamental distinction between mechanisms and logical or strategy operations carried out by mechanisms. We must ask: How deep is this distinction?

Let us take an analogy beyond brains. Consider a fully automatic space vehicle, guiding itself to another planet. It is equipped with sensors, a computer, and means for correcting errors in its course. It has to detect errors as discrepancies from an ideal flight path; but it may not have in its computer a general and consistent account of the planetary system, or its universe. Now we may say with confidence that the course correction jets are *mechanisms*, controlled by the computer. We may also say that a computer is a mechanism, which handles programmes. The machine may suffer malfunctions, and the programmes may have errors which could make the machine give incorrect answers. But the programme is certainly represented with a mechanical system (for example, holes punched in paper tape) and this may go wrong in mechanical ways — the holes may become blocked, the paper may tear, or the tape reader may suffer mechanical failures.

Can the programme go wrong in a *non*-mechanical way? Suppose that, during the flight, an unpredicted comet came into the planetary system, and introduced forces which changed what should have been the ideal flight path. If the computer's model of the universe was not sufficiently general to compute the best path in these changed conditions, disaster might ensue. Some kind of special corrections would be needed, but they may be inadequate or inappropriate. But the resulting error could surely not be ascribed to mechanical error of the space ship — including its computer as part of the ship. Here it is the strategies available to the computer which have become

70

Fig. 21 *Aristotle's illusion. When the crossed fingers are rubbed gently along the nose – you may experience two noses.*

inadequate, or inappropriate, through a change in the situations they have to deal with.

Now suppose that the computer has a sufficient range of strategies to cope with the changed situation; but the sensors are not adequate for detecting the approaching comet which is disturbing the predicted situation. The computer would then continue to control the situation as though there were no comet. Resulting errors would not be due to the computer, but to the inadequacy of the sensors. This would be a straightforward mechanical inadequacy. Or would it? We have argued that stimulation of sense organs is not data, until it is scaled and interpreted according to possible hypotheses. Suppose, then, that the failure of the sensing system is not due to such mechanical limitations as lack of resolution or sensitivity, but rather that the sensed signals were not correctly interpreted, as originating from an object such as a comet? Would this be a mechanical error? Somehow strategies or programmes must be selected for object-recognition: but surely this selection must itself involve strategies. If so, these strategies can be inappropriate. We see this kind of object-recognition inappropriateness in the phenomenon of the hollow face appearing as a normal face: the face-recognising strategies are inappropriate to distinguish the one from the other. What is producing the trouble here is the very high prior probability attached to nose-like shapes being sticking-out objects. If this can happen for us for face recognition, it could happen also for comet recognition by our space ship. I do not see how this can be described as mechanical error – although the space ship and its computer are a mechanism. The point is that this mechanism (and presumably the brain also) is carrying out strategies. If the strategy generates errors we must know its mismatch with the problem to understand the origin of the illusion.

The language we use to describe logical or other operations carried out by machines, is different from a language appropriate to the functions of the machine by which it may carry out operations. It is this distinction, I am suggesting, which divides physiology (or more specifically, neurology) from cognition – and perhaps it justifies psychology as a separate science. It is this distinction which makes us argue that though some illusions have their sources in mechanical-malfunction, others are errors of strategy which may occur though the mechanisms are functioning perfectly.

Before developing this notion of strategy-generated illusions further, we shall look at some examples of illusions which can be attributed striaghtforwardly to 'mechanical' malfunction.

71

R.L. Gregory

Illusions of malfunctioning physiological mechanisms

Figs 22, 23, 24, 26, 28, 31 *Dots (or 'data points) are produced electronically, with a video system in which brief signals from a TV camera are allowed to reach a monitor screen (photographed) at random intervals. Each picture in the sequence shows a doubling of data points. How many data points are required to select the correct 'perceptual hypothesis'? How is this affected by the prior probability of the sampled object?*

Any mechanism can go wrong. But what does this mean? Roughly, it means that it is not carrying out operations with normal reliability or efficiency. A car which has gone wrong may have all manner of deficiencies; and the same is true for the nervous system as we know from all manner of clinical ills. Both for engineering and neural mechanisms, what shows up as symptoms of an underlying fault, or failure of mechanism, depends upon what the mechanism is called upon to do. For example, if the brakes of a car have failed, this will in no way upset performance and may go unnoticed, until there is some need to slow down or stop. Similarly, if the lights have fused, this may go entirely unnoticed until it becomes dark and they are switched on. So too for neurological, or physiological disorders, which may generate illusion. The illusion will only occur — malfunctioning will only show up — if it is playing a significant part in carrying out the necessary operations. (Thus reduced visual acuity will not matter for the headlines of a newspaper though it may limit the reading of small print.)

Physiological mechanisms may be permanently damaged, to produce more or less permanent illusions — though they will show up only in situations calling on these damaged mechanisms. An example is what happens when a lesion prevents the eyes being turned in a certain direction, say to the right. If a person with such a lesion tries to move his eyes to the right, his whole visual world will appear to swing round to the right: in the direction the eyes should have moved. The fault in the eye mechanism (a break in the nerve supply normally contracting extrinsic eye muscles to rotate the eyes) has generated a powerful illusion; which, incidentally is useful in letting us know a lot about why the visual world does not normally swing round when the eyes are moved.[5] This illusion, of course, will not appear until the attempt is made to move the eyes to the right. All illusions are generated only in certain conditions: these conditions may be critical, and so may seldom occur. Thus some illusions might occur with devastating unpredictable suddenness in unusual situations.

Considering now people without neurological disturbances (whether congenital, or due to damage or drugs) we might classify disturbances of neural mechanisms as generators of illusion into two further categories: *mechanism inadequacy*, and *mechanism inappropriateness*.

Any of these three kinds of mechanism-generated illusion can be

72

produced by *mechanism-adaptation.* In most cases this may be regarded as loss of calibration.

Examples of mechanism adaptation: after-images, of brightness or colour; after-effects of movement (the 'waterfall pheomenon'); warm objects feeling cold when the hand has been warmed, and *vice versa* (this can produce a paradox, the same water feeling both hot and cold at the same time); colour changes after looking at bright coloured light; position of the limbs or the apparent weight of objects after carrying a heavy load.

Examples of mechanism inadequacy: the autokinetic effect (small luminous sources apparently moving around in darkness – perhaps the basis of many flying trumpets in seances!) – due almost certainly to inadequacies in the eye movement system which normally allows the world to appear stable during eye movements; false location of sounds by ear when there is false visual information of location; unfamiliar objects being seen as the wrong size or shape through inadequate stereoscopic information, signalled by convergence or disparity.

Examples of mechanism inappropriateness: Phi movement (apparent movement across a gap between two alternately flashing lights) is probably normally useful in that interrupted moving images signal continuous movement; images are interrupted by retinal blood vessels, or by objects passing momentarily behind other objects, such as prey passing behind a tree. This generally useful tolerance to interruptions becomes inappropriate – to generate an illusion of movement – when lights flash with intervals between flashes which could correspond to the motion of an object crossing gaps. Tolerance to gaps generates the movement illusion.

Some distortion illusions may be due to inappropriate (or inappropriate corrections for) sensory adaptation. It is very difficult, however, to establish whether these are 'mechanism' or 'cognitive' errors. The theory of the classical distortion illusions which supposes that they are due to inhibitory effects of neighbouring stimulated cells, shifting the region of maximum activity, may be regarded as distortions produced by inappropriate side-effects of lateral inhibition. Again, it is surprisingly difficult to establish whether these illusions (the Müller-Lyer, Ponzo, Hering, Orbison, etc.) should be placed in this category – or whether they are due to mis-scaling following inappropriate cognitive assumptions, concerning the significance of converging lines. These theories are extremely different in kind, and yet many of their predicted phenomena are similar. This similarity may be accidental.

fig. 44; Ch. 4 figs. 9, 13

73

R.L. Gregory

Illusions of misplaced cognitive strategies

The central notion here is to consider cognitive illusions as formally equivalent to errors generated by misuse of data in science. We considered seven ways in which scientific hypotheses may be inadequate, or inappropriate — and found that perception has these same seven kinds of power and error. This, we argue, justifies the notion that *perceptions are hypotheses*: and that *illusions are failed hypotheses*. We shall now develop this, by taking each of the seven categories in turn, and trying to show how they can generate specific kinds of illusions through misplaced strategies.

1. *Illusions generated by inappropriate data-processing (scaling).*

We have argued that inappropriate assumptions and inappropriate strategies can distort data — to generate scientific errors and perceptual illusions. As we have seen, for signalled events to provide or to be accepted as data, there must be a calibrated detecting system. Generally, also, assumptions about the external world are required to interpret signals as data. This is a subtle matter, for these corrections may have to be modified according to the situation being investigated, or perceived. But of course this must be done on the basis of an *assumed* situation, and the assumptions may be wrong. Here we may return to the case of an astronomer estimating the distance of a star from its apparent brightness, when some of its light may be lost through intervening black nebulosity. An exactly related example for perception is driving in fog, when retinal signals normally related to distance are similarly modified — and it may be impossible to develop 'calibration corrections' in time to avoid disaster.

It so happens that the visual input is especially inadequate with respect to *object distance*. This inadequacy is most unfortunate, because *perceptual hypotheses generally cannot store information of distance*. This must be so, because distance is a contingent matter. Most objects can be at almost *any* distance — and so distance cannot be represented in stored hypotheses. But precise and unambiguous sensory data are only available for near objects, by the accommodation (focussing) of the lenses of the eyes and by the angle at which the eyes converge to meet objects. (Stereopsis, given by the differences of viewpoint of the retinal images to give retinal 'disparity', is not as direct as is often assumed; for disparity must be scaled, by signalled or assumed distance, if it is to give depth information.) The sizes and distances of further objects are extremely important; so we should not be surprised to find that indirect and subtle means are adopted for setting the scale — distance and size — of objects. In the case of pictures, indirect means are all that are available, for (excepting for stereoscopic pictures) they give the one-eyed view offered by distant objects in the normal three-dimension object world. In spite of this we generally see objects with remarkable fidelity in pictures — though with certain systematic distortions, which we should try to explain.

The 'Inappropriate Constancy Scaling' theory of distortion illusions. This theory has its roots in a nineteenth-century notion, due to Thiery (1896), that somehow perspective in pictures upsets apparent size, because distant objects look somewhat smaller than near objects. Thiery's account of apparent size 'following' apparent distance given by perspective will not do, however, for perspective convergence in pictures and illusion figures *increases* apparent size. The theory predicted exactly the wrong answer; but it was a start towards some kind of strategy-generated explanation of distortion.

For a long time it was assumed that apparent size must follow retinal size because each point of the retina was supposed to be linked, one-to-one, with corresponding cortical projection points. But against this, it was realized that an apparently distant after-image looks larger than the same after-image seen as close, 'projected' on a near screen or wall. (The nearly linear increase in the size of after-images with apparent distance is known as Emmert's Law.) Thus Mueler's anatomical point-to-point from retina to cortex argument had to be modified, to account for apparent distance affecting apparent size. The next step, due to Tausch (1954), was to suppose that size constancy was involved in the illusion situation.[27] If perspective features in illusion figures made some features more distant, then, by Constancy, they should be expanded — which they are. The trouble with this is that illusion figures can look perfectly flat and yet appear distorted.

The Inappropriate Constancy Scaling theory was suggested (by the author, exactly ten years ago) to overcome this difficulty.[6] (It is in fact the start of this whole approach to perception and illusion.) It supposes, in the first place, that size and shape constancy are the result of active scaling processes. (There was a long-standing muddle about apparent size and shape being somehow compromises between retinal images and reality: this is a hangover from the direct, or intuitionist, view of perception and is still to be found. In my view it is metaphysical and deeply confusing.) In the second place, it supposes that although size scaling can follow apparent distance

75

R.L. Gregory

Fig. 25 opposite *A normal view of a motorway, showing what the retina receives. If such marked depth cues as convergence give size scaling directly, generally to yield size constancy, then we should expect these features to generate scale distortions when presented on the flat surfaces of pictures or diagrams. This is the basic idea of the 'inappropriate constancy theory' of visual distortion illusions, and is responsible for the Ponzo illusion and the Müller-Lyer illusion – See Chap. 4, figs 9 and 13.*

even with no change in retinal image, it can also be set by *typical depth cues*, even when depth is not seen because it is countered by other information such as the texture of a picture plane. This scaling directly from depth cues was called 'primary', or 'depth-cue scaling'. Something like it is clearly essential if constancy is to be invoked for situations in which there is no apparent depth. This was originally described in the following passage which, since it is quite central, and the starting point of our enquiry, I shall quote:

Inappropriate constancy scaling would produce distortion of visual space, but why should this occur with the illusion figures which are in fact flat, and are generally seen as flat? It is generally assumed that constancy scaling depends simply on apparent distance (as Emmert's Law might suggest); but if we are to suppose that constancy scaling can operate for figures clearly lying on a flat surface, we must challenge this assumption, and suggest that visual features associated with distance can modify constancy scaling even when no depth is seen. If we are to suppose that the (distortion) illusions are due to misplaced constancy scaling, we must suppose that the scaling can be set directly by depth features of the figures, and scaling is not set simply as a function of apparent distance as is generaly thought to be the case.

If perspective or other size-scaling data are presented in situations when they are not in fact related to depth – or are related in atypical ways – then we must expect this strategy to generate corresponding scale distortions. Pictures and illusion figures having marked perspective features seem calculated to upset the system in just this way. Distortions *must* occur, if these features, when misleading, cannot be ignored, or rejected. Gradual rejection could give the decrement of these illusions which may occur with long experience of these figures. This idea of the setting of scale directly, by typical depth features, is an example of scaling 'upwards' from data. We have no awareness of these early stages of perception: but there is far more to perception than what we perceive!

It is apparent that scaling can also be 'downwards', from currently held perceptual hypotheses, changing with changes of hypothesis. Either 'upwards' or 'downwards' scaling should generate distortion illusions, when inappropriate. We may describe 'upwards' scaling as given by rule-following, (for example accepting the rule that converging lines should produce expansion to counter the shrinking of retinal images with increasing object distance). Scaling 'down-

wards' from hypotheses is not given by such rule-following — it is evidently given by 'scale constants' stored in certain object hypotheses.

(a) *Scaling 'Upwards' from sensory signals and data.*

It seems useful to think of scaling from typically depth-related features as scaling 'upwards', from sensory signals and data to the hypotheses — the perceptions. Finally, the selected perceptual hypothesis is scaled for sizes and distances. These will, however, be wrong — there will be distortions — when the scaling assumptions do not apply in a particular case. A dramatic example of this is perspective presented on the flat plane of a picture. There is however good evidence that this is not the whole strategy story of these distortion illusions; there seems also to be:

(b) *Scaling 'Downwards' from perceptual hypotheses.*

In science, data are often scaled according to the prevailing hypothesis — for example, the distance of stars from their apparent magnitude, following hypothetical assumptions — the data changing with hypothesis shifts. The same seems to be true for perception. Scaling can be 'downwards', from the prevailing perceptual hypothesis. Evidence for this comes from what happens when depth-ambiguous objects change apparent orientations, such as wire cubes whose faces apparently switch in depth. The apparently *further* face always looks the *larger* — although there is no change in sensory input (signals) with these shifts of perceptual hypotheses. The change is purely 'central', but yet it produces completely systematic size changes. This can even take place against stereoscopic information.[7]

These scaling changes, related to the prevailing hypothesis or perception, are not limited to changes of size or shape: the 'Gelb effect', of changes of brightness according to what is accepted as shadow may also be interpreted in this way. This is seen most clearly — and again there is no change in the retinal image or other sensory signals — in the curious illusion shown in Fig. 35. These are all, in our view, examples of 'secondary' or 'downward' scaling, modifying data according to features of reigning perceptual hypotheses, and changing with the hypothesis.

2. *Illusions generated by failure to derive object-hypothesis from patterns.*

The adjacent figure is one of a series of pictures of a single object, represented by half-tone dots (produced electronically by a random

78

The confounded eye

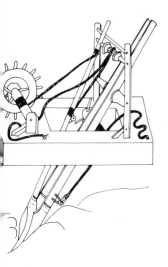

Fig. 27 *Scale distortion in a rectilinear drawing. The base of this medieval machine is drawn with its front and back edges exactly equal – but it appears distorted, the back edge looking too long. Normally the retinal image of its further edge would be smaller than its front – though we know, or assume, it to be rectangular. Viewed directly, this would not appear distorted and the front and back would appear much the same size, in spite of the geometrical shrinking with distance. This drawing is free of perspective – but the observer's brain applies what would normally be an appropriate correction for this shrinking, and as a result the drawing produces violent distortion. This has to be a strategy, or 'cognitive' illusion, for the distortion follows object-knowledge.*

sampling system) so that each dot provides information from the object – which is recognized when there are enough dots – 'data points' – to provide sufficient data for a plausible perceptual hypothesis to be selected. Now, if the object is improbable then more data points are required for its recognition. This is just what we should expect. It may be seen that before the 'correct' hypothesis (perception) is selected, several as-it-turns-out incorrect hypotheses (but also perceptions) are selected, often fleetingly. This is like the well-known 'faces-in-the-fire effect'; and also like the animals, parts of people and so on which we see in the Rorschach ink blots test. Very likely, many of the evocative effects of abstract, and only partially representational, paintings are related to this power of the visual system to select, in tentative form, hypotheses and features of hypotheses. This can give a wonderful richness of experience. Perhaps the artist plays upon submerged hypotheses – evoking them with subtle selection features – to make us see more than is before our eyes.

3. *Illusions generated by misleading laws.*

This is a very large class of illusions. The present can only be 'read', or 'described' in terms of the past: but as things change, generalizations (based on instances) are bound to become inappropriate. It is only very *general* hypotheses, describing *high-level invariances* which can remain appropriate through change. We do not suppose that perceptual hypotheses are of this 'high-level' type – they are the prerogative of science. Hence the importance attached to the most general possible laws, and the most fundamental possible hypotheses. But even these require the assumptions of a deep Uniformity of Nature: some features must be assumed constant. (For example, if the velocity of light has changed since the start of the universe, much of relativity theory, and Hubble's red-shift-expanding universe generalisation, would have to be revised. For related perceptual illusions, we may consider all cases where we assume, from the past, that something is the case when in fact it is no longer the case – hence old people's perception of things.)

An amusing example is, when driving a car: if one presses the accelerator pedal when inadvertently in neutral, the car may seem to *slow down* when it should have *accelerated*. Here, contrast with the expectation from the past has generated an illusion. A similar effect may be experienced on a 'moving staircase' which is in fact stationary – it can be quite difficult to walk up it, for one is 'geared'

79

R.L. Gregory

to its movement. Seeing an after-image as an object is a clear case of an actually queer sensory input being accepted as though it were normal, and accepted as signalling a non-existent object in space. If the eyes are moved, this illusory object *moves with the eyes*, in a most improbable manner. Once false generalizations are established, they can generate bizarre illusions, which may be obviously improbable — or even clearly impossible.

Many illusions in conjuring are probably of this kind: also in flying, or any skill where past regularities are assumed to apply but in fact are not appropriate to the present situation. These may not be due to limitations of the nervous system; they must occur in any conceivable system, biological or machine, forming decisions on data derived from the past.

In science, hypotheses are confirmed or refuted according to a complex web of interacting probabilities. A new observation, or a fact or hypothesis, can shift probabilities for acceptance or rejection in subtle ways, and with influence sometimes across vast distances of science's conceptual field. The traditional classifications of science into physics, chemistry, geophysics, physiology and so on may hide the long-ranging effects of discoveries and ideas.

Do we find that sensory data interact according to their conditional probabilities? Do we find that learned skills (or perhaps the structure of language) impose restraints on such interactions, perhaps similar to the effects of science's structure? These are large questions, which we can only touch upon here; but we must ask whether perceptual interactive effects should be considered in terms of physiological interactions — or whether they are related to probabilities of specific object situations.

The classical perceptual theory which has emphasized interactive phenomena is the Gestalt theory. The Gestalt interactions, and tendencies to preferred forms, were attributed to dynamic properties of supposed 'brain fields'. Cortical field effects were postulated to account for tendency to 'closure', to accept 'simple' perceptual forms, and to fill gaps across boundaries and intervals of time.[18] The Gestalt theory is thus what we would call a mechanism-type theory (though the Gestalt theorists would thoroughly dislike the word 'mechanism', as it would seem to them to imply a lack of the fluidity they are emphasizing). In our terms it is a mechanism-type explanation, because the restraints supposed to generate these perceptual phenomena are attributed to their notion of the physics of brain activity rather than to what the activity is representing. But we could argue that simple forms tend to be accepted for the same reason that simple hypotheses are selected in science — by the

80

principle of Occam's razor. If perceptual interactions are related to changes of probabilities, according to the changing evidence of data, then we could look at the 'Gestalt effects' in a quite different way.

On this way of looking at the matter to recognize a face, a building or a tree, is to assign probabilities to what the various parts may belong to, or be part of. Thus a circle may be the moon, the iris of an eye, the wheel of a car; or it may be part of a very large number of other objects. If the circle has texture or colour, or other features characteristic of some kinds of objects but not of others, then we should expect a preference for, say, the moon rather than an eye. If it is a small circle, then an eye-hypothesis may be favoured over, say, a car, wheel or moon hypothesis . . . and so on. We should also consider interacting probability relations between objects. For example, a circle low down, on what may be accepted as the ground, is more likely to be a wheel than an eye, or the moon. If the sun is shining, the moon hypothesis fades, but it could still be an eye or a wheel. Cartoonists clearly use conditional probabilities to allow us to 'recognise' a few squiggles as objects, within a context which makes them likely. (Thus a restaurant may be indicated by an ellipse to be accepted as a plate: and then the joke about the man with a fly in his soup, or whatever, is understood.) Magritte used our network of prior probabilities to great effect, by painting realistically but with extremely unlikely combinations of objects, sometimes with unlikely relative scales. A good example of this is Fig. 1. Such improbable juxtapositions have a disturbing and sometimes stimulating effect.

It is possible to make an object or a drawing appear as something else, by adding another object or part of an object to change the probability of the original — which may then appear quite different though its pattern of stimulation is unaltered. An example is the drawing of a tree in Fig. 29. Now look at Fig. 30. This is the same 'tree' drawing but it looks quite different. The added data — the 'cigarette' — transforms the 'tree'. When irrelevant, what is accepted as data may generate an illusory shift such as misidentification of objects. Although this seems to have been hardly at all considered by writers on human perception (because perceptions are not generally regarded as hypotheses?) conditional probabilities have been incorporated into an important computer program for object recognition.[11] It will, like us, come to wrong answers in atypical situations.

For an exactly parallel case in science, consider the data of the post holes found in the archaeological 'dig' for early huts, shown in Fig. 32. Here the data affect the probabilities of alternative hypotheses (round huts, square huts and so on) and the hypotheses affect

Fig. 29 *Just a tree?*

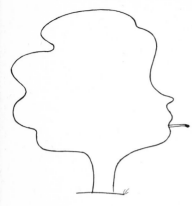

Fig. 30 *The same tree but with an addition which changes its probability of being simply a tree. Conditional probabilities seem not to have received sufficient attention in perceptual theory; but are, at least intuitively, appreciated by artists, and could be the source of many illusions. Conditional probabilities are involved in object recognition by computers and are of the first importance in relating data to hypotheses.*

what will be accepted as data. Some 'post holes' are rejected by both groups of archaeologists – we may assume because they do not fit any preferred hypotheses. This, in turn, is exactly paralleled by the perceptual experiment illustrated in the series of photographs starting with Fig. 22, showing electronically generated data points used for measuring the data required to elicit perceptual hypotheses. (This was developed by Robert Williams, working in the author's laboratory.)

All this seems to lie at the heart of perception, as it does of science. Conditional probabilities give data power; but this same power, it seems, can generate systematic and dramatic errors in science, and illusions in perception. The Gestalt writers pointed out important perceptual phenomena, but if we are right, their interpretations of these phenomena (including their laws of 'closure', 'good figure', 'common fate', and so on) are fundamentally wrong. They are not properties of brain fields: they are characteristics of perceptual hypotheses generally appropriate to objects.

4. *Illusions generated by mis-linking data and facts.*

There are perceptual inferences from what is probable – the size-weight illusion is an example. In unusual circumstances, this generates deviations from fact to give illusion. In pictures this is part of the power of line or shaded shape to represent objects.

There is now considerable evidence for 'preprocessing' procedures for deriving data from sensory signals, for these are perhaps never adequate to control behaviour or give perception directly. When these procedures are carried out, in some conditions they may even produce false links within data, and between data and facts even as basic as contours, often regarded as primary 'bricks' of perception. The linking is so complex that it is hard to find any basic bricks.

It is likely that many of the 'Gestalt Principles of organization' are symptoms of the way in which data are linked to form hypotheses. We may now look back at these demonstrations and see them in the light of a very different philosophy. We would no longer wish to say that analysis of perception is impossible; rather we seek adequate concepts and evidence of the structure of perception – of how data are linked – so that we can analyse it and its processes.

Perhaps we must wait upon developments in the science of Machine Intelligence (or 'Artificial' Intelligence) to gain deeper insight into the logic (valid and fallacious) of brain function. If so, machines will teach us humanity.

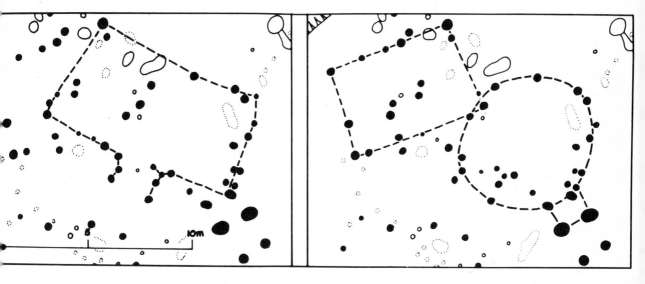

Fig. 32 *Archaeological post holes and hypotheses of huts. The black dots are holes found in an actual archaeological dig. Some may be post holes, others rabbit-holes or whatever. One group of archaeologists selects a set of the holes as post holes – data – and rejects others as irrelevant. They then join their data to form hypothetical early huts. Other archaeologists select some different holes as 'data', and form different hypothetical huts. Here we see the influence of hypotheses on what are accepted as data. This is a two way process – in science and in perception. This is a very different way of interpreting some of the Gestalt effects of perceptual dot grouping, and is central to our approach; for we regard perceptions essentially as hypotheses.*

5. *Illusions generated by ambiguity.*

Inadequate data produce what is often called 'perceptual ambiguity'[2][5] Since all data are open to many interpretations, the problem becomes: Why is perception ever *non*-ambiguous? Data which allow alternative hypotheses of roughly equal probability, generate *spontaneous switching of perceptions*. This is a particularly interesting *phenomenon of perception*, which brings out the importance of selection of hypotheses on the basis of their relative probabilities. Perception is, in this sense, a kind of betting.

The same sensory data may be in some situations ambiguous, in others not – for the general context can affect prior probabilities. It is quite easy to set up ambiguous dynamic situations, and these are especially interesting. For example, the objects viewed by shadow projection exhibit all manner of interesting effects, as redundant information (surface texture and so on) is removed by the shadow-projection technique. In the first place, *direction of rotation* is always ambiguous. Any figure seen as three-dimensional will spontaneously change its apparent direction of rotation (generally every few seconds) as the figure alternates in depth. Now, apart from this, what happens with *familiar* objects is quite different from what happens with *unfamiliar* objects – for which there can be no adequate available perceptual hypothesis. Suppose we start with a familiar object, say a wire cube. This is seen to rotate *as a rigid object*, the apparent lengths of the edges, and the angles of the corners, being maintained. If we remove parts of the cube, say one

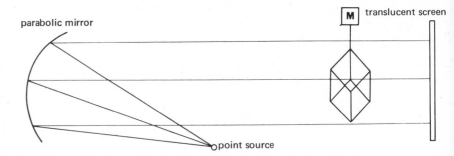

edge after another, then it gets more and more labile. For example, a pair of faces, joined by a single edge, will not remain parallel, but will frequently appear to rotate separately, or slide across each other in various ways. A single edge, at right angles to a single face, will swing round its corner where it is rigidly attached, as the face becomes normal to the observer: but this does *not* happen for the same edge of the complete, or nearly complete, cube. So this is not a matter merely of geometry; but rather of what assumptions are adopted for accepting sensory inputs as data for supporting, modifying or rejecting hypotheses.

These demonstrations reveal some of the 'unitary' assumptions which are accepted for building object-hypotheses, on limited data. We find for example that: (i) *parallelism is conserved*, while (ii) *right-angularity is not conserved*. This, however, takes us to a somewhat different issue — the logical structure and 'building blocks' of perceptual hypotheses — about which as yet we know very little. These dynamic ambiguities are highly suggestive for showing what data are necessary for establishing perceptual hypotheses of familiar objects (such as cubes); and for discovering the basic assumptions which are, (at least tentatively) accepted for building and selecting all perceptual hypotheses from visual data.[7]

Consider Fig. 34. This looks like a pair of faces, somewhat different from each other. Actually the right-hand picture is a photograph of a normal face; but the left-hand picture is not — this is the *hollow mould* of the right-hand face. The nose is *not* sticking out, as it appears to be: it is hollow, going inwards. This extremely powerful effect holds with any lighting, and against a great deal of countermanding sensory data — provided one hypothesis only is extremely likely. This is best demonstrated not with a photograph of, say, a hollow face; but with the hollow mould itself. It continues to appear as a normal face until closely approached, with both eyes giving full stereo depth information. When the observer then withdraws a little, it will suddenly return to appearing as a normal face — though he *knows* it is hollow. So we discover that intellectual knowledge of such perceptual situations does not always correct perceptual errors. In other words, perceptual hypothesis-making is not under intellectual control. If the perceptually depth-reversed face is rotated — or if the observer moves round it — the face apparently *rotates in the wrong direction*. Motion parallax is being interpreted according to the false hypothesis — to generate a dramatic illusion, which is improbable. So both the texture depth data from the hollow face, and the resulting illusion of motion, are inadequate as data to correct the hypothesis — against the extreme improbability of a face being hollow.

It is perhaps logically confusing to say that data are ambiguous. It is hypotheses which may be ambiguous, when data are insufficient to decide between alternative hypotheses. Whether available data will suffice depends upon the prior probabilities of alternative hypotheses in the running for selection. There are many interesting and important effects related to rivalry and spontaneous switching between alternative hypotheses. An example is shown in Fig. 35. These phenomena give a unique opportunity for establishing what is associated with perceptual hypotheses, and what with data (or 'cues')

Fig. 34 *A normal face* left *and a hollow replica or mould* right. *Both appear as normal faces. The probability of hollow faces is so low that it is almost impossible to see the mould correctly.*

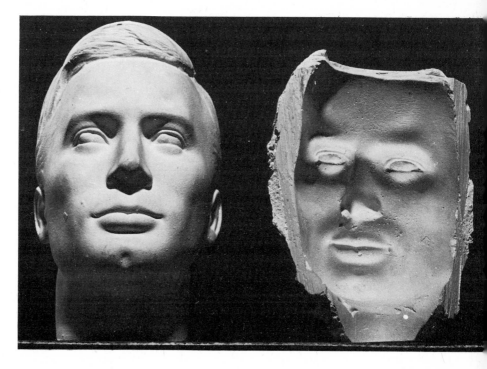

85

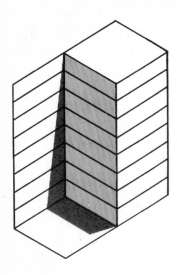

Fig. 35 *A dark region, or a shadow? This is a depth-reversing drawing of brick walls, with a 'shadow' painted on the wall. But it is only a plausible shadow for one orientation of the figure (for the sun is always above, shining down). To most observers of this figure, the grey region looks almost black when it could not be a shadow, and almost transparent and light when it could be a shadow cast by light from above. This changes with each depth-reversal of the figure — and so cannot be set by depth or any other sensory cues, for they are not changing. The 'shadow' is tied to one of the alternative perceptual hypotheses which are selected by this figure.*

monitored by the senses: for, with hypothesis-switching, the data remains the same, but perception changes — so any changes must be 'central' and attached to specific hypotheses. This reminds us of the archaeologists and their post holes. Hypotheses affect data, and data affect hypotheses. Spontaneous switching, or entertaining of alternative hypotheses, allows reappraisals to be made. This is the essentially dynamic quality of perception — and (at its best) of science.

6. *Illusions generated by paradox*

Here we have two classes of illusion: (*a*) Those produced when a selection of incompatible data is presented (as in 'impossible' pictures,[2][3] such as Fig. 36), and (*b*) those due to paradoxical selections made by the observer from a non-preselected situation (such as the 'impossible triangle object'[7] of Fig. 37). Preselection of data is the prerogative of the artist and the scientist — this is indeed what they have in common. The first form of paradoxical perception is far more common than the second — at least in our society where artists and scientists are so active!

(*a*) *As presented.* Paradoxes can be created by juxtaposing data in ways that would not normally — or could not — occur. Paradoxes can also be created by combining concepts (or words) in odd ways. For example, if I were to say 'There is a square circle', you might well assume that I had made a verbal mistake, that I did not know the language, or that I was using these words in an irresponsible or provocative way. Similarly, if a *picture* appears paradoxical, this could be due to the artist putting together incompatible depth cues or other features which could not occur for natural objects. The 'impossible triangle' figure, devised by Lionel and Roger Penrose, is probably the simplest and clearest example of such a visual paradox. The artist Maurice Escher has made extremely effective (if disturbing) use of these effects in his extraordinary graphic work. We assume that the object world cannot itself be paradoxical. So paradoxes are characteristic of *descriptions* —– including pictures and hypotheses — not of reality.

If we find that a scientific hypothesis is paradoxical, this is a sure sign that it must be reconsidered, and restructured, for it cannot be representing reality. But now consider a perceptually paradoxical object. An artist may combine incompatible features in a quixotic way, to create a paradox; but if it is an untampered *object* (not painted, viewed in normal lighting, and so on) which appears

86

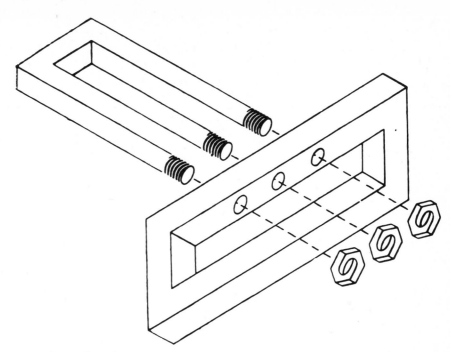

Fig. 36 *This is a simple line figure but appears extremely confusing. The confusion is cognitive. We are unable to form consistent hypotheses as to what objects these lines represent.*

Fig. 37 *Paradoxical object. This gives the same pattern or information to the eye as the Penrose impossible triangle (Fig. 20). This is however a photograph of an actual object – which itself appears just as odd! The 'solution' is seen in Fig. 38. The paradox is generated by a false assumption – that the three edges of the object lie on a plane. In fact they do not, as is clear from Fig. 38.*

paradoxical – then, though the *perception* may be paradoxical, the *object* cannot be paradoxical. This implies that we have selected a paradoxical hypothesis, for a *non*-paradoxical *object*. This is a matter not of a paradoxical *presentation* of data, but rather of producing an internal paradox from data freely selected from the world.

(b) *As selected.* The triangle object (shown as a photograph in Fig. 37) appears impossible. (For the full effects, and to avoid confusion, the object itself should be considered, rather than its picture.) From the critical viewing position, from where the two ends of the object optically join, it appears as an *impossible* triangle. It appears, in fact, the same as the impossible triangle *picture* of Fig. 20. It follows, then, that here we have a solution to the picture-paradox of Fig. 37 – but the solution is not discovered by the perceptual hypothesis system. Even stranger, once discovered, the valid solution is not available to the perceptual hypothesis-generator – for the perception remains paradoxical though intellectually we know a perfectly reasonable solution to the paradox.

By examining Figs. 37 and 38 carefully, we can spot why our perceptual hypothesis is paradoxical. We *assume*, incorrectly, that the two ends of the object lie at the same distance, and are in physical contact. In fact they lie at different distances, and are only *optically* in contact. Having accepted this single false assumption – which it is difficult or impossible to resist – we at once generate a paradoxical perception; for the other features, such as the perspec-

87

tives of the corners, are incompatible with the sides lying in a plane. What is happening is that a three-dimensional object is being 'described' perceptually with an hypothesis assuming it to be on a two-dimensional plane except for the corners, which receive three-dimensional treatment incompatible with the overall two-dimensional account. This generates the perceptual paradox which resists our intellectual understanding.

We should be puzzled to account for both (i) this perceptual acceptance of an obviously *improbable* hypothesis (it must be extremely improbable if it is, or appears, impossible!), and (ii) the selection of the *highly probable* 'face' hypothesis, rather than the correct hollow mould, against a great deal of sensory data (texture gradients, stereo disparity and so on) supporting the correct but unlikely mould against the probable but false face which is seen. (This situation itself may appear intellectually paradoxical!)

Consider again that hypotheses in science are built and selected by following rules of inference, from more or less unitary data and assumptions. Now once a false assumption is accepted, although it generates what may appear paradoxical, it may be difficult or at the time impossible to replace it with anything better. The same can occur if inappropriate kinds of inference, or sets of rules, for hypothesis-building are accepted. So surely we can understand why the face hypothesis is accepted because it is probable, though the impossible triangle hypothesis is accepted though it is clearly improbable. Normal rule-following from the typical face-like features of the mould (the outlines of the eyes, nose, mouth, etc., being very like those of a normal face) generates a face hypothesis; which is so probable, against *contenders* that countermanding data (from the texture gradients and so on) are rejected as insufficient to justify any other – including the true – hypothesis. Just this rejection of data occurs in science, in related cases, and usually this is justified, for all data are fallible and so should be challenged and sometimes rejected. This is another case of data being modified (or selected) *downwards* from hypotheses.

In the case of the impossible triangle a single false assumption – that the *optically* touching ends are *physically* touching, and so lie at the same distance – generates a perceptual hypothesis which is paradoxical. Evidently the perceptual hypothesis-generator does not have elaborate check procedures; so we are stuck with this paradox. We may go further and suppose that it is largely because perception is fairly crude in its hypothesis-generation that science, with its sophistication, has developed and proves so useful.

Fig. 38 *The truth of Fig. 37 is revealed! But although we now know the truth, we cannot see it. Fig. 37 still looks just as odd.*

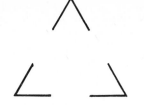

Fig. 39 *A triangle with gaps.*

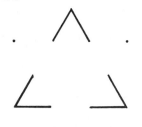

Fig. 40 *A faint illusory triangle may be visible, its corners touching the dots and covering the gaps.*

Figs 41 and 42 *The illusory triangle is stronger. A photographic negative of this figure gives a darker-than-dark illusory figure. Smaller angles to the sectors produce a concave figure below. We regard this illusion as due to a false fiction, postulated to account for the gaps.*

7. *Illusions generated by creativity.*

Perception is essentially the postulating of objects from strictly inadequate data. We may say, then, that behaviour is controlled from perceptual *postulates* rather than directly from sensory *data*. We have found that object-hypotheses can be ambiguous, distorted or paradoxical. They can also be false fictions.

As we have pointed out, there are many effects (such as 'faces-in-the-fire' and the Rorschach ink-blot test) where fleeting objects are 'seen' though not present. This, indeed, occurs in some degree whenever pictures represent objects – faces, ships or whatever – from marks on canvas or paper. This is essential for graphic art to be possible. It would be particularly interesting if apparently basic visual features – such as contours and brightness differences – could be generated. Can illusory 'data' be created simply by setting up sufficiently high probabilities that they *should* be present?

Consider Figs. 40, 41. The triangular shaped area of enhanced brightness, with sharp contours, is illusory. There are no such physical contours, or intensity differences. They do not seem to be generated by peripheral contrast effects (such as by lateral inhibition), and it is difficult to suppose that these contours are due to selection of striate feature detectors (by the inline edges of the sectors) for we get no such effects with, say, a simple broken triangle though there are lined-up features in this case. Also, we can generate curved illusory contours in this way, but it is unlikely that if there were curved line detectors, they would be selected by such out-of-line features. Earlier writers have suggested 'Gestalt closure' for these effects:[26,16] but even if this were accepted as a *modus operandi*, the generated figures can have poor Gestalt shapes[8] such as, indeed, the *concave* illusory triangle in Fig. 42.

It is important to note that object-recognition involves separating an object from its background. Now *absence of part of an expected background* is evidence of a *nearer masking object*. Could it be that these effects are due to postulating a nearer object – on the basis of the evidence of the gaps in the figures when these are improbable? An important implication is that *absence* of stimuli – when the absence is improbable – can be data for perception. This is indeed a formal objection to the classical stimulus-response paradigm. It is however a principal power of hypotheses. We also find[8,9] that distortion illusions, of full strength, can be generated across illusory areas, or contours. Is this a 'mechanism' or a 'strategy' situation? These phenomena could be crucial for deciding. This is an example of the

R.L. Gregory

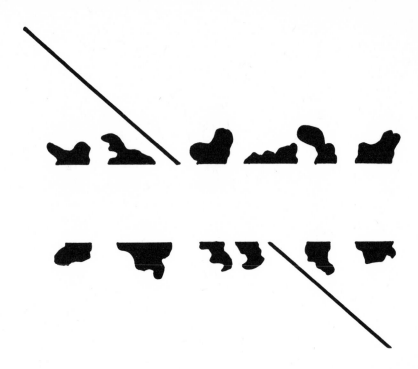

Fig. 43 *Distortion illusions can be produced across illusory contours. Unless it is established that these figures evoke neural mechanism exhibiting lateral inhibition (which seems at present unlikely) such a 'mechanism' theory is rejected by these effects; since they parallel distortion illusions with explicit contours. Stimulus contours are not necessary for any of these distortions.*

power of illusions as research tools at the edge of our present knowledge.

Perception, illusion and reality

If apparently basic visual features, such as contours, can be generated by perceptual hypotheses, we should accept with great caution the notion that peripheral physiological activity is closely related to perceptual phenomena, or to much behaviour. This is, (perhaps unfortunately) a consequence of the entire 'hypothesis' paradigm. But if this is true we must learn to live with it.

We have argued that perceptual hypotheses can – like the hypotheses of science – be uncertain, ambiguous, distorted, paradoxical and fictional in the sense of going beyond fact, sometimes to generate error. But we suppose that none of these can apply to physical reality. Facts are, or they are not. Facts, or physical events, cannot be uncertain, ambiguous, distorted or paradoxical: and they cannot go beyond themselves, to be fiction. We may speak loosely of a line being distorted or bent; but we mean by this that it differs from some other line, real or ideal. It is not facts, it is description, which can be distorted, ambiguous or paradoxical. This has several implications. In the first place, behaviour (leaving aside verbal

90

The confounded eye

Fig. 44 *This is a Hering
illusion without the usual
straight lines distorted by
radiating lines. Instead,
there are corresponding
gaps in the radiating lines
– which appear displaced
just as the explicit lines
appear bent in the usual
figure. This shows that a
lateral inhibition 'mechanism-type' theory will not
do, if explicit stimulation
of the retina with inter-
secting lines is necessary
for lateral inhibition.
These effects have not received sufficient attention
by theorists of illusion. It
is to be hoped that the
necessary neurophysio-
logical experiments will
soon be undertaken, to fill
conceptual gaps between
'mechanism' and 'strategy'
in perception.*

behaviour for the moment) is, like any other set of movements or interactions between objects, part of the normal world of object-facts. One's hand is an object just like any other object; and so it, or its movements, cannot be ambiguous or paradoxical. So, if we were to limit the notion of illusion to behaviour, we would have no reason to use these descriptions. But if we regard perception as some kind of internal account of the object world, then perception can be said to have these properties, when there is illusion. Consider similarly the physiology of the brain. The brain is an object in the same sense that hands are objects. Physiology is concerned with the physics of neural function. But we have just said that this cannot have these curious characteristics of illusions. So how, in any direct sense, can illusions – or indeed perception – be regarded in terms of physio-logical processes? This is where our notion of strategies or oper-ations, of more or less logical kinds, carried out by the physiological mechanisms, come in. If brains can describe states of affairs, or possible states of affairs, the 'descriptions' may be logically impos-sible, though the brain mechanisms are not.

We find a similar situation in language. I can say, 'There is a square circle', but I cannot make my hand move in such a way that it follows a square circle. My speech can be paradoxical, ambiguous and so on – but this is not so for mechanisms or non-symbolic behaviour. What I can experience in illusion states cannot always be carried out in behaviour. But in the symbolic behaviour of art we might communicate by shared internal illusion.

We know far less about the structure of perceptual than of scientific hypotheses. It would be rash to suppose that these hypotheses will be similar in their detailed structure, for science is certainly far more analytical than is perception. Probably we should only expect surface similarities; and these we have found. Science makes use of formal definitions, of laws and allowed operations of logic and calculation. Should we expect these – except as it were *operationally* – in the brain's hypotheses?

Science uses and operates with symbols – is this so also for brains? Perhaps in an important sense it is. Perhaps we should think of brain states as *representing* descriptions, operations, concepts and hypo-theses. If so – and this conclusion seems forced upon us – we are left with the totally unsolved problem: How do brain states represent? Here we need to – though unfortunately we do not – understand the relation between the physiology of brain states and their power to represent – could this be similar to the power of symbols?

91

R.L. Gregory

Fig. 45 *A new illusion. This striated rightangular parallelepiped object is made of the children's construction toy 'Leggo'. It appears to expand away from the observer — contrary to perspective. This is so for the actual model — try making it — as well as the photograph. Possibly the many crossed contours set size scaling appropriate to a longer object.*

Some of our illusion phenomena suggest something of how perceptual hypotheses are organised. The main clue comes from the ambiguous figures, such as Necker cubes. They show more than the important fact that scaling can take place downwards, from hypothesis to data. The fact that they spontaneously change — from one orientation to another, or to a different object — but with only a limited repertoire, for any given figure or object is what is so suggestive. It implies that not only must there be in operation the current or reigning hypothesis — which is the present perception — but also there are more or less ready-formed rival hypotheses, waiting to challenge and overthrow the reigning hypothesis. An overthrow may occur without new data or any external trigger — it may be a purely internal coup. These coups — these spontaneous perceptual changes — alternate between viable possibilities. The two orientations of the Necker cube are roughly equally probable for an object which is indeed a cube. But there are plenty of other-shaped objects it could be: indeed, strictly there is an infinity of alternative three-dimensional shaped objects for any given plane projection such as a retinal image. This means that the contending hypotheses are not arbitrarily chosen — they are always (or at least nearly always) plausible candidates, with high probabilities of being at least as appropriate as the reigning hypothesis. It is possible for contenders having somewhat lower probabilities to effect the coup and become for a time the reigning hypothesis.

Is it justified to regard these contending rival hypotheses as fully formed? I think that it is; for how else could they compete in the select company of challengers to the reigning hypothesis?

Does creation spring from sources of illusion?

Should we describe all fiction and fantasy as illusion? I think that there are good reasons for classifying fictions as different from the distortions, ambiguities, paradoxes and so on which we have considered so far. We regard illusions as systematic errors: but it is not correct to regard fiction as necessarily in error — though it may depart from *acknowledged* fact. Works of fiction, such as novels, are mainly true. They describe conversations and behaviour of beings, with the human number of heads and arms, in a broadly similar world, and with much the same fears and hopes experienced by ourselves and our friends. All this corresponds to 'facts about people'. In a novel, there may be a 'Mrs Jenkins living at No. 29, Greek Street': when as we discover, by calling, in fact a Mrs

93

R.L. Gregory   Blenkinsop lives there, and the house has three stories instead of two. But these are small errors when we consider how much (even in a science-fiction novel) corresponds with earthly fact. So evidently it is a mistake to equate 'fiction' with 'false', so we should not regard fiction in quite the same way as we regard illusion — though the *sources* of illusions and imaginative creation may be the same.

Illusions, we believe, can be produced by inference-procedures and rule-following generating systematic departures from fact. But it is important to note that divergence from accepted fact may not be error — it could turn out to be largely or even wholly true. Further, the generation of novelty requires deviation from what has been accepted. This is a necessary condition for inventing new solutions to old problems. To judge that a perception is illusory we must hold an hypothesis of what is in truth the case — but this hypothesis may always be in error. So what seems illusion may sometimes turn out to be truth. We can only be certain that a perception is illusory when it violates logical requirements for what can be fact: so we know that any perception which is ambiguous, or paradoxical, must be at least in part illusory. But this logical criterion applies only to *experience* of illusion, and not to actions of behaviour: for behaviour cannot be logically impossible, except when it is symbolic, as for language. (But then it is the symbols which are contradictory or ambiguous, not the means by which they are expressed.) All we can say with certainty of illusions which do not violate logic is that they are deviations from what is accepted as fact. So all we can do is to pit what we think we perceive against what we think we know: but either, or both, may be false. The more basic concept is deviation from what is accepted as fact. A deviation may be an illusion or it may be a discovery. Illusions, we believe, can be generated by inference-procedures and rule-following, which though they may build and select valid hypotheses can also generate departures from fact. But it is important to see that divergence from accepted fact need not produce error or illusion — it can generate discovery.

Any perception clinging totally to what was, must fail just so far as the present differs from the past it represented. This can only be avoided by continually inventing a fictional future — which must be partly novel and may be true — if illusions of perceptual inertia are to be avoided. In these perceptual processes we may see the sources of discovery and invention. Here, also, we may see the artist playing upon and evoking our powers to invent other worlds. The power of perception to deviate from accepted fact cannot be safe. It can leap to land upon the familiar, the unknown or spawn its own creations.

94

References

1 Adrian, C. (1928), *The Basis of Sensation*, London.
2 Charpentier, A. (1891), 'Analyse experimentale de quelques elements de la sensation de poids', *Arch. Physiol. norm. path. 3*, 122.
3 Coppen, F.M.V. (1941), 'The differential threshold for the subjective judgement of the plastic and plastic properties of soft bodies', *Brit. J. Psychol. 32*, 3, 231-247.
4 Gelb, A. (1929), *Handbook of Normal and Pathological Physiology 12*, 594.
5 Gregory, R.L. (1958), 'Eye movements and the stability of the visual world', *Nature, Lond. 182*, 1214.
6 Gregory, R.L. (1963), 'Distortion of visual space as inappropriate constancy scaling', *Nature, Lond. 119*, 678.
7 Gregory, R.L. (1970), *The Intelligent Eye*, London and New York.
8 Gregory, R.L. (1972), 'Cognitive contours', *Nature, Lond. 238*, 5358, 51.
9 Gregory, R.L. (1973), 'A look at biological and machine perception', in Michie, D., (ed.) *Machine Intelligence 7*, Edinburgh.
10 Grose, R.F. and Birney, R.C. (eds.) (1963), *Transfer of Learning*, New York.
11 Guzman, A. (1971), 'Analysis of curved line drawings using context and global information', in Meltzer, B. and Michie, D. (eds.) *Machine Intelligence 6*, Edinburgh.
12 Helmholtz, H. von (1867), *Handbook of Physiological Optics* (English translation ed. Southall, J.P., 1963, London and New York).
13 Hubel, D.H. & Wiesel, T.N., (1962), 'Receptive fields, binocular interaction and functional architecture in the cat's visual cortex', *J. Physiol. 160*, 106.
14 Ittelson, W.H. (1962), *The Ames Demonstrations in Perception*, Princeton.
15 Kanizsa, G. (1966), 'Margini quasi-percettivi in campi con stimulazioni omogenea', *Rivista di psicologia 49*, 7.
16 Kant, I. (1781), *Critique of Pure Reason*.
17 Koffka, K. (1935), *Principles of Gestalt Psychology*, New York.
18 Köhler, W. (1920), 'Physical Gestalten', Ellis, W.H. (1938), *Source Book of Gestalt Psychology*, London.
19 Köhler, W. (1940), *Dynamics of Psychology*, London and New York.
20 Kuhn, T.S. (1962) *The Structure of Scientific Revolutions*, Chicago.
21 Medawar, P.B. 1969, *Induction and Intuition in Scientific Thought*, London.
22 Necker, L.A. (1832), 'Observations on some remarkable phenomena seen in Switzerland; and an optical phenomenon which occurs when of a crystal or geometrical solid'. *Phil. Mag.* (3 ser). *1*, 329.
23 Penrose, L.S. & Penrose, R. (1958), 'Impossible objects: a special type of illusion', *Brit. J. Psychol. 49*, 31.
24 Ross, H.E. and Gregory, R.L. (1970), 'Weight illusions and weight discrimination: a revised hypothesis', *Quart. J. Exp. Psychol. 22*, 2, 318.
25 Rubin, S. (1915), *Synoplevede Figurer*, Copenhagen (Eng. tr. in Beardslee, D.C. and Westheimer, M. (eds.) (1958), *Readings in Perception*, Princeton).
26 Schumann, F. (1904), 'Einige Beobachtungen über die Zusammenfassung von Gesichtseindrücken zu Einheiten', *Psychol. Stud. 1*, 1.
27 Tausch, R. (1954), 'Optische Täuschungen als artifizieller Effekt des Gestaltungsprozesses von Grössen und Formenkonstanz in der natürlichen Raumwahrnehmung', *Psychol. Forsch. 24*, 299.

Fig. 1 *Chrysalis of the blue butterfly, Spalgis epius, of the Oriental Region mimicking the face of a rhesus monkey. (After Aitken)*

3 *Natural Deception*

H. E. Hinton

If an animal is seen, felt, smelt, or heard by another that can eat it or exploit it in some way, a basis already exists for the evolution of deception, and nearly all animals resort to deception for protection. Distasteful or poisonous animals often advertise their presence by bright colours, and they seem to be the only exceptions to the general rule: their problem is not to deceive but to represent themselves for what they are.

Strict neutrality does not exist in nature. Every characteristic of an animal is on balance either to its advantage or disadvantage. When the relations between an animal and its environment change so that some characteristic ceases to have a selective value, it is sooner or later lost. Even if it is not 'actively' selected against and it is in some ways biologically neutral, it nevertheless requires energy for its production and so is a disadvantage. It is because of this that it is not only possible but objectively correct to think that every characteristic now has a selective value or has had one in the recent past. Where there is a selective value there is a function, and it is therefore not naive to assume, with the proviso already noted, that every characteristic of a living plant or animal has a function although the nature of the function may continue to baffle us even after long and arduous experiment.

Deception is most readily appreciated by us when it concerns colour and shape. But behaviour may play a key role, and smell, taste, and sound are also often involved. Any region where animals are numerous provides a wide panorama of deception, ranging from resemblances so slight as to be scarcely noticeable to those so perfect that their very perfection provokes disbelief in the uninitiated. The origin of all these deceptions seems clear enough: geneticists have calculated that a chance resemblance so slight as to save the animal in only one out of about ten thousand encounters with predators will in the long run tend to be preserved and elaborated.

The structure and form of an animal are very often determined by

97

selective pressures that have nothing to do with deception. However, it appears that all colours of all animals that are normally visible to others are determined by either the requirements of deception or advertisement. This may be illustrated by a simple example. All insect pupae that are concealed in cells or cocoons are whitish or brownish, the difference in colour depending entirely upon the degree to which the cuticle is hardened by tanning. Melanins and compounds concerned with tanning the cuticle give it its brownish colour. No concealed pupae are camouflaged or have warning colours. On the other hand, all exposed pupae are either camouflaged in some way or have warning colours.[16] The exceptions to this rule are only apparent exceptions that strengthen it rather than invalidate it. For instance, the pupa of the magpie moth has bright warning colours and is enclosed in a cocoon. However, the meshwork of the cocoon is sufficiently open so that the pupa within can be seen without difficulty. Experiments show that the pupa is distasteful to many birds.

Most animals that are exposed to the view of their enemies have somehow to contrive not to be recognized. And most instances of deception involve modifications of colour, and sometimes also structure, that make animals unrecognizable although plainly in view. For instance, a large number of quite unrelated animals live on lichen-covered bark and they too resemble lichens on bark. The most common modification for deception is a colour that blends into the background. Sometimes local races of a species differ according to local differences in the colour of the background. In others, the colour changes with season so that seasonal changes in the colour of the surroundings are matched. Some, like the chameleon, are able to alter their colour immediately in response to the colours of different places. Species that are unable to alter their colour may choose to stay only in those places where they blend into the environment.

In very many animals concealment is effected chiefly by counter-shading so that the normal visual clues by means of which solid objects are recognized as such are lost. In some semi-transparent fish countershading may even extend to the internal organs. Many others are disruptively coloured: strongly contrasting colours break up continuity of surface and recognizable outline so that concealment is effective because the appearance of form is destroyed.

Examples of these and other methods of deception are illustrated in the section given below on special protective resemblances. Other examples may be found in Cott's[5] classic book on adaptive colouration.

98

Plate 8

Many animals have multiple defence systems but normally employ only one of them unless an attack is pressed home. A pet yellow-bellied toad I found in Bulgaria provides a good example of this sort of thing. When it is lying in a muddy patch in wait for its prey, the colour of its pimply back blends so well with the mud that it is hard to distinguish it. If I poke it gently it hollows its back and raises its front and hind feet so that the palms are uppermost. Each palm has bright yellow markings, a typical warning colour, but a true and not a false warning colour because the toad is a very poisonous animal. If it is further disturbed, it secretes a bitter, strongly smelling, poisonous fluid. Sometimes it also flips over onto its back exposing the extensive bright yellow marking of its belly. With such an array of defences one might expect the toad to be highly successful, which it is.

Mimicry and warning colours

It is usual to speak of a resemblance between two or more animals (or plants) that involves warning colours as mimicry. A resemblance that does not involve warning colours, such as that between some butterflies and leaves, is generally spoken of as a special protective resemblance. Two kinds of mimicry are often distinguished. Batesian mimicry is that in which a harmless and edible species resembles a harmful non-edible species sufficiently so that it is sometimes mistaken for it by a predator and so escapes. Müllerian mimicry occurs when two or more distasteful or harmful species resemble each other. Predators have to learn by experience which are the distasteful animals. When two or more distasteful species resemble each other, fewer of each are damaged or killed as the predators learn to leave them alone. We may therefore suppose that there is always some selective pressure for converting a Batesian type of mimicry into a Müllerian type.

Although it is customary and sometimes practically useful to distinguish between two kinds of mimicry, Batesian and Müllerian, it must be remembered that such categories necessarily involve the behaviour of third parties, the signal-receivers, towards the mimic and its model. As soon as we consider the signal-receivers, it becomes clear that the distinction between Batesian and Müllerian mimicry can only be made in respect to particular signal-receivers. This necessarily follows because, as anyone who has fed predators knows, their tastes differ very markedly: what is distasteful or otherwise objectionable to one will be much sought after by another. Thus

99

H.E. Hinton

what is good Batesian mimicry so far as one predator is concerned is Müllerian mimicry for another predator if the model and what we have supposed to be the mimic are both distasteful to it. What in the past have been described as Batesian mimics turn out to be Müllerian mimics in respect to some predators; and it may even be that none of the numerous recorded instances of so-called Batesian mimicry always belong solely to this category. We also have to remember that the feeding habits of the predators may differ greatly with season and the relative abundance of other food: when food is scarce they may eat the mimic that they left strictly alone when other food was abundant. In short, even with respect to a particular predator there may be a switch between Batesian and Müllerian types of mimicry according to season.

Sometimes much is made of the distinction between mimicry and crypsis (meaning concealment or camouflage). For instance, a caterpillar that looks like a dead twig is said to be cryptic, but there is no worthwhile distinction between this phenomenon and mimicry of a living poisonous animal: both models are rejected by predators, because for one reason or another they do not like to eat them. The argument may be pursued a little further. Counter-shading, disruptive colouration, and so on, enable the animal to blend into its background. Here again there appears to be no fundamental distinction between being coloured and shaped to resemble an individual object in the environment and being coloured and shaped to fade into the background. Of course the selective pressures that result in either camouflage or mimicry do not differ in principle. It seems necessary to say this because some professional biologists who do not cavil when faced with an example of camouflage will do so when confronted with an example of mimicry, even going so far as to claim that there is a difference in principle between the phenomena. Some might say that in both crypsis and mimicry the prey is seen but not distinguished by the predator from something inedible (dead twig) or from something distasteful (poisonous animal), whereas in camouflage the prey is not seen at all. However, a well-camouflaged animal is in fact seen but not distinguished from its background.

A distinction must be made between resemblances that have selective value and those that do not. A resemblance that has no selective value is fortuitous. Statements about mimicry that are later shown to have been based upon fortuitous resemblances do not affect the validity of the theory of mimicry.

Statements about mimicry or about warning colours are informative statements to which a literal meaning can be attributed because they are not consequent upon some definition. One might therefore expect that such statements can be falsified, or verified, or both. However, in actual practice such statements can never be falsified and can only be verified under some circumstances. The reason for this is as follows. Perhaps most biologists accept the Haldane-Fisher calculations to the effect that a character that confers a selective advantage of as little as 0.01 per cent will in the long run tend to be preserved and developed. For instance, Haldane has shown that a simple dominant with a selective advantage of only 0.1 per cent will establish itself in 50 per cent of the individuals of a population in 5,000 generations. Now, even if the first figure cited is too low by an order of magnitude, it is hardly likely that an experiment on the efficacy of mimicry or warning colours could be designed to have an error as low as 0.1 per cent. While it is not necessary to agree with the assumptions on which the calculations of Haldane have been made, nevertheless the general, and I think the correct, view is that a feature that in the long run confers only a very small degree of advantage in the struggle for existence will be preserved.

Oddly enough, many biologists who hold the view that a character will be preserved that affords protection one in ten thousand times will nevertheless proceed to carry out an experiment not designed to test a possibility within two orders of magnitude of the figure they accept in another, as it were, compartment of their mind. I am unaware of any experiments made on mimicry or warning colours that do not show a positive significance beyond the five per cent level. And there is good reason for this. In this subject the experimenter only chooses examples to test when he is reasonably convinced of the outcome on more general grounds. In short, people do not engage on experiments *in vacuo* but only to verify or falsify some preconceived notion, and it so happens that the selective advantage necessary to preserve a character is far too small to be tested by any means that in practice are available. In this connection it may be noted that among the most unshakeably held propositions are precisely those that in principle are not subject to verification or falsification by experiment, e.g. the proposition that man and fish once had a common ancestor.

Many readers will be familiar with some examples of mimicry such as that between the common drone fly (*Eristalis*) and the honeybee. Here one example will suffice to illustrate some general principles. *Danaus chrysippus* is one of the best known and most widely distributed butterflies. It evidently invaded Africa from the Oriental region: there are no species-groups of *Danaus* peculiar to Africa. The

Fig. 2 *The drone fly, Eristalis*

Fig. 3 *The honey bee, Apis*

great number of butterflies and moths that mimic it in Africa testify to an invasion of some antiquity. It was apparently a common insect in Egypt in the recent past, and seven butterflies that appear to be this species are represented in a Thebian fresco about 3,500 years old in the British Museum.

Its large size and reddish wings margined with black spotted with white make it very conspicuous. It is also poisonous. Its larva feeds on plants of the milkweed family. From these it obtains and stores heart poisons (cardiac glycosides), which are strong emetics for birds. These poisons from the plant persist in the pupa and adult. Because *Danaus* is a large, conspicuous, and poisonous butterfly we might expect it to have some mimics, but the number comes as a surprise: I know of 33 kinds of butterflies and moths that are either Batesian or Müllerian mimics in Africa and 5 in the Oriental Region. In the latter region, in contrast to Africa, many species of *Danaus* are available as models, and this is probably why there are so many fewer mimics of *chrysippus* in the Oriental Region.

The different kinds of milkweeds (Asclepiadaceae) vary greatly in the amount and kinds of cardenolides they have. Because of this, the poisonous quality of the adult butterfly depends upon the species of milkweed its larva ate. This has been elegantly shown by Brower[4] for American species of *Danaus* and related butterflies: some are ten times stronger emetics for bluejays than others, according to the species of milkweed eaten in the larval stage. Besides some butterflies, many beetles, bugs, and other kinds of insects obtain their poison from the plants on which they feed and store it with little or no alteration. On the other hand, there are a great many poisonous insects that synthesize their own specific poisons, as do ants, bees, and wasps.

Many have noted the fact that among animals birds have exceptionally long memories. Sometimes a single experience of a distasteful or poisonous insect will be remembered for most or all of their lives, particularly by members of the crow family. Some normally poisonous insects, such as those that obtain their poisonous and distasteful attributes from plants, can be made edible by feeding them on non-poisonous plants. Such insects of course retain their warning colours. By making bluejays hungry, it is sometimes possible to get them to feed on a monarch butterfly (*Danaus plexippus*) that has been made non-emetic by the method noted above. When this was done, the reaction of the bluejays was most significant. Instead of swallowing the now harmless butterflies rapidly, they would peck them and swallow the pieces gingerly, often regurgitating them

Fig. 4 *Mimicry. The poisonous Danaus chrysippus centre left - is mimicked by the female Hypolimnas misippus centre right. The subspecies of Danaus, dorippus bottom left is mimicked by the female of the sub-species of Hypolimnas bottom right. Hypolimnas misippus male top*

before finally swallowing them.[4] These and other experiments with animals clearly show that a species of insect rejected because it is in some way unpleasant is remembered much longer than is a species that had no unpleasant consequences after being eaten.

In Batesian mimicry the edible mimics are less numerous than their distasteful models, as first noted by Bates himself. The predators should learn as little of the mimics as possible. If they were to find a high proportion of mimics as compared with models, they would learn less quickly or not at all if edible mimics greatly outnumbered their distasteful models. Many mimics are polymorphic; that is, the same species has two or more colour forms. In some species the sexes of the mimic are alike and both are polymorphic. In others the sexes are unlike and one or more or even all forms of the female may be mimics. The advantages of polymorphism, especially for a Batesian mimic, are twofold. Firstly different forms are not tied to the same model but can mimic the most common and poisonous model of their particular area. Secondly, it enables the mimic to increase its total number of individuals and still remain relatively scarce in comparison with its models.

Mertensian mimicry is a term coined[43] to describe what is supposed to be a distinctive type of mimicry found among coral snakes with bright red, yellow, and black bands. It is claimed that some species are so poisonous that predators cannot learn to leave them alone because all that try to attack them are killed. It is therefore said that such species are protected against the attempts of predators to eat them because they mimic similarly coloured but less poisonous species. That is, the deadly species gain immunity by resembling less deadly species which the predators have learnt to leave alone. But this argument seems absurd because no snake is so poisonous that all animals bitten by it are killed. We must remember that predators often have both natural and acquired immunity against snake and other venoms. The mongoose, hedgehog, and pig all have a high degree of natural immunity to snake venoms: gram for gram the mongoose has about 50 or more times the natural immunity of a mouse for cobra venom, and my pet mongoose seems hardly disturbed when bittten by the common viper.

Intraspecific mimicry

Two different kinds of intraspecific mimicry may be distinguished: the signal-receivers may be members of the same species or they may belong to another species. The best known examples of signal-receivers that belong to the same species as the mimic are found among cichlid fishes and baboons.

The developing embryo of a fish extracts the oxygen it requires through the eggshell from the ambient water. It is therefore necessary to circulate the water around the eggs and avoid the formation of a thick diffusion boundary layer, particularly in those species that lay in ponds and lakes rather than in rivers. Many methods of circulating water around the eggs are used by fish. Among cichlid fish the primitive method of caring for the eggs appears to be to fan the water over eggs laid in some kind of nest. The fanning may be done by either sex or both. However, a great many cichlid fish are mouth-brooders. As the fish breathes, a current of water flows through the mouth so that not only are the eggs well-aerated but they are also protected from enemies. In the less specialised species, the male squirts semen over the eggs after they are laid. After a period that may be as long as several hours or even a day, the female sucks up the now fertilized eggs. Wickler[42] points out that in some African species of *Tilapia* the females suck up the eggs about ten minutes after spawning, whereas other species hardly wait as long as two minutes to do so. In such African species as *Haplochromis burtoni*, the eggs are sucked up by the female immediately she spawns and before the male has had time to fertilize them. In those species in which the female sucks up the unfertilized eggs, the male has spots on its anal fin that in size and colour closely resemble the eggs. The male waits until the female has collected her eggs and then turns on one side, releases its sperm into the water, and spreads its anal fin so that the egg-like spots are displayed. The

Fig. 5 a: a cichlid fish of the genus Haplochromis. b-e: anal fins of Haplochromis and related fishes. e: anal fin of Schubotzia, which is closely related to Haplochromis. We may suppose that when the interval between the time that the female laid eggs and picked them up became very short, a few of the eggs were sometimes not fertilized. It was at this stage in evolution that egg dummies first began to develop on the anal fins of the male. The female attempts to suck off the egg dummies and in doing so sucks up sperm that fertilizes the eggs in her mouth. (Figs. b-e after Wickler)

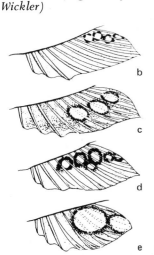

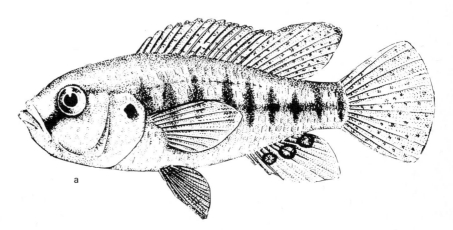

female tries to suck up the dummy eggs on the anal fin, and in so doing sucks up sperm that fertilize the eggs already in her mouth.

The females of many kinds of baboons have the ano-genital region swollen and brightly coloured, especially at oestrus. The female presents her backside with the tail up or to one side as an invitation to the male to mate. But this behaviour pattern is also regularly used to inhibit attack from other members of the group of either sex. And it is used as a kind of greeting to any higher ranking member of the group. The swelling and colouration of the backside of the female is particularly conspicuous in those species that have the most aggressive and quarrelsome males.

Now the males of many baboons have backsides that in form and colour closely resemble those of their females. Males with modified backsides are known only in those species in which the female has a modified backside. In the hamadryas baboons the backside of the male very closely resembles in both colour and form that of the female in oestrus. The functional significance of this mimicry by the male of the backside of the female becomes evident when the behaviour of the males is examined. The males never make use of their backside swellings as an aid to mating. Instead, they employ their backsides just as females do when they wish to inhibit aggression by another individual: males present their backsides to males higher in the peck-order of the group, and they will also present their backsides to females that rank higher than themselves.

A very unusual instance of intraspecific mimicry where the signal-receivers are members of other species is found among some psephenid water beetles.[17] Their larvae are often called water pennies. Fish occasionally feed upon them, but it seems they have difficulty in detaching them from the stones and so usually do not bother to do so. The pupae are glued to stones beneath the surface of the water. The species of *Eubrianax* retain all but the last three segments of the larval cuticle. The shed segments of the larval cuticle are replaced by hard pupal structures which from a dorsal view so closely mimic the missing parts of the larval cuticle that the latter appears to be complete. Thus, from a dorsal view a fairly close examination is required to distinguish the pupa from the larva. In the species of *Psephenoides* the mimicry of the larva by the pupa is further developed: the larval cuticle is entirely shed and the whole dorsal surface of the pupa resembles the larva (Figs. 6 and 7). The resemblance to the unusually modified eighth and ninth abdominal segments of the larva is achieved not by a comparable modification of structure but only by a colour pattern. The selective value of this

106

mimicry seems to be that fish confuse the pupae with the larvae and so sometimes or often leave them alone. However, if the pupae are also difficult to detach, fish only have to remember one pattern instead of two, and so each stage of the insect reinforces the protection achieved by the other.

Special protective resemblance

In an earlier but not distant age examples of the protective colours and shapes of animals testified to the wisdom of the Creator and revealed to simple piety the immediate finger of God. Since the middle of the nineteenth century both the same examples and very many new ones have been used to buttress the theory of natural selection. The growth of experimental biology, especially after the first quarter of this century, led to the gradual replacement of biologists with wide field interests by a new class of professionals who were laboratory men more interested in the exploitation of the new technology than in the relation of the whole organism to its environment. The enormous growth and sophistication of instruments for testing and analysis, developed to a large extent by chemists and physicists, enabled the new biologist to ask questions which he had never seriously done so long as the means for their solution were not available.

During the last decade or so interest has markedly revived in the relations of whole organisms to their environment and how they survive natural hazards, a revival of interest no doubt stimulated by increasing awareness of diminishing natural resources and the

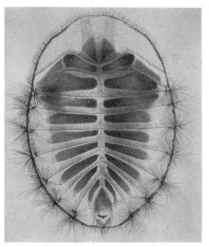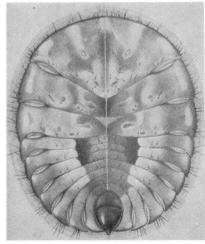

Figs 6 and 7 *pupa of the water beetle, Psephenoides gahani mimicking its larva*

H.E. Hinton   problems created by pollution. But now experimental methods are used to test hypotheses produced in an earlier age largely by inductive reasoning.

The gradual replacement of the naturalist by the professional in positions of power and influence in the field of biology, and the consequent neglect of problems that had previously held attention, seemed by some to require justification. And it is not surprising that this often took the form of virulent attacks upon the credulity and intelligence of the adherents of what was considered to be one of the most extravagant theories of the old-fashioned biologists. In his justly famous book *On Growth and Form* D'Arcy Thompson[38] has this to say of the theory of protective colouration:

> Only for a moment let us glance at a few instances by which the modern teleologist accounts for this or that manifestation of colour, and is led on and on to beliefs and doctrines to which it becomes more and more difficult to subscribe.
>
> Some dangerous and malignant animals are said (in sober earnest) to wear a perpetual war-paint, in order to 'remind their enemies that they had better leave them alone'. The wasp and the hornet, in gallant black and gold, are terrible as an army with banners; and the Gila Monster (the poison lizard of the Arizona desert) is splashed with scarlet – its dread and black complexion stained with heraldry more dismal. But the wasp-like livery of the noisy, idle hover-flies and drone-flies is but stage armour, and in their tinsel suits the little counterfeit cowardly knaves mimic the fighting crew.
>
> The jewelled splendour of the peacock and the humming-bird, and the less effulgent glory of the lyre-bird and the Argus pheasant, are ascribed to the unquestioned prevalence of vanity in the one sex and wantonness in the other.
>
> The ptarmigan and the snowy owl, the arctic fox and the polar bear, are white among the snows; but go he north or go he south, the raven (like the jackdaw) is boldly and impudently black.
>
> ... And a flock of flamingoes, wearing on rosy breast and crimson wings a garment of invisibility, fades away into the sky at dawn or sunset like a cloud incarnadine.

This kind of argument sounds formidable and is sometimes convincing to zoologists who have made no close study of animals in their natural environment but are more interested in exploiting the capacities of new gadgets than in animals. A widely practised

108

technique of vilification is that which seeks to include what is to be vilified in a category of events already discredited in order to avoid the difficulty of dealing faithfully with the argument. Teleological argument is discredited: if the theory of protective colouration be described as teleological the unwary may think there is no need to look further into the matter and so the gratuitous nature of the classification may escape their notice.

Another example of illegitimate argument is to lump dissimilar cases together under the pretension that the same evidence applies to each. That Thompson does just this is evident when he asks why if other animals are white in the arctic the raven should be black and successful. But each animal has its own special relations with the outside world. The raven is an omnivorous scavenger with few or no enemies in the arctic and thus no selective pressure is exercised against its black colour as is against any other colour but white in the ptarmigan and, for different reasons, in the arctic fox, polar bear, and snowy owl. His argument could be used to maintain that the poison glands of snakes are of no value to them because non-poisonous snakes are also successful.

Great theories like great causes attract extravagant enthusiasts. An unscrupulous attack upon a theory may usually be recognized for what it is by a feature that is common to nearly all such attacks: the central theme of the theory and the chief evidence is ignored but instead the extravagancies of already discredited adherents are demolished with gusto. This kind of intellectual sleight of hand, and it is no more than this, is glaringly evident in his passage relating to the colour of flamingoes, which is from the justly discredited work of Thayer. Thompson feels called upon to cite some field naturalists in support of his argument — not Darwin, Müller, Bates, Wallace, nor any of the great nineteenth- or twentieth-century naturalists, but Theodore Roosevelt!

It is particularly interesting to note that as the instances of mimicry and other kinds of protective resemblance are subjected to rigorous experiment, the interpretations of the earlier naturalists are by and large found to be correct. The reason for this is simple. Briefly, it is that the knowledge of structure and function of the meanest and most ignorant of biologists vastly exceeds that of animal predators. The visual spectrum of man and the chief vertebrate predators — lizards and birds — is similar. Thus, when an animal with some kind of protective resemblance is seen from near enough so that the question of visual acuity is not involved, it seems reasonable enough to believe that anything that will deceive the naturalist will

109

also deceive a lizard or bird. For instance, I have studied insects for some forty years, and I am of the unshakeable opinion that if a beetle can deceive me into thinking that it is a wasp it will certainly also deceive a lizard or bird.

It should be possible to predict the kinds of models most often involved in special protective resemblances. The models should be inedible, or dangerous, or both to the predators. Furthermore, objects that are to serve as models for many different kinds of animals should be both numerous and widely distributed. It seems reasonably certain that leaves, sticks, and twigs provide the largest number: they are very common in most environments and they are inedible to most predators. It might be expected that stones would be common models, but they are rarely used as such for a number of reasons. Most important is their absolute immobility as compared with leaves and twigs, which makes it especially hazardous for an animal resembling a stone to move at all. A further disadvantage is that stones in one locality often appear very different from those in nearby localities, whereas leaves and twigs are much the same anywhere. A still further disadvantage is that the colour and reflectivity of stones often changes greatly, as compared with leaves and twigs, when they are wetted by rain.

Of all the features shared by vertebrates the least dissimilar one is the eye, and among natural objects the inherent conspicuousness of the vertebrate eye is unusual. It thus follows that the eye is the most common and widely distributed feature of vertebrates available as a model for a small animal like an insect. The vertebrate eye has the further advantage that it is very small as compared to the rest of the body and so the discrepancy in size between the eye-spot of an insect and the eye of a vertebrate is small.

There is another great advantage in a vertebrate eye as a model. For the reason already noted, the large eye-spot on a small animal like an insect suggests to the predator that a much larger animal is looking at it. Also the mere act of being peered at by an unknown animal often induces an avoidance reaction. Everybody knows that to be peered at is disturbing. Little is known of the relation of eye-spots of, say, insects and vertebrates. It would seem that what is normally used as a model is a generalised vertebrate eye, and almost always one with a round pupil. If the eye is a particularly alarming feature, it might be expected that in vertebrates themselves the eye would tend to be concealed. And this is indeed the case. Concealment of the eyes in vertebrates is effected in many different ways. The iris may be cryptically coloured and resemble the general pattern of the head, a camouflage that sometimes extends to the membrane investing the eye. More often a pattern is used to mask the eye so that it appears to be part of the pattern that surrounds it. For instance, many frogs have a black lateral stripe on the head that includes most or all of the eye. Such stripes are very common in fishes and snakes. Occasionally the stripe that masks the eye may be vertical, as in some fish. Although the most perfect examples of patterns that obliterate the eye tend to be found among lidless animals like fish and snakes, numerous examples of eye obliteration by disruptive patterns occur among birds and mammals. Disruptive patterns that obliterate the eye even occur in a few insects such as grasshoppers.

It has been convincingly shown by experiments that birds are in fact alarmed and draw back when suddenly confronted with the eye-spot of an insect. For instance, Blest[2] found that yellow-hammers and other birds were greatly alarmed when a peacock butterfly opened its wings and suddenly displayed its eye-spots. By using dummies he was able to discover the kind of eye-spots that most alarmed his birds.

We may briefly allude to other advantages of eye-spots. When they do not confer immunity, the attack of the predator tends to be directed towards them. Many animals, especially insects, have eye-spots far from the delicate and essential parts of the body. The result of this is that a sudden and unavoidable bite from a predator is likely to be on a part of the body that can be readily sacrificed, such as a piece of the hindwing of a butterfly or moth. Sometimes the eye-spot is only part of a dummy head at the hind end of the body, a head that if it fails to prevent the predator from attacking at least directs the attack to a non-critical part of the body and may also confuse the predator as to the direction of movement of its prey.

Fig. 8 *A blue butterfly, Pseudolycaena marsyas, of South America, with a false head. (After Hingston)*

Of the common poisonous animals I suppose that apart from snakes none are so widely feared and excite as much aversion among humans as spiders. But this fear of spiders is an irrational one, a phobia called arachnophobia. Although all spiders without exception are poisonous, only about a dozen species in all the world are sufficiently so to harm large animals. Our irrational fear of spiders is seen for what it is as soon as we consider them as models for other small animals: I know of not a single certain instance of another animal mimicking a spider! The fact is that spiders are juicy morsels for very many lizards, birds, and other predators. As a consequence of this, spiders provide very many examples of camouflage and special protective resemblances. For instance, no ant mimics a spider

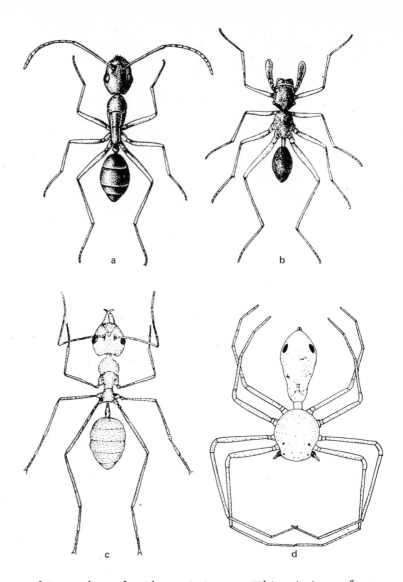

Fig. 9 *Spiders mimicking ants. a: Camponotus compressus and its mimic (b), a species of Myrmarachne. c: Oecophylla smaragdina and its mimic (d) Amyciaea forticeps. (After Berland)*

fig. 9

fig. 10

but a fair number of spiders mimic ants. This mimicry of ants may involve little more than behaviour: the spider runs about like an ant and deceives us into thinking it is one. But when we catch it and hold it still we find there is little resemblance between the two. On the other hand, some spiders are much modified to look like ants. In some the front looks like the front of the ant, whereas in others the back looks like the front of the ant.

Sometimes the mimicry is achieved not by a modification of the body of the spider but because the spider runs about carrying a dead ant on its back just as one often sees ants carry dead ants. What is here mimicked is an ant carrying a dead ant. Some of the spiders

112

prey on the ants they mimic. Some writers refer to this as aggressive mimicry. This particular kind of mimicry probably does not assist the spiders in catching ants. In those instances I have observed I became convinced the mimicry was directed against casual predators that would leave the ants alone. Sometimes the term aggressive mimicry is used for instance where there is mimicry of the food of the prey. Several kinds of fish and a turtle, *Macroclemmys temmincki*, have a dummy prey. The tip of the tongue of the turtle has two red-spotted appendages that resemble worms and can be twitched by muscular contractions. The turtle lies with its mouth open and snaps up any fish that attempt to gobble up the worms. Catfish, angler fish, bat fish, and others have dummy worms which lure their prey to them. Nothing seems to be gained by speaking of such instances as aggressive mimicry.

Resemblance to droppings of other animals

Droppings of caterpillars, birds, and lizards are very common objects in nature, and it should occasion no surprise that a fairly large number of small animals like spiders and insects mimic them. I have already said that the chief attribute of stones that restricts their use as models is their absolute immobility. Droppings are also immobile, but with the important difference that their mimics are on leaves and branches which themselves move in the breeze.

The dropping mimicked may be small or large, fresh or dry, or more or less intact or splashed as if fallen from a great height. The latter are often mimicked by geometriid and depranid moths. Clearly, only a moth that sits with its wings open is likely to mimic a bird dropping that has splashed. Nearly all mimics of bird droppings are broadly elliptical in section. Moths that mimic cylindrical bird droppings achieve the effect by wrapping their wings like a cloak around their bodies, and of course by having the appropriate colour.

The size of the excreta plays a very important part in its selection as a model. For instance, we would hardly expect very small beetles to resemble bird droppings which are always much larger than themselves, and they do not do so. Instead, they resemble small droppings like those of caterpillars. In most parts of the world, and especially in north temperate regions, the size of bird droppings is right for most kinds of caterpillars, at least while they are young. However, many caterpillars are an inch and a half to three inches or more when full grown. Bird droppings that size are very uncommon on leaves. The problem of growing beyond a reasonable size for a

Fig. 10 *A spider carrying a dead ant and mimicking an ant carrying another ant. (After Hingston)*

113

bird dropping is solved in a very remarkable manner. During its first few instars while it is still relatively small it may mimic a bird dropping, but in the penultimate or last instar it appears in a totally new garb. It may now have bright warning colours. Even its habits undergo a drastic change. It no longer rests during the day exposed on the upper surface of a leaf as a bird dropping would be but rests on a stem or twig or on the undersurface of a leaf. Different kinds of caterpillars vary as to the instar in which an obligatory switch away from a resemblance to a bird dropping is made. In some it is the second or third instar, but in many species of swallow-tails (*Papilio*) it is the last (fifth) instar that is different. Sometimes the switch is to warning colours, as in the caterpillar of the alder moth, or it may be to camouflage colours, as in some species of *Papilio*. Obligatory switches in behaviour and structure during development are common in other insects besides caterpillars. Such changes in a mantid (see fig. 11) have recently been described in some detail.[1]

A number of leaf beetles of the genus *Chlamys* in Central and South America so closely resemble the droppings of caterpillars that one has to squeeze them to tell the difference. A few of those I found are listed by Cott[5] (p. 331). In 1971 I was in a forest in Venezuela and saw what I at first took to be a caterpillar dropping near the base of a leaf in a position where it might well have rolled. I was instantly reminded of experiences with *Chlamys* in Mexico thirty-seven years before, and I picked up the object. But this time it was a membracid bug, not a beetle!

An East Indian crab spider, appropriately named *Ornithoscatoides decipiens*, rests on a fine web on the upper surface of a leaf. 'Thus resting with its white abdomen and black legs as the central and dark portions of the excreta, surrounded by its thin web-film representing the marginal watery portion become dry, even to some of it trickling off and arrested in a thickened extremity such as an evaporated drop of water would leave . . .'[9] Several other spiders are known to mimic bird droppings. The significance of this has, I think, been misunderstood by Cott and other writers, who think the mimicry is to deceive insects into approaching closely. It is true that some hesperid butterflies and other insects are sometimes attracted to fresh bird droppings, and indeed spiders that mimic bird droppings sometimes catch such insects, but this is not I think the chief selective value of the resemblance. It is much more likely that the mimicry is to deceive the predators of spiders. This is certainly so of all the so-called allurement colours and shapes of crab spiders: their resemblance to flowers is strictly for the birds and lizards. When they

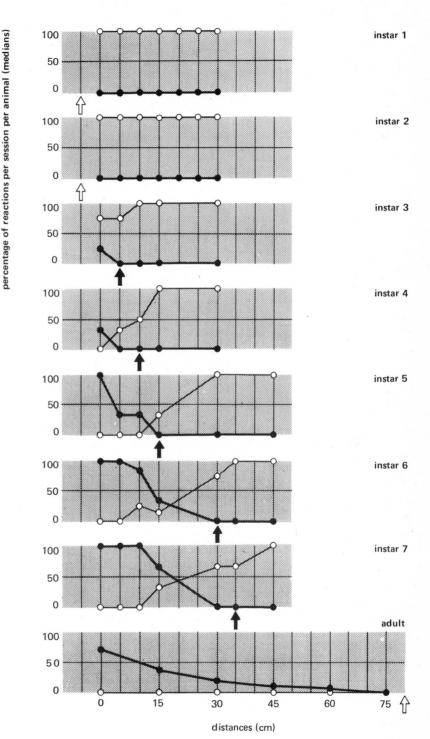

Fig. 11 *Switch from cryptic reaction (open circle) to defensive display, or deimatic reaction (solid circle) during development of the praying mantid, Stagmatoptera biocellata, when confronted with a cow-bird, Molothrus bonarensis. In the first two larval instars when the animal is small the only response, however close the bird, is an attempt to conceal the important clues by means of which predators recognize it. This is the cryptic reaction. A defensive response appears in the third instar, and from the third to the seventh larval instars the bird has to be further and further away (black arrows) to evoke a cryptic reaction. By the time the animal is an adult it exhibits only a defensive reaction. (After Balderrama and Maldonado)*

115

are examined by ultraviolet it becomes evident that they are very conspicuous to insects, which, unlike birds, can see in the ultraviolet. Those that I have examined in the ultraviolet are very conspicuous, and they will be so to insects, all of which can see in the ultraviolet.

Resemblance to twigs

Many kinds of insects resemble twigs of their host plant so closely than an experienced entomologist has difficulty in distinguishing insect from twig even when peering closely. Among the best known of these mimics of twigs are looper caterpillars (Geometriidae). Their bodies are long and narrow and their resemblance to a twig of their host plant is further enhanced because they are the same colour and have bumps and markings on their bodies that look like buds and leaf scars. Most of them are unusual in lacking all but the two hind pairs of prolegs. When they are not feeding they grasp the stem with their prolegs only and extend their bodies at an angle. Their immobility and position further contribute to their likeness to twigs. One species on a cypress in my garden always remained during the day on a dead stem extended from it at the same angle as the dead twigs. Its colour was the same. At night it left the dead stems and fed upon the green leaves but before morning always returned to rest on a dead stem.

fig. 12

In these caterpillars form and colour and behaviour all contribute to the resemblance. De Ruiter[37] tested the ability of jays and chaffinches to distinguish between caterpillars and twigs. Rows of twigs of the host plant were placed on the floor of the experimental cage, and dead or live caterpillars were mixed at random among the twigs. Once a bird had found a caterpillar, either because it had stepped on it or because it had moved, it would immediately begin to peck for a time at other twigs. In nature the insects that resemble twigs are usually far from one another and not in close groups. Thus any bird finding one by chance and therefore pecking at other twigs would be discouraged long before it came upon another insect. The resemblance between the caterpillars and twigs of their host plant is highly specific. In de Ruiter's experiments caterpillars placed among twigs of similar size but from other species of plants were immediately recognized by the birds. The results of these experiments show that there is a strong selective pressure for a more and more perfect resemblance both in behaviour (immobility) and form and colour. Objections to the theory of mimicry are sometimes made on the grounds that the mimicry is more perfect than it need be to be effective and that the resemblance is therefore fortuitous and not

Plate 8 *Live Hercules beetles, Dynastes hercules. The specimen on the left is in the yellow phase when the spongy layer in the wing-cases is filled with air. The specimen on the right is in the black phase when the spongy layer of the wing-cases is filled with liquid.*

116

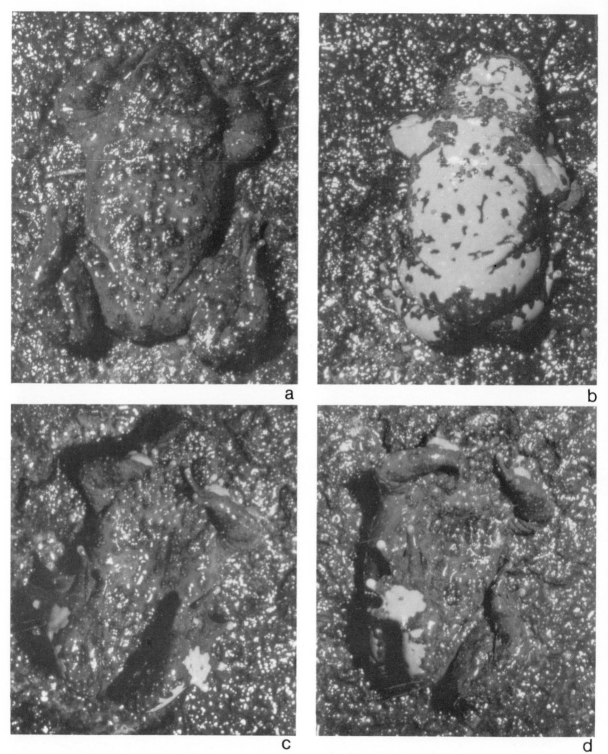

Plate 9 *Yellow-bellied toad on a patch of mud.* a: *dorsal view;* b: *ventral view;* c and d: *posture when threatened, with back hollowed and palms uppermost showing the patch of bright yellow.*

evolved because of its selective advantage to the organisms concerned.

Resemblance to an animal already eaten by parasites

Caterpillars of a number of unrelated families in many parts of the world attach to the surface of their pupal cocoons much smaller empty cocoons that resemble the cocoons of parasitic wasps.[16] After consuming the pupa, the brood of some species of parasitic larvae emerge and spin their own little cocoons on the surface of their host's cocoon. Birds tend not to open such parasitized moth cocoons because they learn that within there is little or nothing but the skin of the pupa left, and the individual parasites are not large enough to repay the effort of opening their cocoons.

The way in which the caterpillars make the false cocoons is much the same in different families. The larva voids *per anum* a globular pellet. The pellet is then attached by a silken cord to the inner roof of the cocoon. After this, the larva bites a hole in the cocoon near the point of attachment of the cord and pushes the pellet out through the hole. When the pellet is on the outer surface of the cocoon, the larva repairs the hole through which it was pushed. During this process, the larva reverses its position in the cocoon, and, after a short pause, a second pellet is voided and fastened in the same way to the opposite end of the cocoon. The number of pellets or false cocoons thus formed varies, but sometimes more than forty are formed on one cocoon. Some African arctiids and bombycids make similar false cocoons on the surface of a loose silken network beneath which they spin their pupal cocoon.

There are two other interesting ways in which pupae deceive predators by having the appearance of being already consumed. An African lycaenid butterfly, *Agriolaus maesa*, has markings and depressions on its surface that resemble the exit holes of parasites.[16] Another species in the same family, *Teratoneura isabellae*, is so clothed with whitish hairs that it appears to be heavily attacked by moulds.[16]

Resemblance to an animal attacked but discarded as distasteful

A nymphalid butterfly, *Limnitis populi*, always pupates on the upperside of a poplar leaf and always in a very exposed position, at the edges of woods and never in them, that is, in just those places most frequented by birds. Before pupation the caterpillar attaches

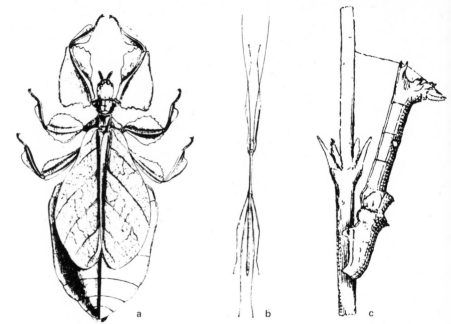

Fig. 12 *a and b: two stick insects of the family Phasmidae. The one on the left, Phyllium scythe, resembles a leaf. The antennae are very much shortened and quite unlike their usual form in the family seen on the right, Bacteria tenuis. c: the caterpillar of the early thorn moth, Selenia bilunaria, which resembles a twig. (a and b after Westwood, c after Poulton)*

a   b   c

the stalk of the leaf to the twig with silk, and the leaf cannot fall if it later becomes detached. A silken mat is spun on the upper surface of the leaf, and the edges of the leaf are bent upwards so that only the upper part of the pupa can be seen from the side. The pupa is in the centre of the leaf with its head towards the tip. It is whitish yellow with numerous black spots. On the base of the abdomen there is a large swelling that is orange-yellow, shiny, and semi-transparent. The cuticle behind the swelling is matt, whereas that in front of it to the head is highly polished. The appearance of the pupa suggests that a bird or another animal has broken the base of the abdomen entirely destroying the upper part of the first segment so that the cuticle with the black spots is scattered about or floating on the expelled yellow liquid.[33] Part of the contents of the pupa have oozed out to form the large and semi-transparent swelling, and, because the head end is inclined downwards towards the tip of the leaf, some of the liquid has flowed forwards over the fore part of the pupa, which is highly polished and appears to be covered by a liquid film. Behind the swelling, however, the surface is matt, nor would any liquid be expected to flow in this direction, which is against gravity. Birds and other vertebrates have to learn the significance of warning colours by experience: in nature a small percentage of animals with warning colours are attacked and then discarded because they are found to be distasteful or poisonous.

120

Resemblance to a monkey's face

The pupae of three species of blue butterflies have attracted some attention because of their resemblance to the face of an anthropoid. The pupae are generally found on twigs and branches or on the upper surfaces of leaves. The Indian *Spalgis epius* looks like the common rhesus macaque of its region, whereas the African *Spalgis lemolea* looks like one of the species of *Cercopithecus*.[18] When I took a pupa to the zoo I had no difficulty in identifying the particular monkey it resembled: it was *Cercopithecus patus*, a species common where the pupa occurs.

fig. 1

It seems too much to attribute to coincidence the fact that the Oriental species looks like a common Oriental monkey and the African one like a common African monkey. The chief argument against such resemblances being anything but fortuitous is the difference in size between mimic and model, the pupa being only 4.5 to 6.5 millimetres long. But we have to remember that a high proportion of insectivorous birds hunt by the method of 'rapid peering'; they peer at objects from several different angles in rapid succession. Their binocular field is probably usually so narrow as to be of little practical importance, and perception of solidity and distance is gained by evoking parallax. But with birds as with us and other vertebrates, the apparent distance of a *familiar* object is determined by the size of its image upon the retina. The method of rapid peering of insectivorous birds is going to mean that from time to time a bird will suddenly have a close up frontal view of one of these pupae.

The more we experiment with and know about the structure and habits of animals the less we are able to attribute to 'accidents'. The Japanese crab, *Dorippe japonica*, resembles one of the Sumurai. It is edible but it is not eaten. It has often been cited as a clear and indisputable instance of a purely fortuitous resemblance, but Huxley[24] says: 'The resemblance of *Dorippe* to an angry traditional Japanese warrior is far too specific and far too detailed to be merely accidental: it is a specific adaptation which can only have been brought about by means of natural selection operating over centuries of time, the crabs with more perfect resemblances have been less eaten.'

Resemblance to the head of an alligator

In Brazil and nearby countries there are several species of bugs of the

Fig. 13 *a: head of the bug, Fulgora lucifera from Brazil. b: a spectacled caiman from Brazil*

genus *Fulgora* that reproduce the most prominent features of an alligator.[34] The front of the head is hollow and much enlarged. The proportions of the head differ somewhat among the different species, but all have a nasal prominence in front, a large false eye behind, usually with a white mark that simulates specular reflection from a real eye, and false teeth produced by a combination of colour and relief. Some of the teeth appear to protrude over the lower jaw just as they do in the alligator.

Apart from conveying the appearance of an alligator, I have been unable to discover any functional significance for these extraordinary and profound modifications of the head. The sucking mouthparts of the bug are behind the part of the head shown in the photograph. There seems to be nothing to quarrel with the common and simple view that the selective value of the modifications of the head of the bug lie in deceiving birds and monkeys into believing that they are facing a real alligator, an animal adept at seizing birds, monkeys, and other animals that incautiously approach the edge of a lagoon or river. In many of the ponds and lagoons in the interior of Bolivia and Brazil I found alligators almost as common as newts in ponds in England, and I soon learnt not to shoot birds likely to fall into the water because I was hardly ever able to retrieve them before they were snapped up by alligators.

It would seem that the only real objection to the view that these bugs mimic alligators of the genus *Caiman* is the difference between the sizes of the two, but this apparent difficulty has been dealt with when discussing the mimics of monkeys. The species of *Fulgora* are particularly interesting in other ways. Their colour is such as to blend well with the bark of certain trees, and this may well be an effective defence before a bird or monkey approaches near enough to resolve the features of the head. If, despite all, the attack is pressed home, the bug opens its wings and displays a large and brightly coloured eye on each hind wing.

Deception by addition of adventitious material

By clothing themselves with material from their surroundings many animals pass unnoticed by their enemies. Flat-fishes scatter sand over their bodies so that little more than their eyes are exposed. Some oribatid mites and small beetles plaster mud on their backs and so become indistinguishable from their background. The animals that deceive in this way often renew or add to their clothing from materials ready at hand, with the result that changes in their immediate environment are often reflected in the appearance of their covering. Crabs, insects, and other kinds of animals may exercise great care in just how the adventitious material is arranged on their body so that the best camouflage is obtained.

A looper caterpillar from Borneo fastens flower buds to the long spines of its body so that it comes to resemble an inflorescence. The flower buds are renewed as they wither. The larva of the blotched emerald moth changes its camouflage with the season: in the summer it fastens fragments of the leaves of its host plant to its hooked bristles but after hibernating for the winter it uses scales or husks of oak or oak buds in the early spring. A particularly interesting kind of deception is practised by some South American spiders that carry a dead ant on their backs. The resemblance of the spider to an ant carrying a dead ant is reinforced because the spider runs about in a jerky ant-like manner.[3]

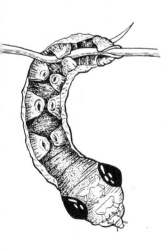

Fig. 14 *The larva of a S. American hawk moth, Leucorhampha, mimicking a snake. (After Hingston)*

123

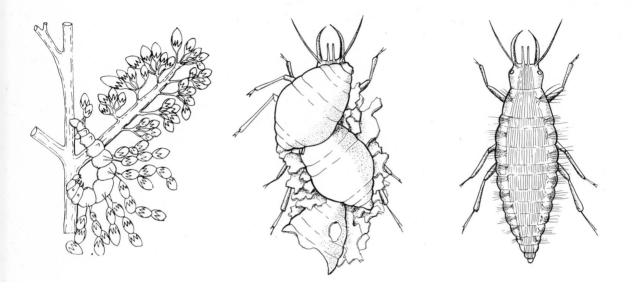

Fig. 15 above *Looper cat-erpillar from Borneo. The caterpillar fastens flower buds to its long spines and so comes to resemble the inflorescence on which it lives. (After Shelfond)*

Fig. 16 *Larva of a green lacewing, Chrysopa. The larva fastens the remains of its prey, in this instance aphids or greenflies, on to its back and so conceals itself from animals that might otherwise attack it. (After Hingston)*

Sometimes animals deceive by growing other animals or plants on their bodies. A scorpaeonid fish from India, *Minous inermis*, has a coat of polyps of *Stylactis minoi*, a hydroid that is apparently restricted to this fish. This is also an example of mutualism or symbiosis: the fish is camouflaged by the hydroid and in turn provides it with a place to grow. A Japanese and a European hermit crab have a similar association with another hydroid, but in these instances the hydroid grows on and conceals the mollusc shell in which the crab lives. Symbiotic associations are well known between crabs and sea anemones that have warning colours and are very distasteful to fish. These crabs thus exploit the fact that fish learn not to attack the anemones.

In recent years it has been discovered that in the lowland rain forests and the high moss forests of New Guinea no less than three different subfamilies of weevils grow veritable gardens of crypto-gamic plants on their backs and sometimes also parts of their legs.[1][2] These gardens consist of various species of fungi, algae, lichens, liverworts, and mosses. The plants are usually grown in what appear to be especially modified pits surrounded by stiff hairs. The plants growing on the beetles are similar to those usually found on the surface of the leaves and bark of the plants on which the insects feed and so provide an effective camouflage. The miniature gardens of cryptogamic plants carried about by the weevils, especially species of *Gymnopholus*, are not free of pests: besides bacteria and protozoa, a

124

sessile rotifer, a nematode, and an oribatid mite live on the cryptograms. A colydiid beetle, *Dryptops*, of New Guinea is also known to grow lichens on its back.[12]

Protective resemblance achieved by altering the surroundings

fig. 14

In most instances of special protective resemblance, the animal resembles some object that is normally avoided or ignored by predators – a caterpillar looks like a snake or a butterfly like a dead leaf. However, it is sometimes not the animal that comes to resemble an object that for one reason or another is relatively immune from attack. Instead the animal alters its surroundings so that it blends into them or else makes a number of dummies of itself that increase its chances of escaping attack. Orb-weaver spiders provide many beautiful examples of this.[14,15] These large and usually soft-bodied animals are juicy morsels for a wide range of predators. Perhaps most

fig. 19

of them live concealed nearby and only rush onto the web when an

Fig. 17 *Various ways in which orb-weaver spiders protect themselves from predators by altering their surroundings. a: Gasteracantha brevispin from the Andaman Islands. b: Uloborus sp. from Baghdad. c: Cyclosa sp. from India. d: Tetragnatha baculiferens from Burma. (After Hingston)*

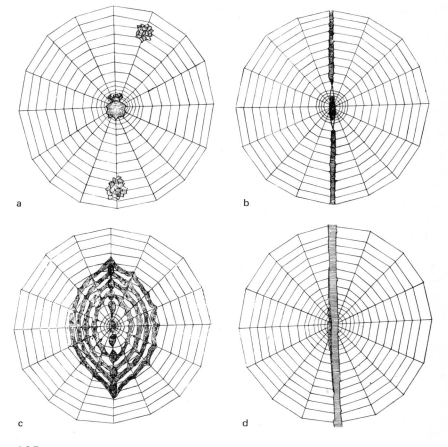

H.E. Hinton

insect becomes entangled. However, many live on the web itself. In this very exposed situation it is perhaps not surprising to find that an unusual variety of devices has been evolved that assist in avoiding attack. In addition, many have very hard and spiny bodies, a most unusual feature among spiders.

Hingston[14,15] has made a special study of the protective devices of orb-weavers, and a few of these are noted here. The spider shown in fig. 17a collects and binds together the insects it has sucked dry to form two heaps coloured like itself. Thus a bird or another enemy has only one chance in three of catching the spider the first time. *fig. 17* *Uloborus* constructs a flocculent band drawn out here and there by the anchoring threads. The band is absent on the hub of the web. The spider rests on the hub with its first two pairs of legs thrust out in front and the last two pairs behind. The colour, size, position, and immobility of the spider combine to make it appear part of the band. *fig. 17* Another spider makes a vertical string of pellets of silk and remains of insects, and it may even add pieces of seeds and bits of leaves to the pellets. It also spins four concentric ribbons around the hub. These are white and very conspicuous, and attachments to the anchoring threads break up the shape of each ribbon. The spider is completely lost to view in this complicated system of pellets and *fig. 17* ribbons. *Tetragnatha* has a withered piece of stick in its web. It presses itself against the stick with which it blends exactly, the first two pairs of legs being extended forwards and the hind pair backwards. The short third pair of legs is used to clasp the stick. If the stick or web is touched, the spider remains motionless, relying on its camouflage, but if it is further disturbed it runs along the stick or drops to the ground. Another species of the same genus collects a *fig. 19* dead curled leaf and fastens it to the centre of the web. It hides in the leaf. Various species of *Argiope* make silvery white zigzag ribbons in their webs, sometimes in a straight line interrupted only by the hub or in a Y- or X-shaped pattern. The zigzag bands form a pattern *figs. 18,19* that confuses not only by its bright colour but also because of its numerous angles. Attention is thus taken away from the spider, which in any event has been given a very unnatural and unspider-like shape because the zigzag bands appear to be continuous with its body. In many of these species the back of the spider also has bright silvery markings, and these add to the impression that the bands and the spider are one body.

In some ways the most interesting of all the spiders described by Hingston is *Cyclosa tremula* of Guyana. The spider rests in the centre of the hub and has a striking white and black disruptive pattern. It

Fig. 18 *Zig-zag patterns of white distract attention from the spider itself, which rests at the centre of the web, four legs forward, four legs backward. Argiope argentata from the Mato Grosso.*

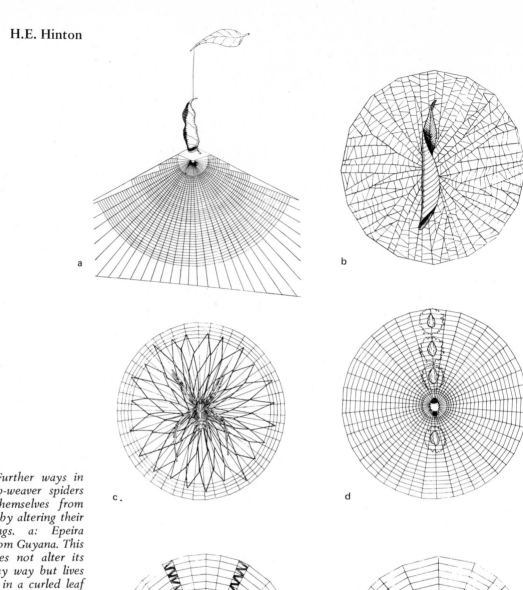

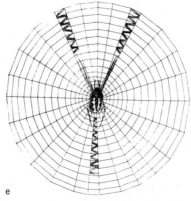

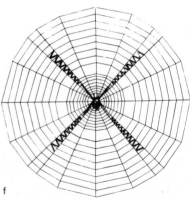

Fig. 19 *Further ways in which orb-weaver spiders protect themselves from predators by altering their surroundings. a: Epeira gregalis from Guyana. This spider does not alter its web in any way but lives concealed in a curled leaf nearby from which it rushes out when an insect becomes entangled in its web. b: Tetragnatha foliferens from the Nicobar Islands. c: Argiope cuyunii from Guyana. d: Cyclosa tremula from Guyana. e: Argiope catenulata from Burma. f: Argiope pulchella from India. (After Hingston)*

makes pellets of insect remains bound with silk. The pellets are in a vertical line that bisects the web, one in front of the spider and three behind. The spider thus appears to be a black and white pellet in a line of equidistant grey pellets. Around each pellet is a wavy thread that mimics the hub of the web. The disruptive colour of the spider is very different from that of the greyish pellets. However, if the spider is threatened, it raises itself a little from the surface of the hub and vibrates its body sufficiently rapidly so that the black and white patches cannot be resolved and the spider therefore appears grey like the pellets.

Deception by groups of individuals

Relatively few instances are so far known in which another object is mimicked not by an individual but a group of individuals. Several species of bugs of the genus *Ityraea* in Africa aggregate together in such a way as to mimic an inflorescence of lupin. One of these, *Ityraea nigrocincta*, has green and yellow forms. Some observers claim that the green forms tend to rest at the top of the stem and the yellow forms below them, thereby increasing the resemblance to an inflorescence, because the individual flowers open progressively and green buds are often present at the tip while yellowish flowers are already open lower down. Related bugs with similar habits are recorded from India and Ceylon. Young caterpillars may crowd together and collectively resemble a bird dropping, e.g. *Triloqua obliquissima* of Uganda. In Guyana there is a membracid bug, *Bolbonota*, the female of which sits on its nest. Both female and nest are very conspicuous and easily mistaken for one of the numerous crops of a small white fungus common in the vicinity.[13]

Many aposematic (warningly coloured) animals effectively increase their conspicuousness by aggregating together: 'The more we are together the more conspicuous we shall be.' For instance, most hawk moth larvae are solitary and are camouflaged, but a high proportion of the aposematic species tend to aggregate in groups consisting of many individuals. Some aposematic fish, such as the silurid *Plotosus angullaris*, swim very close together making a large and very conspicuous black ball. In Mexico I have seen bushes loaded down with aposematic cantharid beetles (*Chauliognathus proteus*). It is now known that some of the species that form such aggregations, e.g. lycid beetles, secrete a special pheromone that functions to bring the individuals together and is called an aggregation pheromone.[8] Many distasteful butterflies that fly alone during the day roost at night

129

massed very close together. At night the warning colours of the individuals in these sleeping assemblages are not so apparent but their scent and form make it easy for predators to recognize them for what they are, and in any event a predator has only to try one to leave the whole lot alone.

Emission of light for deception

Natural light is used in a large number of ways: the larvae of some midges use it to attract their prey, fireflies and other beetles use it to beckon the opposite sex, some animals use it to warn and intimidate their enemies, and by some it may perhaps be used to light the way. Here I am concerned with its use by some female fireflies to lure males of other species which they promptly eat.

A number of fish that live in the deep sea or at intermediate depths have light producing organs, called photophores, along their flanks or ventral surfaces. The light produced is directed by a system of mirrors and/or lenses in the direction in which the shadow of the fish would naturally fall.[6] When their shadows are obliterated the fish are difficult to see from below. Perfect camouflage in this way would necessitate replacing exactly all of the light absorbed by the upper part of the body of the fish. If the camouflage is to be good, the light emitted by the photophores should have the intensity and spectral composition of the sunlight penetrating to the same depths. Obviously camouflage of this kind is not possible just below the surface because near the surface the light of the photophores is not intense enough to compete with that from the sun. It has been shown that light produced by the photophores passes through colour filters so that it exactly matches the wave lengths of the sunlight that penetrates to the depth at which the fish live.[6]

Argyropelecus affinis is a laterally flattened hatchet fish that lives at depths of 300 to 500 metres. The light from its photophores matches over a wide range of angles of viewing the daylight around it. Daylight intensities of light fall by a factor of about 10 for every 60 metres increase in depth. Thus, if an *Argyropelecus* moved up from a depth of 500 metres to one of 300, the intensity of the light produced by its photophores should increase over 100 times. *Chauliodus sloani* lives deeper in the sea. Its photophores are smaller, and they have to produce less light to do the same job of camouflage. For effective camouflage it is of course necessary for the fish to alter quickly the intensity of the light it produces in order to allow for differences in sunlight caused by clouds.

H. S. Barber long ago suggested that females of the carnivorous firefly *Photuris* might mimic flashes of *Photinus* females and thus lure *Photinus* males so they could eat them. Lloyd[28] has shown that Barber was indeed right. Males of various species of *Photinus* emit as they fly about a flash pattern that is simple and constant at short, fairly regular intervals. *Photinus* females remain on the ground and respond to the flash pattern of males of their species by flashing. This exchange of flashes enables the males to find the females. There are many different species of *Photinus*, but the length of the flash, flash rate, and number of pulses in the flash pattern enables the female to distinguish the males of its own species from other males. On its part, the male is assisted in identifying the right species of female by the time she takes to flash back after receiving his signal.

Males and females of *Photuris* also locate each other by flash signals. The females of this genus are unusual in that they eat other beetles. Lloyd has found that several species of *Photuris* not only have specific flash patterns that attract their own males, but also others that mimic the flash patterns of *Photinus* females. Female *Photuris* are thus able to induce *Photinus* males to approach them, which they then eat. The intensity of the flashes from *Photinus* females is less than that from *Photuris* females, but when a *Photuris* female is luring a *Photinus* male it reduces the intensity of its flashes so that they correspond more closely to the signal the male *Photinus* would expect from its own female. There is some evidence that some species of *Photuris* can mimic more than one species of *Photinus*.[28]

Colour changes

Very many animals have evolved the capacity to change their colour according to outward circumstances. The change in colour may be relatively slow and irreversible. Such changes are often called 'morphological' colour changes. The same developmental stage may irreversibly change colour, but more often irreversible colour changes occur between different stages of the same species. For instance, caterpillars of many swallow-tail butterflies may look just like a bird dropping when they are little but when they reach a certain size they suddenly assume bright warning colours.

The relatively rapid and reversible colour changes undergone by many invertebrates and vertebrates are called 'physiological' colour changes. They are brought about by the rapid concentration or dispersion of pigment granules within cells and not by the contraction or expansion of the cells themselves. The cells that contain the pigment granules are called chromatophores. They occur in leeches, polychaete worms, crustaceans, echinoderms, molluscs, fishes, amphibians, and reptiles. The common chameleon changes colour by dispersing or concentrating pigment granules in its chromatophores. Chromatophore cells are branched and are often closely associated in groups called chromatosomes. When the chromatosome has more than one type of pigment granule, the granules in some branches may be concentrated or dispersed while those in others are stationary. The very rapid and spectacular colour changes of the squid and other cephalopods are brought about in a unique way. Their so-called chromatophores are elastic spherical cells full of pigment. When muscles attached to the pigment cells contract, each cell is pulled out into a disc many times its original diameter.

Oddly enough, although most kinds of animals are insects, none have chromatophores of the branched-cell type so widely distributed in the animal kingdom, and very few are able to change their colour rapidly and reversibly. One of the most curious of these is the aquatic larva of the phantom midge *Chaoborus*. It can vary its buoyancy and so the depth at which it floats in the water. It does this by varying the size of two pairs of large air sacs, one pair in the thorax and the other in the abdomen. When it is over a bright sandy bottom, light reflected from the air sacs does not make it conspicuous. The matter is quite otherwise when it is floating over a dark muddy or leafy bottom, when reflection from the air sacs would result in four very bright and conspicuous spots. Modified fat body cells I have called chromatocytes are present on the outer surface of the air sacs. These cells have a dark pigment. When the larva moves over a dark bottom, the chromatocytes flatten out and completely cover the air sacs so that they are no longer conspicuous. But if the transparent larva now swims into water over a sandy bottom, the four blackish spots look very conspicuous. What now

Fig. 20 *A tracheal air sac of Chaoborus crystallinus with (a) chromatocytes in the dark-adapted condition, (b) partly light-adapted condition, and (c) light-adapted condition. After a day or so on a light background the chromatocytes aggregate into even smaller groups. The air sacs are in the metathorax and the seventh abdominal segment. (After Dupont-Raabe)*

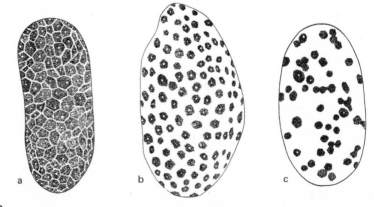

132

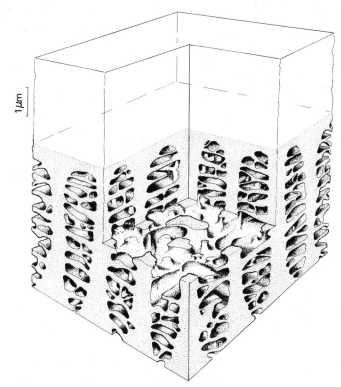

1 μm

Fig. 21 *Diagram of the structure of the yellow spongy layer of the wing-cases of the hercules beetle, Dynastes hercules. The outer transparent layer is unshaded. (After Hinton and Jarman)*

happens is that the chromatocytes round up and disperse so that there is once more a reflection from the air sacs and the whole larva is again inconspicuous. The change in colour shown in fig. 20 can occur in 10 to 30 minutes, and it is under endocrine control.[7]

The Hercules beetle of Central and South America is perhaps the second largest insect in the world. We have recently found out how it changes the colour of its hard wing-cases from yellowish to black and back again to yellowish within a few minutes. The outer layer of the wing-case is transparent and about 0.003 of a millimetre thick. Below this is a yellowish spongy layer about 0.0005 mm. thick. The cuticle below the yellow sponge is black. When the yellow sponge is full of air it is optically heterogenous and reflects yellow light back through the transparent layer. When the yellow sponge is liquid-filled it becomes optically homogenous and the black cuticle below is seen. Epidermal cells well below the yellow sponge are responsible for filling it or emptying it of liquid and therefore for changes in the colour of the wing-cases.

Normally the colour depends upon the ambient humidity, black in high humidities and yellow in low. The result of this is that the wing-cases are black at night when the humidity is high and yellowish

fig. 21

Plate 9

133

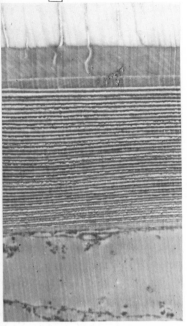

1 μm

Fig. 22 *The 44 × 2 inter-ference layers of the wing case of the African tor-toise beetle, Aspidomor-pha tecta*

during the day when it is low. The selective value of this appears to lie in the fact that at night there is usually enough light so that a beetle with yellow wing cases will be more easily seen by predators than one with black wing-cases. During the day this is reversed: a beetle with yellow wing cases, particularly if it is feeding on fruit, will be less conspicuous than an entirely black one. Changes in colour are usualy not under central nervous control. However, beetles sometimes become yellow when they should have been black, and it thus appears that central nervous control of colour change can override local autonomous control.

In warmer climates tortoise beetles are common on the upper surfaces of leaves. Some look like irridescent golden drops, others like opals. Electron micrographs through their wing cases show that their colour arises from multiple-layer interference. In most there is little change in colour with changes in the angle of the incident light, which shows that the mean refractive index must be high. When the beetle is poked or otherwise disturbed, it changes colour. This change in colour is effected by varying the moisture content of the thin films and thereby their thickness. For instance, the species shown on the left side of •Plate 10 changes from pale gold to reddish copper. The change of colour takes two or three minutes, which is odd because they must often be damaged or eaten by predators before the red warning colour appears.

The significance of the gold or opal colours is not evident: some predators may see them as warning colours. A friend said that they looked like drops of water, a suggestion I dismissed without much thought. However, sometime later when looking into a cage in which I was breeding cockroaches I had recently brought back from Australia, I thought one of my tortoise beetles had somehow got in and was on a cabbage leaf. But my beetle turned out to be a drop of water. There are insects that undoubtedly mimic drops of water. One of these is the pupa of a crane fly (*Geranomyia*) that is enveloped in a hygroscopic mucoprotein. It hangs down from the ends of palm leaves in rain forests and looks just like a hanging drop of water.[15] The disturbing thing is that not only does imagination tend to run riot but on further investigation one finds that nature has out-stripped the most fevered imagination.

Diffraction gratings

During the past three years D.F. Gibbs and I[19,21,22] have discovered diffraction gratings in a large number of insects. I have

134

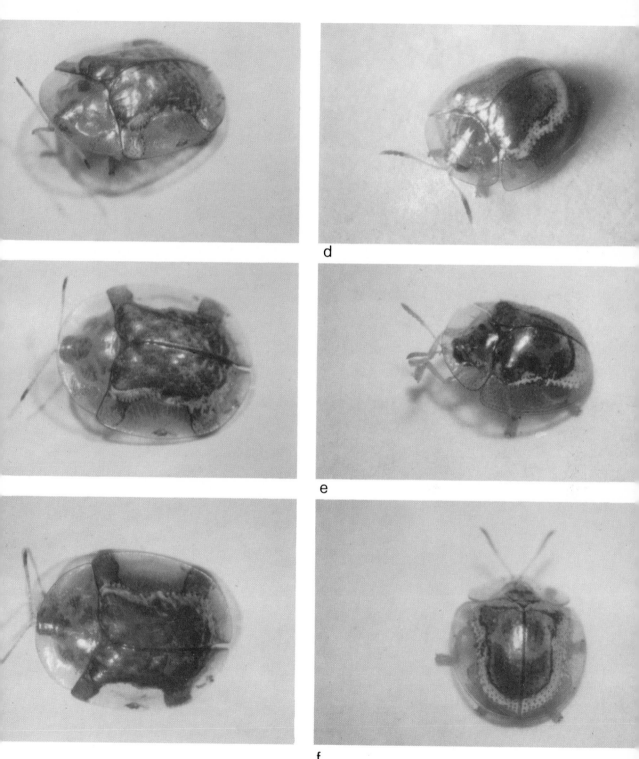

d

e

f

Plate 10 *Colour changes of tortoise beetles.* a-c: *changes made in about two minutes by the African Aspidomorpha tecta.* d-f: *colour changes of an unidentified tortoise beetle from Trinidad.*

a

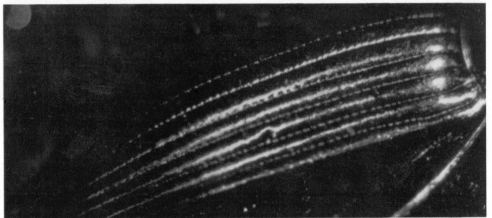

b

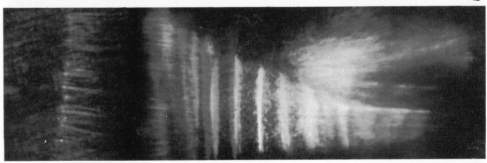

c

previously noted the fact that it becomes difficult to estimate the distance away and therefore the size and the shape of an object when its appearance, i.e. its reflectance or both its reflectance and colour, change rapidly with the angle at which it is viewed. This difficulty arises irrespective of whether the attacker is estimating distance by stereoscopic vision or by evoking parallax. A diffraction grating not only provides a warning colour but also, because some of the light reflected from the grating is specularly reflected (zero order), with a reflectance that makes it more difficult for the attacker to estimate distance. A diffraction grating thus produces an unusual combination: a warning colour that at the same time deceives about distance and shape. When reflectance and colour change with small differences in angle of viewing the effect on vision is comparable to sliding out of control when trying to walk on a very slippery surface.

Before the selective advantage of diffraction gratings in a few animals is considered, the physical principles of this way of producing colour may be briefly noted. When white light falls on a plane surface that has a large number of straight parallel lines that may be grooves or ridges, each line will scatter the light over a wide range of angles. The light reflected in any particular direction will be light scattered from each of the lines. Light from different lines will usually have travelled a different distance both before and after scattering by the lines. The difference in the distance travelled by light from adjacent lines is the path difference. Because light is a kind of wave, the path differences result in phase differences. Thus, as the crest of a wave is arriving from one line, a trough may arrive from an adjacent line and so cancel the effect. However, if the path difference is a whole number of wavelengths, crests from adjacent lines, and therefore from all lines, will always arrive together. That is, they will be in phase and there will be a great increase in brightness. If the path difference is $n\lambda$ where λ is the wavelength and n is a whole number, it can be shown that $n\lambda$ is related to the angles of incidence and emergence of the light, θ_1 and θ_2, by the formula $d(\sin\theta_1 - \sin\theta_2) = n$ where d is the distance apart of adjacent lines.

When $n=0$, $\theta_1 = \theta_2$ for all wavelengths. This corresponds to ordinary specular reflection from a flat surface with no grooves. In this context n is called the 'order' of the spectrum, and when $n=0$ the spectrum is referred to as the 'zero order spectrum', but it is not really a spectrum. When $n=\pm 1$ there is a first order spectrum and the angle of emergence of the beam depends upon the wavelength. The shorter wavelength light always emerges in a direction closer to zero order than the longer wavelength light. In the spectra of other orders

Plate 11 *Colours produced by diffraction gratings.* a: *the ground beetle,* Iridagonum quadripunctum *(grating structure shown in fig. 23);* b: *the ground beetle,* Loxandrus lucidulus *(grating structure shown in fig. 23);* c: *stridulatory file of the mutillid wasp,* Mutilla europaea. *Five orders may be seen on either side of zero order (file structure shown in fig. 23). In the mutillid wasp the radius of the stridulatory file is small and the grating lines are far apart with the result that the spectral bands are narrow. In the two ground beetles, on the other hand, the radius is much greater and the grating lines are more narrowly separated with the result that the spectral bands are much broader than in the wasp.*

the blue is also nearer to zero order and the red furthest from zero order. The spectra become wider and usually fainter as n increases. Thus, as n increases the spectra overlap more and more – only the first order is completely free of this overlap – and the resultant mixed wavelengths form less and less saturated colours at large deviations from the zero order.

The angular width of the spectra depends on the distance apart of the lines of the grating. A coarse grating, that is, one with widely spaced lines, results in small angles of deviation and small dispersion. For any grating spacing and wavelength there are values of n so large that no angles can be found to fit the formula given above, and when the grating lines are close together only one or two orders may be visible. When the lines are separated from each other by less than half a wavelength no spectra at all are produced except of course the zero order, which, as previously noted, is not a spectrum. High orders from coarse gratings may be visible in principle but not in practice because of insufficient intensity. The distribution of brightness between the various orders depends upon the precise shape of the grooves or lines, and even low orders may be dim or absent.

A plane grating is thus much like a plane mirror, but, in addition to the ordinary image, it produces a sequence of images smeared out into spectra in a direction at right angles to the lines. These images are seen collectively only when the grating subtends a sufficiently large angle to the eye. In diffuse light, for instance when the sky is heavily overcast, spectra from the different parts of the source may overlap so much that little if any colour can be seen. Unlike colours produced by diffraction gratings, those produced by thin film interference remain brilliant in diffuse light.

The more regular the periodicity of the grating, the sharper are the maxima and minima of reflectance of a particular colour. It is for this reason that the more perfect the grating the more the predator is likely to be confused, providing that the angular separation between diffraction maxima is relatively small compared with the range of angles over which the predator views the insect when estimating distance.[19]

The diffraction gratings of beetles are by no means as perfect as we might have expected them to be. This imperfection is of itself most interesting and requires an explanation. We know that the epidermal cells that form the ridges or grooves of the grating can make lines that are remarkably regular. For instance, the ridges of the stridulatory file of the mutillid wasp and many other insects may be as regular as if they were ruled mechanically. It seems unlikely

fig. 23

138

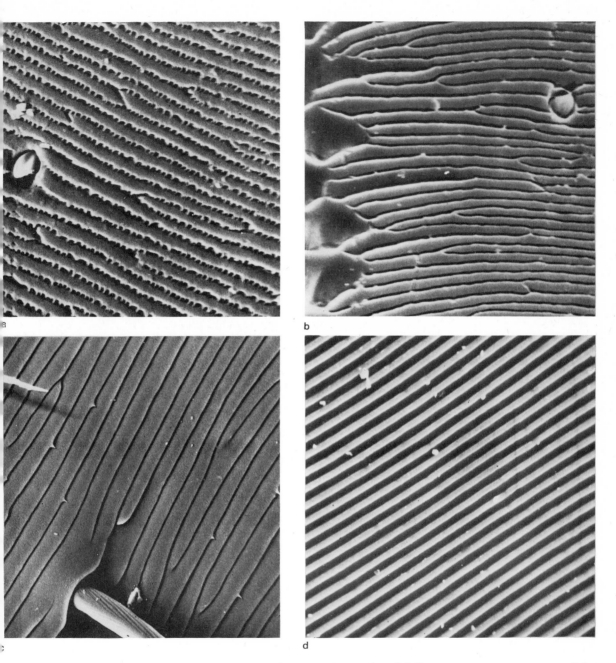

Fig. 23 *Scanning electron micrographs of diffraction gratings. Wing cases of the ground beetles, Iridagonum quadripunctum (a) and Loxandrus lucidulus (b). For the colours they produce see Plate 11, a and b. c: base of coxa of middle leg of the rove beetle, Quedius ochripennis. d: stridulatory file of the third visible abdominal tergite of the mutillid wasp, Mutilla europaea. For colours produced see Plate 11, c.*

139

that all diffraction gratings of beetles have irregularities and dislocations simply because they are all still evolving and have not reached the required state of perfection. Many of these beetles have on other parts of their bodies stridulatory files that do not function as diffraction gratings but have parallel ridges that lack irregularities or dislocations. It therefore seems that some other reason has to be found for this lack of perfection in the form of diffraction gratings of beetles. I have previously suggested[19] that a less perfect grating has a slight selective advantage over a perfect one in that a perfect grating might produce too sharp a peak of reflectance when reinforcement occurs. A very bright reflectance could well act as a beacon and so outweigh the benefits of confusing distance. It would, of course, only act as a beacon to the kind of casual predator that was not repelled by the colour. In this connection it must be remembered that there are very many kinds of animals with warning colours that are normally concealed but can be suddenly revealed when attack is imminent.

Diffraction gratings are common among beetles, where they have been independently evolved a hundred or more times. Apart from beetles, the stridulatory files of mutillid wasps and some spiny orb-weaver spiders also function as diffraction gratings. The irridescent colours of all other animals, e.g. the feathers of birds, scales of lizards, and so on, result from constructive interference produced by thin films. Other animals often have structures that at first sight appear to be diffraction gratings but nevertheless do not function as such. For instance, the scales of the wings of moths and butterflies usually have ribs of the right periodicity to produce diffraction colours. But because the individual scales are too irregular in profile, the spectra produced by different parts of the same scale, or by adjacent scales, overlap and summate to white light.

As already noted, in diffuse light when the sky is overcast the spectra from different parts of the grating may overlap so much that little if any colour can be seen. For the best production of colours, the grating must be illuminated by parallel light such as is produced from a small distant source like the sun. Because of this we may suppose that the selective pressure for evolving diffraction gratings for warning colour and deception about distance will increase with the number of hours of sunshine. It thus appears to be no accident that the highest percentage of beetles with diffraction gratings is found in the sunniest parts of the world, although a few also occur in north and south temperate regions.

Having said so much in general terms about diffraction gratings, we may now look briefly at two groups of beetles. Nearly all of the ground beetles of the family Carabidae that have diffraction gratings are either nocturnal or live on the ground among grass roots or concealed in other places. Most of the time they are in the shade where there may be little parallel light. In their normal environment the brown or black colour of their cuticle harmonizes with the background. However, from time to time they have to cross open patches of ground where they are exposed to sunlight, and it is at such times that their warning colours and specular reflectance are advantageous. It should be noted that an insect with a diffraction grating has to a considerable extent an 'all or none' warning colour. In dim diffuse light the colour of the cuticle may be procryptic and inconspicuous, but as soon as it is exposed to the sun warning colours appear. These ground beetles could not solve their particular problem by evolving interference colours because these would still be brilliant in diffuse light and so would make them conspicuous even when they are not fully exposed to the sun. A pattern of warning colours formed by pigments in the cuticle would also render them conspicuous even in dim light.

In nearly all beetles the grating lines on the dorsal surface are normal to the major axis, although a few exceptions are known. However, some of the tropical species of whirligig beetles (Gyrinidae) of the genus *Gyretus* are unique in having grating lines that are at right angles to each other.[22] The grating lines of the thorax of *Gyretus* are always parallel to the major axis, whereas those of the wing-cases and head are normal to the major axis. These beetles live in small or large aggregations on the surface of ponds and streams. The upper part of their body is exposed above water. When hunting for food they swim in circles. Because the head, thorax and wing-cases (elytra) are three convex parts, there will be three different highlights (zero order) when viewed from certain angles at any particular incidence. At some angles there will therefore be three streaks of spectra that are slightly differently oriented. However, when on one of the parts of the body, i.e. the thorax, the grating is normal to that of the other two parts, the orientation of the streak of spectra will nearly always be very different.

If we rotate a horizontal grating about a vertical axis and view it at grazing incidence, the apparent rotation is large when the lines appear vertical to the eye and small when they appear horizontal. When a whirligig beetle with grating lines at right angles to each other on different parts of its body is swimming in circles, a predator viewing it from the side will see the spectra on the head and elytra

141

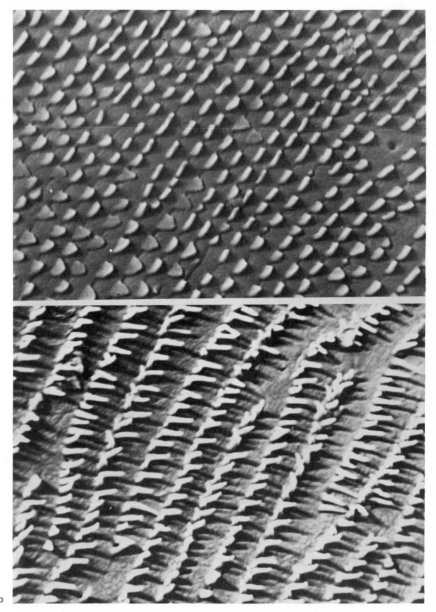

b

Fig. 24 *Scanning electron micrographs of the diffraction gratings of the wing cases of the scarabaeid beetles, Homalotropus sericeus (a) and Sericesthis micans (b). In the Scarabaeidae, microtrichia in the form of slender spines or flat triangles are rather regularly spaced along any one of the main grating lines. However, the spacing of the microtrichia of one grating line does not correspond well with the spacing of the microtrichia on adjacent lines. The effect of this irregularity is to degrade the resolution of the corresponding spectra; and in the species so far studied the resolution of spectra in a direction across the major axis is negligible.*

rotate faster than the spectra on the thorax. But when the predator views the beetle from before or behind, the spectra on the thorax will then appear to rotate faster than those on the head and elytra. A beetle that is circling will thus present a predator from many angles with spectra that on at least part of its body are relatively rapidly shifting their position. In some whirligig beetles all of the grating lines on the dorsal surface have the same orientation, and these species will present a predator with relatively rapidly shifting spectra from only half as many angles of viewing. In beetles that do not move in circles there would appear to be less advantage in having grating lines on the dorsal surface normal to each other, and none are known to have such lines.

Exploitation of ultraviolet in deception

The light that reaches the surface of the earth from the sun extends from the far infrared to about 300 nanometers (1 nm = 10 A), wavelengths shorter than this being completely absorbed by the atmosphere, chiefly the ozone layer. However, man is only sensitive to waves from about 400 nm to about 780 nm, and this is what we call the visible part of the spectrum. So far as we know, the visible part of the spectrum of other vertebrates is near enough the same, although a young chicken is sensitive to waves as short as 395 nm. Of course some vertebrates are more sensitive to a particular part of the spectrum than are others. For instance, many birds discriminate better in the yellow part of the spectrum than man but are less competent in the red than man. Except for primates, most mammals are unable to discriminate wave lengths and so have no colour vision. This is related to the fact that most are nocturnal, and the capacity to distinguish colours has little selective value for a nocturnal animal. For instance, nocturnal carnivores like cats lack colour vision, but mongooses that hunt by day can see colours as can some squirrels.

In insects the cornea of the eye transmits ultraviolet and the retina is sensitive to it. Most insects that have been tested have a peak of spectral sensitivity at about 350 nm and another between 490 and 500 nm, although the peak in the visible is as low as 450 nm in some and as high as 550 nm in others. The sensitivity of most insects ceases at about 600 nm unless very extreme intensities are involved. Some butterflies, a firefly, and a very few others are sensitive to red. As we have said, no light below 300 nm reaches the surface of the earth. However, Lutz and Grisewood[31] used a special arc and a quartz spectrograph to produce light of 254 nm, and they were able

H.E. Hinton

to show that *Drosophila* flies were sensitive to it. Thus these flies are sensitive to a much shorter wave length of light than either they or their ancestors can ever have experienced.

The capacity of insects to see further into the violet side of the spectrum than vertebrates is exploited by them in a number of different ways. We are here chiefly concerned with the way it permits unrelated insects living in the same region to see specific and sexual colour differences among themselves while at the same time they evolve warning colour patterns that are identical in the part of the spectrum visible to vertebrates. We are also concerned with a similar phenomenon among flowers: the evolution of identical warning colours in the visible while still competing for pollinators in another part of the spectrum. In short, the selective pressure for the evolution of a common type of warning pattern against vertebrates need not conflict with the pressure to maintain specific and sexual colour differences because the latter can be developed in another part of the spectrum.

The common terms used in talking about colour can be defined very briefly. Intensity means the amount of energy of the stimulus, and it may be defined either in terms of energy (watts) or number of quanta. When the energy of the light rays is the same, the number of quanta increase with wave length, but when the quanta of the light rays is the same there is a decrease in energy content with increasing wavelength. Brightness is distinguished from intensity, and it is measured subjectively by us and in experiments on animals by their behaviour. Brightness depends both upon intensity and wavelength, and some wavelengths produce a stronger reaction than others. When the intensities of two wavelengths are the same, the brighter one is the one that is more effective as a stimulus. The light rays are not themselves coloured but they elicit sensations of colour, and when we talk about light of different colours that is what we mean. It is thus clear that we also have to distinguish between colour and the wave length of the stimulus. Two stimuli of quite different wavelength content may appear the same to an animal. For instance, to us a pure spectral light of 580 nm seems to be the same yellow as an appropriate mixture of 520 nm and 640 nm. Light of different wave lengths may elicit the same sensation of colour, e.g. 650 nm and 750 nm both appear red to us. Spectral efficiency describes the magnitude of the response plotted against different wavelengths when the energy is kept constant. In most recent work on colour the number of quanta are kept constant.

A group of different species that occur in the same region and share the same pattern of warning colours is called an aposematic assemblage. In most such groups, especially if they are large, some species may be clearly related to each other and others may belong to different orders. As explained before, it is a great advantage for the different members of the group to look exactly like each other. By so doing any particular predator has fewer patterns to learn and so each species of the assemblage escapes with fewer casualties. And it is possible for them to look like each other in the visible part of the spectrum if they can use the ultraviolet not only as a means of recognizing their own species but also as a means of recognizing the opposite sex. Such visual signals are particularly important for insects active during the day. A few members, all diurnal scarabaeid beetles, of an aposematic assemblage from the Oriental Region are shown below.

In most of the day-flying scarabaeids belonging to the genera *Glycosia* and *Glycyphana* the yellow spots of the wing-cases absorb ultraviolet, but in *Glycyphana horsfieldi* the yellow patches strongly

Fig. 25 *Members of an assemblage of warningly coloured insects from the Oriental Region. The three species shown here are day-flying scarabaeid beetles. a and d: Glycyphana horsfieldi. b and e: Glycosia tricolor; c and f: Glycyphana binotata. From above they all look much alike in the visible. The light patches on the wing cases of G. horsfieldi strongly reflect ultraviolet, whereas the light patches on the wing cases of the other species absorb ultraviolet. When seen from the side (d-f) the three species may be immediately distinguished in both the visible and ultraviolet by the differences in the white spots on the sides of the abdomen. These white patches are insect whites that reflect all wavelengths in the visible as well as those far into the ultraviolet.*

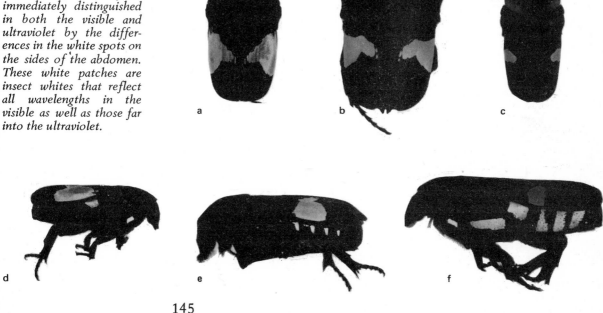

Fig. 26 *Scanning electron micrographs of the fine hairs that reflect insect white on the abdomen of the scarabaeid beetle Glycyphana binotata. See Fig. 25.*

Fig. 27 *Reconstruction of part of a wing scale of the male of the butterfly, Eurema lisa. The laminate ridges projecting upwards are the interference films responsible for the ultraviolet reflection. The pigment granules responsible for the yellowish colour of the scale project downwards in to the air space within the main body of the scale. (After Ghiradella et al.)*

0.5 μm

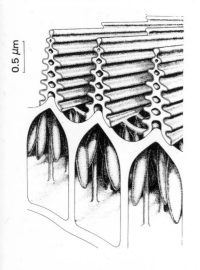

reflect ultraviolet. The colour pattern of all is more or less identical from above. The white patches on the sides, however, are very different in the three species. Now this white is both vertebrate white and insect white, that is, it reflects all wave lengths in the visible spectrum of both vertebrates and insects. Thus these species of scarabaeid beetles can recognize members of their own species both in the visible and ultraviolet.

A great many moths and butterflies have patterns made up of patches of scales that absorb ultraviolet and patches that strongly reflect ultraviolet. Ultraviolet patterns have been most studied in butterflies of the family Pieridae, and in these, as in so many other butterflies, the patterns of the two sexes are different. In all other insects that I have so far examined, scales that reflect ultraviolet do so because they contain an ultraviolet reflecting pigment. However, the scales of many Pieridae are quite exceptional in that their ultraviolet reflection is in fact an interference colour produced by many thin films in the ridges of the scales. We[11] have shown that layers of cuticle about 85 nm thick of a refractive index of about 1.6 alternate with air layers (refractive index 1.0) also about 85 nm thick. The mean refractive index is therefore low (1.3), and as a consequence colour is very dependent upon angle of viewing. Many Pieridae produce brilliant irridescent colours exactly as do the well-known *Morpho* butterflies of Central and South America, the essential difference being that the interference colours of *Morpho* are in the visible part of the spectrum whereas those of the Pieridae are only in the ultraviolet part and therefore visible only to other insects. When a butterfly with structural ultraviolet is flying, bright flashes will be continually emitted as the wings beat through the appropriate angle of viewing.

It is well known that courtship in many butterflies is initiated by the male which depends on visual signals from the wings of a female of its own species. In some pierids it has been shown that the visual signal is the ultraviolet pattern of the female. There is a considerable amount of evidence for the view that the ultraviolet pattern of the male plays an important part in successful courtship, but I know of no unambiguous experimental evidence for this.

Some pierid butterflies belong to aposematic assemblages, and here, as in the scarabaeid beetles mentioned above, the butterflies recognize members of their species and of the opposite sex by means of visual signals to which vertebrates are completely blind. One of the particularly interesting things about pierid butterflies is the fact that ultraviolet reflection is sometimes structural in both sexes

146

Fig. 28 *Brimstone butterfly, Gonepteryx rhamni. Male upper side (a) and under side (b) photographed in visible light and upper side (c) and under side (d) photographed in the ultraviolet, 365 nm. Female upper side (e) and under side (f) photographed in the ultraviolet, 365 nm.*

147

(*Hebomia*), structural only in the male and pigmentary in the female (*Colias, Eurema, Gonepteryx*), or produced by pigments in both sexes (*Euchloe, Pieris, Aporia*). There seems to be no instance in which scale structure is responsible for ultraviolet reflection in the female and only pigment in the male.

Mazokhin-Porshnyakov[32] points out that the ultraviolet reflection coefficient of the white spots of nocturnal moths is very high, ranging from 25 to 55 per cent. He also refers to work that claims that the light at night is very rich in ultraviolet, ' . . . about 75 per cent, on account of the moon . . .' He therefore suggests that the ultraviolet reflections of nocturnal moths play a part in recognizing the opposite sex. However, the ultraviolet component of the albedo of the moon, as measured from space, is surprisingly small: it is less than 2 per cent as compared with 7½ per cent in the visible and over 10 per cent in the infra red. Clearly much of the sun's ultraviolet reflected from the moon will be absorbed by the atmosphere. It thus seems safe to assume that there is so little ultraviolet at night that there must be some other reason for the ultraviolet patterns of nocturnal insects. All nocturnal insects of course have to be somewhere during the day. Some years ago I discovered that the white patches and bands of *Aedes* and other mosquitoes strongly reflected ultraviolet. I assumed[20] that just as mosquitoes and other insects may have a disruptive pattern in the visible they also have one in the ultraviolet. For instance, the alternate white and black bands on the legs of *Stegomyia* and other mosquitoes constitute a disruptive pattern. Because the white is also an insect white and the black absorbs ultraviolet, the banding of the legs is a disruptive pattern for both insects and vertebrates. I do not mean to suggest that all ultraviolet reflection from nocturnal insects has to do with disruptive patterns for protection against diurnal predators: its significance is still an open question.

Ultraviolet patterns of flowers

As long ago as 1793 Sprengel suggested that the dark patches at the bases of the petals of many flowers serve as honey guides. Although his views were generally accepted throughout the nineteenth century, they were not confirmed by experiment until this century.[26,27] In many kinds of flowers nectar guides that are dark in the visible also absorb ultraviolet and so appear coloured to the insect, e.g. in the pink flowers of the wood sorrel. In other flowers the nectar guides are not visible to us but also absorb ultraviolet more strongly than

Fig. 29 *Photographs of three kinds of yellow flowers in the visible on the left and on the right in the ultraviolet. The honey guides are not visible to us. To insects the honey guides will be a different colour from the rest of the flower because they absorb ultraviolet and reflect yellow, whereas the rest of the flower reflects both yellow and ultraviolet. In the photographs taken at 365 nm the honey guides are black because they absorb all ultraviolet. Top pair: Greater Celandine, Chelidonium majus. Middle pair: Lesser Celandine, Ranunculus ficaria. Lower pair: Bulbous Buttercup, Ranunculus bulbosus*

148

other parts of the petals and so are recognizable to insects. In still other flowers, the nectar guides reflect ultraviolet and the other parts of the petals absorb it, and thus it is the reflectance of ultraviolet rather than its absorption that distinguishes them for the insect.

Richtmyer[35] and Lutz[29,30] described the ultraviolet patterns of many kinds of flowers, and it is now a commonplace that most flowers that appear very similar to us, or to other kinds of vertebrates, have strikingly different patterns in the ultraviolet and are therefore distinguished from afar by insects. For instance, a number of quite different composites will often be found growing close to each other. The uniform yellow tint of their flowers, and the absence of dark central or radial markings, makes it difficult for us to distinguish them until we view them in the ultraviolet when for the first time we become aware that each has a conspicuously different pattern. In composites the pigments responsible for the nectar or honey guides are usually flavonol glucosides, which reflect yellow and absorb ultraviolet.[39]

figs. 29,30

fig. 30

Because insects are sensitive to ultraviolet they can distinguish between flowers or other objects that have the same colour in the visible spectrum but absorb or reflect different percentages of ultraviolet or have different patterns of ultraviolet absorption. A white flower or any other white object that absorbs ultraviolet will appear coloured to an insect, and the insect can distinguish such objects from otherwise identical ones that reflect ultraviolet although the two may appear identical to us. Thus an insect not only can distinguish between objects solely on whether they reflect or absorb ultraviolet but may possibly distinguish between them according to the percentage of ultraviolet reflected or absorbed. Furthermore, even when the total amount of ultraviolet reflected from two flowers is the same, they may nevertheless appear very different to an insect if they have different patterns, say on the petals, based solely on local differences in ultraviolet reflectance. It thus seems that irrespective of any colour flowers may have in the visible part of the spectrum, the physical basis exists for flowers to exploit an enormous range of colour and pattern in the ultraviolet part of the spectrum in order to attract pollinators.

Fig. 30 *Photographs of three kinds of flowers in the visible on the left and on the right in the ultraviolet (365 nm). Top pair: Sorrel, Oxalis articulata, a pink flower with honey guides absorbing all light in both the vertebrate and insect spectrum. Middle pair: Tick-seed, Coreopsis, a yellow flower. Lower pair: Leopard's-bane, Dorinicum plantagineum, a yellow flower.*

Significance of the bright colours of flowers

A naturalist would assume that any small animal coloured as brightly as a flower would have a selective advantage in being so conspicuous: it would be poisonous or dangerous in some way or else would be mimicking another animal dangerous to casual predators. He would, of course, take account of the natural environment of the animal, a precaution necessary because some apparently conspicuous animals are not in fact easily recognized in their natural environment. For instance, fish with yellow and black stripes that help them fade into the bright colour scheme of the coral reefs in which they live.

Are we to subscribe to the universal belief that among nearly all living things brightly coloured flowers are an exception? That their vivid reds and yellows do not warn the casual predator away but beckon him to feed? Let us for a moment consider an alternative explanation, and one that will throw new light on the significance of their ultraviolet patterns. In no instance does the success of a species of plant seem to depend upon having its flowers eaten by an animal, although the adequate distribution of a number of species depends upon their seeds being eaten and passing undigested through the alimentary canal of an animal.

It is hard to think of the bright colours of flowers as warning colours because they please us and we seek them out and even breed plants solely for the colour of their flowers. But the aesthetic sense now largely responsible for our attitude to flowers is very recent in evolutionary terms and clearly evolved very late, possibly not until the Pleistocene or about 100 million years after the appearance of brightly coloured flowers.

There are two kinds of mimicry, Batesian and Müllerian. We have seen that many assemblages of animals consist of a number of different poisonous or distasteful species with the same aposematic colours and a number of harmless species similarly coloured. The colours of the latter are called pseudaposematic or false warning colours. For any colour pattern to be effective as a warning one it is of course necessary for some members of the assemblage to be distasteful or poisonous. Therefore, if we are to consider that the bright colours of flowers are warning colours it is essential to show that a 'reasonable' number of flowers are either themselves distasteful or poisonous or are on plants that have these properties.

So many factors are concerned in the effectiveness of warning colours that what might be considered a reasonable percentage of obnoxious forms in one assemblage may not afford effective protection in another. However, the percentage of distasteful or poisonous plants is high enough to quell any serious doubts about the theory on these grounds. For instance, there are just over 1800 kinds of flowering plants (angiosperms) in the British Isles. By 1954 no less than 111 were known to be responsible for cases of serious

152

poisoning or death among livestock.[10] Thus no less than 6 per cent of flowering plants in the British Isles are known to cause serious poisoning or death of livestock. No less than 26 of the 126 families of flowering plants include species known to be occasionally fatal to livestock.

The proportion of poisonous plants seems to be at least as high in other countries. For instance, in 1932 Watt and Breyer-Brandwijk[41] listed 452 poisonous species in South Africa, including those that are strong emetics or purgatives. If these constituted only 6 per cent of the species there would be 7,500 kinds of flowering plants in the region, which is probably an overestimate. Among the poisonous species are 53 that are sometimes fatal to animals and 37 known to have killed humans.[41] Another 500 species are used as medicines. Of these, the many kinds used as aphrodisiacs are almost certainly external irritants, as are all other known aphrodisiacs. The compounds used in modern medicine are nearly all toxic if taken in more than the prescribed quantities, and it seems reasonable to add many if not most medicinal plants of South Africa to the list of plants toxic to some animals. The figure of 500 excludes a fair number used to cure barrenness, impotency, bed-wetting, and other conditions.

All that the theory now advanced requires is that the plant be sufficiently distasteful so that it is sometimes or often avoided. The figures that I have mentioned do not, for instance, include nettles that are largely immune from the attacks of herbivores because of their mildly poisonous hairs. It seems evident that the percentage of obnoxious plants will be very much greater than 6 if we rightly include such plants as nettles and those avoided because of their taste or other properties but which are not sufficiently poisonous to have seriously damaged livestock.

It may be objected that although the leaves and other parts of many plants are poisonous their flowers are often harmless. This is not as weighty an objection as it seems for a variety of reasons.

Animals that experience a distasteful object tend to recognize it by its most conspicuous features, which in plants are frequently the flowers. Furthermore, once animals associate something unpleasant with a brightly coloured object they do not only leave that object alone but tend to avoid edible objects that happen to be nearby. For instance, it has been shown[36] that a crow given the aposematic caterpillar of a cabbage white butterfly remembered the aposematic colour scheme of the caterpillar for nine months, although during this time it was offered no other aposematic species and so there was no reinforcement. After nine months it rejected on sight other caterpillars with somewhat similar aposematic colours. Even when hungry it refused to pick up or eat non-aposematically coloured caterpillars when these were placed close to an aposematic caterpillar. By placing edible caterpillars near an aposematic one it was found that the aposematic caterpillar gave protection to as many as 15 harmless and cryptically coloured caterpillars.[36] Experiments with birds show that some begin by testing even when their aposematic patterns are very little different from those they know, but in due course they begin to generalize and leave all aposematic insects alone. There is, of course, another kind of generalization that arises simply because of the failure of some predators to discriminate between related but dissimilar patterns.

As soon as it is evident that we cannot dismiss the view that flowers have warning colours on the grounds that not enough kinds of plants are obnoxious, other objections come immediately to mind. Herbivores are important enemies of plants, but like most mammals they have no colour vision. On the other hand, birds have excellent colour vision, and nectar is an important part of the diet or even the chief food of over 1,600 species or about 19 per cent of all birds.[25] The fact that flowers are not present on plants for part or much of the year seems to be a further serious objection to the theory.

Flowering plants originated before the Cretaceous, and by the latter half of that period all of the principal groups of dicotyledons were already present. The dominant groups of herbivores in the Cretaceous were iguanodons and ceratopsian reptiles, and, so far as is known, all reptiles have good colour vision. It therefore appears probable that one of the chief selective pressures responsible for the evolution of brightly coloured flowers were herbivorous reptiles with good colour vision. Mammals did not become dominant herbivores until after the Cretaceous with the appearance of the Condylarths in the middle Paleocene, that is, long after the diversification of flowering plants. Throughout the Tertiary different groups of mammals succeeded each other as the dominant herbivores: Hyracoidea in the Oligocene, giraffes in the Lower Miocene, but antelopes and their relatives did not become dominant until the Pliocene. To summarize, mammals were at best insignificant herbivores at the time when the chief groups of flowering plants were evolved, and their lack of colour vision is therefore irrelevant when the origin of the bright colours of flowers is being considered.

Although herbivorous mammals are unable to discriminate wavelengths independently of brightness, flowers with a colour pattern usually also have a pattern of brightness that may enable mammals to identify them. The warning colours of their flowers are only one way in which plants defend themselves. Other means of defence are odour, taste, poisonous substances, hairs, spines, and lignification of the tissues. For instance, a stinging nettle is generally avoided by cattle, horses, sheep, and even voles. The poisonous alkaloids in ragwort usually cause this plant to be left severely alone by rabbits and larger herbivores. Herbivores learn to distinguish plants irrespective of their flowers. In South Africa cattle, sheep, and goats are killed by eating *Dimorphotheca caulescens*, but livestock introduced into the veld where the plant grows eventually learn to recognize it and avoid eating it.[41] Sometimes cattle and horses develop a craving for a poisonous plant and seek it out, a fact made use of by stockbreeders when they wish to identify the plant concerned: an animal turned out again into the same pasture will often lead one directly to the plant.[10] Cattle and horses are known to develop a craving for such poisonous plants as buttercups, bryony, woody nightshade and laurel, and they are able to distinguish them when they are not in flower.

Birds are warm-blooded reptiles with excellent colour vision. Although they originated in the early Cretaceous or before from a stock that also gave rise to the crocodiles, the kinds of birds that are associated with flowers did not evolve until sometime in the Tertiary, that is, long after the evolution of the chief groups of flowering plants. It is thus evident that birds are in no way concerned with the early evolution of brightly coloured flowers.

By the second half of the Tertiary, if not before, certain groups of birds had clearly evolved *pari passu* with the flowers they pollinate. It may be reasonably assumed that before birds began to feed upon nectar, they were attracted to flowers by the presence of insects. Only after a long history of feeding upon flower-inhabiting insects did they begin to rely more and more upon nectar. The subsequent evolution of the relation between birds and flowers is easy to trace, at least in broad outline. We may dwell briefly upon the symbiosis that now exists between many birds and flowers before dealing with a critical question for our theory, namely, how is it that flower-pollinating birds are undoubtedly attracted to colours that are warning colours for most other vertebrates?

The relations between birds and flowers provide a continuous spectrum of mutual adaptations, ranging from those in which neither flower nor bird show any symbiotic adaptation at a morphological level to those in which both flower and bird exhibit marked

H.E. Hinton

morphological changes. We would expect this because morphological changes in living organisms are nearly always preceded by behavioural changes. When the association between flowers and birds has a long history and insects no longer play a part in pollination, the flowers tend to have little or no odour. This seems to be related to the fact that birds generally have a poor sense of smell. Among some of the pollinators, such as humming birds, the olfactory nerve is much reduced or even completely degenerate, e.g. species of Colibri. More nectar tends to be produced than in insect-pollinated flowers, e.g. a bromelid, *Puya chilensis*, has 0.5 to 0.75 grams per flower, and as much as a quarter of a litre can be collected from a single plant.[25] Furthermore, the amount of sugar in the nectar tends to be much less than in insect pollinated flowers: the nectar often has only about 5 per cent sugar, whereas honeybees are not generally attracted to nectar with less than three times this amount of sugar. Many of the highly specialized bird pollinators have long and curved bills as do many humming birds and honeycreepers. Their tongues are often exceptionally long and either split at the apex, as in many humming birds that can form an apical tube with the split tongue, or have an apical brush of long, hair-like papillae, as in some of the honeycreepers and parrots. In this connection it is interesting to note that many bats that pollinate flowers also have apical brushes of papillae on their tongues. The flowers and adjoining parts tend to be much tougher in bird- than in insect-pollinated flowers. For instance, some of the eucalyptus flowers pollinated by parrots are extensively lignified.

The colours of flowers pollinated by birds tend to be pure spectral colours. The preferred colours are red, orange, and yellow, followed by blue, violet, white, and finally cream. In some regions flowers pollinated by birds are very frequently red, as in tropical America. It may be noted here that, apart from some butterflies, few insects are sensitive to red, and, speaking very generally (because sometimes both insects and birds may play a significant part in pollinating the same kind of flower), insects are not much attracted to flowers pollinated by birds. In this connection, the rarity of pure red among orchids is particularly interesting because orchids are primarily pollinated by bees. The few orchids that have various shades of red are either pollinated by butterflies, e.g. species of *Disa* and *Epidendrum*, or by birds.[40]

The peak of specialization is reached by humming birds, which are an exclusively American group. Some of their specializations have already been mentioned. Humming birds obtain much of their protein from insects found either in the flowers or caught on the wing. Their young are reared chiefly on insects, but the birds mainly visit flowers for nectar, and, related to the fact that they feed on the wing and do not land on flowers, many of the flowers pollinated by them are pendant.

Angiosperms are primitively pollinated by insects, and all other methods of pollination — birds, bats, wind, water — are secondary. For insects to be replaced by birds presupposes that for many kinds of flowers there is a selective advantage in birds rather than insects as pollinators. Although a few of the bird pollinators, e.g. some parrots and Meliphagidae, extensively damage flowers, the great majority do not. The chief selective advantages of having birds as pollinators depends on a variety of factors. For instance, birds have a much longer working day, from first to almost last light, whereas insects are not active until long after sunrise and usually cease long before sunset. Also birds work throughout the year and live for several years, whereas insects tend to be strictly seasonal, short-lived, and much more affected by bad weather than birds. So long as it is exclusively pollinated by insects, a plant cannot usefully flower except in the insect season, but when pollinated by birds it is freed of any restriction of this kind.

If our theory is correct that the bright colours of flowers, especially the reds to which most insects are blind, are warning colours for vertebrates, we have to suppose that in the first instance certain birds were attracted to flowers because of the presence on them of large numbers of easily accessible insects. Now it is a fact that some birds are attracted to the warning colours of bees and wasps, and, like the bee-eaters (Meropidae), specialize on feeding on these poisonous insects. These birds are therefore attracted to patterns of yellow and black, red and black, and so on, that is, to patterns of bright colours that not only serve as warning colours for nearly all other vertebrates but also for most birds. It thus seems that some groups of birds have reversed their normal reaction to the bright colours of flowers just as they have done to the bright colours of certain Hymenoptera. Let us for a moment glance at the matter from the plant's point of view. It produces a flower that has to be pollinated. In order to be pollinated it must attract animals competent to pollinate it by colour, odour, or shape, or by some combination of these. It must therefore advertise the presence of its flowers, but in such a way that undesirable animals are repelled. To a large extent flowers have clearly managed to resolve these two apparently contradictory requirements.

157

References

1 Balderrama, N. & Maldonado, H. (1973), 'Ontogeny of the behaviour in the praying mantis', *J. Insect Physiol. 19*, 319-336.

2 Blest, A.D. (1957), 'The function of eyespot patterns in the Lepidoptera', *Behaviour II*, 209-256.

3 Bristowe, W.S. (1941), *The Comity of Spiders*, London.

4 Brower, L.P. (1969), 'Ecological chemistry', *Sci. Am. 220*, 2, 22-29.

5 Cott, H.B. (1940), *Adaptive Coloration in Animals*, London.

6 Denton, E.J., Gilpin-Brown, J.B. & Wright, P.G. (1972), 'The angular distribution of the light produced by some mesopelagic fish in relation to their camouflage', *Proc. Roy. Soc. Lond. (B). 182*, 145-158.

7 Dupont-Raabe, M. (1957), 'Les Mécanismes de l'adaption chromatique chez les insectes', *Arch. Zool. exp. gén. 94*, 61-294.

8 Eisner, T. & Kafatos, F.C. (1962), 'Defense mechanism of arthropods. X: A pheromone promoting aggregation in an aposematic distasteful insect', *Psyche, Camb. 69*, 53-61.

9 Forbes, H.O. (1885), *A Naturalists's Wanderings in the Eastern Archipelago*, London.

10. Forsyth, A.A. (1954), 'British poisonous plants', *Bull. Min. Agric. Fish. Fd H.M.S.O. 161*, 1-111.

11 Ghiradella, H., Aneshansley, D., Eisner, T., Silberglied, R.E. & Hinton, H.E. (1972), 'Ultra-violet reflection of a male butterfly: interference color caused by thin-layer elaboration of wing scales', *Science, Wash. 178*, 1214-1217.

12 Gressitt, J.L. (1969) Epizoic symbiosis. *Ent. News 80*, 1-5.

13 Haviland, M.J. (1926), '*Forest, Steppe and Tundra. Studies in animal environment*, Cambridge.

14 Hingston, R.W.G. (1927), 'Field observations on spider mimics', *Proc. zool. Soc. Lond. 1927*, 841-858.

15 Hingston, R.W.G. (1932), *A Naturalist in the Guiana Forest*, London.

16 Hinton, H.E. (1955a), 'Protective devices of endopterygote pupae', *Trans. Soc. Brit. Ent. 12*, 49-92.

17 Hinton, H.E. (1955b), 'On the respiratory adaptations, biology, and taxonomy of the Psephenidae, with notes on some related families (Coleoptera)', *Proc. zool. Soc. Lond. 125*, 543-568.

18 Hinton, H.E. (1958), 'On the pupa of *Spalgis lemolea* Druce (Lepidoptera, Lycaenidae), *J. Soc. Brit. Ent. 6*, 23-25.

19 Hinton, H.E. (1970a), 'Some little known surface structures', *Symp. R. ent. Soc. Lond. 5*, 41-58

20 Hinton, H.E. (1970b), Algunas pequenas estructuras de insectos observadas con microscopio electrónico explorador', *Acta politec. méx. 10*, 181-201.

21 Hinton, H.E. & Gibbs, D.F. (1969), 'Diffraction gratings in Phalacrid beetles', *Nature, Lond. 221*, 953-954.

22 Hinton, H.E. & Gibbs, D.F., (1971), 'Diffraction gratings in gyrinid beetles', *J. Insect. Physiol. 17*, 1023-1035.

23 Hinton, H.E. & Jarman, G.M. (1973), 'Physiological colour change in the elytra of the Hercules beetle, *Dynastes hercules*', *J. Insect Physiol. 19*, 533-549.

24 Huxley, J. (1957), *New Wine in New Bottles*, London.

25 Jaeger, P. (1959), *La Vie éntrange des fleurs*, Horizons de France, Paris.

26 Knoll, F. (1956), *Die Biologie der Blüte*, Berlin.

27 Kugler, H. (1955), *Einführung in die Blütenökologie*, Stuttgart.

28 Lloyd, J.E. (1969), 'Flashes of *Photuris* fireflies: their value and use in recognizing species', *Florida Ent. 52*, 29-35.

29 Lutz, F.E. (1924), 'Apparently non-selective characters and combinations of characters, including a study of ultraviolet in relation to the flower-visiting habits of insects', *Ann. N.Y. Acad. Sci. 29*, 181-283.

30 Lutz, F.E. (1933), ' "Invisible" colours of flowers and butterflies', *J. Am. Mus. nat. Hist. 33*, 565-576.

31 Lutz, F.E. & Grisewood, E.N. (1934), 'Reactions of *Drosophila* to 2537Å radiation', *Am. Mus. Novit. 706*, 1-16.

32 Mazokhin-Porshnyakov, G.A. (1969), *Insect Vision*, New York.

33 Portischinsky, I. (1890), 'Caterpillars and butterflies of St Petersburg Province (Lepidopterarum Rossiae biologia)', *Horae Soc. ent. ross. 19*, 50-97.

34 Poulton, E.B. (1924), 'The terrifying appearance of *Laternaria* (Fulgoridae) founded on the most prominent features of the alligator', *Proc. ent. Soc. Lond. 1924*, x1iii-x1ix.

35 Richtmyer, F.K. (1923), 'The reflection of ultraviolet by flowers', *J. optic. Soc. Am. 7*, 151-168.

36 Rothschild, M. (1964), 'An extension of Dr Lincoln Brower's theory on bird predation and food specificity, together with some observations on bird memory in relation to aposematic colour patterns', *Entomologist 97*, 73-78.

37 Ruiter, L. de (1952), 'Some experiments on the camouflage of stick caterpillars', *Behaviour 4*, 222-232.

38 Thompson, D'A.W. (1942), *On Growth and Form*, Cambridge.

39 Thompson, W.R., Meinwald, J., Aneshansley, D. & Eisner, T. (1972), 'Flavonols: pigments responsible for ultraviolet absorption in nectar guide of flowers', *Science, Wash. 177*, 528-530.

40 Van der Pijl, L. & Dodson, C.H. (1966), *Orchid Flowers. Their pollination and evolution,*

41 Watt, J.M. and Breyer-Brandwijk, M.G. (1932), *The Medicinal and Poisonous Plants of Southern Africa, being an account of their medicinal uses, chemical composition, pharmacological effects and toxicology in man and animal,* Edinburgh.

42 Wickler, W. (1962), 'Zur Stammesgeschichte funktionell korrelierter Organ- und Verhaltensmerkmale: Ei-Attrappen und Maulbrüten bei afrikanischen Cichliden', *Z. Tierpsychol. 19*, 129-164; 256.

43 Wickler, W. (1968), *Mimicry in Plants and Animals*, London and New York.

159

Fig. 1 *To perceive the bird in this picture the eye needs to classify some parts of the pattern as background and some as the animal. It may be that the pictorial recognition difficulties observed in some cultures are essentially of this nature. More complex problems arise when a picture makes several mutually exclusive classificatory schemes possible.*

4 Illusion and Culture

Jan B. Deregowski

Symbols constitute a whole spectrum of devices for communicating reality, ranging from purely arbitrary words to frankly representational pictures. Such expressions as 'Strzeż się psa' or 'Graesset måa ikke betraedes' are utterly incomprehensible to those unfamiliar with the code used. Even in a familiar tongue, 'when we endeavour to make a full and accurate verbal description of even the simplest things, such for instance as an ordinary kitchen can-opener, we accumulate such an enormous and complicated heap of [words] that it becomes practically impossible for anyone but a highly trained specialist to understand what we have said'.[37] In these circumstances we reach for a sketch pad, and have an excellent historical justification for doing so, for it is held that only after the introduction of prints (about A D 1400) did exchange of technical information begin to gather momentum and the development of modern technology commence.

And yet, a picture by an ancient Egyptian is unlike a picture by a Renaissance painter. Such cross-cultural differences pose a host of questions about the relative merits of various styles. Anthropological and cross-cultural studies suggest some possible answers.

Over two and a half centuries ago Taylor[64] in his 'work necessary for painters, architects etc. to judge and regulate designs by' explained that the veracity of a painting is the direct result of the extent to which light reflected from its surface approximates to the light which would be reflected from the depicted object. This very principle is embodied in those aids to drawing which rely on a translucent screen which intercepts reflected light and leaves the artist only the task of recording the pattern which the intercepted light makes. Devices of this kind were once much in vogue for teaching the rules of perspective;[27] recently, however, the same approach has been successfully used in teaching pictorial perception to a group of African adults.[11] Such an analysis of pictures suggests that there exists an optimum way of depicting an object, which can

161

Jan B. Deregowski

be arrived at by consideration of purely physical principles of propagation of light. Gibson[26] agreeing with this view remarks:

> It does not seem reasonable to assert that the use of perspective in paintings is merely a convention, to be used or discarded by the painter as he chooses. Nor is it possible that new laws of geometrical perspective will be discovered, to overthrow the old ones. It is true that the varieties of painting at different times in history, and among different peoples, prove the existence of different ways of seeing, in some sense of the term. But there are no differences among people in the basic way of seeing, that is, by means of light, and by way of the rectilinear propagation of light.

An important touchstone by which this statement, as well as other postulates about psychological precepts, can be judged is provided by cross-cultural research; a comparative study of processes of culturally different groups. If the laws of pictorial perception are as definite as Taylor suggests, then little difference between such groups should be observed; but if important differences are observed they need to be elucidated, perhaps by taking into account other than purely physical factors.

Some observations on non-Western cultures

Before considering cross-cultural evidence — a word of warning. Most cross-cultural studies confound culture with other factors, such as genetics and ecology. Hence many of them, in the days when a different terminology was *à la mode*, would have been described as 'racial' — in the non-evaluative sense of the term. Beveridge's[6] paper, for example, on 'Racial differences in phenomenal regression', if it had been published today, would certainly have had the term 'racial' replaced by 'cross-cultural'. Yet even if one cannot always definitely attribute an observed effect to a particular cause, this does not invalidate the data entirely. It would be the consequence if such an attribution were the sole object of study, but this is not the case. Many a psychologist is interested in a process rather than an individual or a social group. In studying a process, such as remembering, learning, or maternal behaviour, he, by tradition, spans many species, from things that crawl or swim to things that walk and things that fly. Surely, then, he should also study the behaviour of various subgroups within the same species. Further, many cross-cultural studies have been criticised on a variety of grounds. Yet

162

unless these criticisms suggest a systematic error, they do not invalidate conclusions drawn, but allow these studies to provide mutual support. Thus if responses of a sample of Eskimos show no significant correlation between two psychological tests, and the same result is obtained in Nigerian clerks and workers, one is probably justified in accepting this evidence as a tentative suggestion (and all scientific findings are tentative to a greater or less degree) that the phenomena are independent. An alternative explanation, that there prevails, in the examples quoted, such a combination of genetic and ecological factors as to obscure a real correlation, remains, in the circumstances, a less elegant, and less attractive, alternative. The importance of studying various populations lies in the very fact that they present unique combinations of variables which may, and occasionally do throw an entirely new light on phenomena.[38]

Old missionary reports sometimes contain observations which, though lacking the sophistication of controlled experiments, are sufficiently well described to offer a rich ground for hypotheses. Thus difficulties in perception of pictures found in some social groups, whose systematic investigation was begun about fifteen years ago, had been reported over seventy years ago by Dr Laws[5], a Scottish missionary active in Nyasaland:

> Take a picture in black and white, and the natives cannot see it. You may tell the natives: 'This is a picture of an ox and a dog'; and the people will look at it and look at you and that look says that they consider you a liar. Perhaps you say again, 'Yes, this is a picture of an ox and a dog.' Well, perhaps they will tell you what they think this time! If there are boys about, you say: 'This is really a picture of an ox and a dog. Look at the horn of the ox, and there is his tail!' And the boy will say: 'Oh! yes and there is the dog's nose and eyes and ears! Then the old people will look again and clap their hands and say, 'Oh! yes, it is a dog.' When a man has seen a picture for the first time, his book education has begun!

Fraser[24] had similar experience as shown by the following description of an African woman groping in search of meaning in a picture:

> She discovered in turn the nose, the mouth, the eye, but where was the other eye? I tried, by turning my profile, to explain why she could only see one eye but she hopped round to my other side to point out that I possessed a second eye which the other lacked.

163

Nor are such observations confined to the past. Bitsch, a Danish explorer, recently encountered similar difficulties in Pigmies from Ituri in the Congo.

However, one can also find contradictory evidence in reports from Africa:

> The first picture flashed on the sheet was that of an elephant. The wildest excitement immediately prevailed, many of the people jumping up and shouting, fearing the beast must be alive while those nearest to the sheet sprang up and fled. The chief himself crept stealthily forward and peeped behind the sheet to see if the animal had a body, and when he discovered that the animal's body was only the thickness of the sheet, a great roar broke the stillness of the night.[49]

Similar, but not as dramatic, responses to pictorial material have been described by Doob[22] and by Thomson.[66] Thomson showed to Wa-taveta women 'a few photographs of some of their charming white sisters'. These photographs 'were a source of great delight. They actually supposed them to be living beings, and if told that they were asleep, or were having chop, they were quite satisfied.' No recognition difficulties there.

Thus the difficulties appear to vary perhaps in kind, perhaps merely in degree, but as rigid experimental procedures of empirical psychology have not been used one cannot be sure of their validity or meaning.

The problem foreshadowed above can be broken into several interrelated constituents.

Problems of pictorial recognition

An inability to perceive that a pattern of lines and shaded areas on a flat surface describes some aspect of the real world would form such a basic obstacle to pictorial perception that further difficulties simply could not arise. This situation can best be conveyed to a reader by figure 1, in which cues to a meaningful organisation of the pattern have been much reduced and which, therefore, looks very much like abstract design. The possibility that such an inability might be present is suggested by the laborious way in which the African women described above pieced together a picture of a human head, and by Dr Laws' observation. More complex difficulties may also arise; a depicted object may be recognised as something other than the artist had intended because of the difference of the cultural

164

Illusion and culture

Fig. 2 *The duck-rabbit offers us two alternative schemes for perceptual organization, each leading to a meaningful figure.*

background of the artist and the viewer. Furthermore, interpretation of cues conveying pictorial depth may prove an obstacle. These cues tell the observer that the depicted objects, although presented on a flat surface – that of paper or a screen – are not to be perceived as being in the same plane and equidistant from the observer.

A duck-rabbit, one of the pet creatures of psychology, which has waddled or hopped from the pages of a German humorous weekly to Wittgenstein's philosophical seminar, has its cultural counterpart in fig. 3. When subjects from East Africa were invited to say what they saw in this simple drawing, they described it as a family group in which a young woman carries upon her head a four-gallon tin – a common sight in those parts. Such an interpretation occurs to but a few 'Western' observers, who generally see the drawing as portraying an indoor scene, a rectangular window being just behind the young woman's head. The artist presents observers with two important cues: the *pictorial depth cue* provided by the corner of the room which, to a 'Western' observer, reinforces the *cultural cue* of a rectangular window. Many African subjects, as will be shown later, do not

Fig. 3 *A window or a petrol can? An indoor or an outdoor scene? Perceptual skills and cultural experience determine what one sees in this picture.*

165

Jan B. Deregowski

respond to the pictorial depth cues as strongly as Western subjects do. Moreover the cultural cue of an intended window was to them contradictory to such a depth cue, since it was not a window at all but a four-gallon tin. (The reader, if of Western cultural background, may wish to try to 'Africanize' himself for a while by covering the Y-shaped representation of the corner of the room with a piece of paper, thus leaving himself with only the cultural cue: this may enable him to see the four-gallon tin he did not see before.) If such simple drawings are misunderstood, what guarantee is there that the assumption is true, which is so often tacitly made in popular campaigns of health education, safety, agricultural instruction, etc., that pictorial representation constitutes a universal tongue? Empirical search for an answer to this question has yielded some interesting and useful results.

As far as pictorial recognition is concerned, the evidence is rather scanty. Apart from the reports already quoted, there are observations by Herskovits[30] concerning a bush Negress, who failed to recognize her own son in a photograph; and by Waburton,[68] who found that Ghurkha recruits often failed to recognize pictures even of objects they knew quite well. Similar observations have been made in Nigeria[3] and South Africa.[39,7] On the other hand, Mead[51] found no comparable difficulties in Samoa. Mead's work, in turn, is difficult to reconcile with a study by Forge,[50] who found that the Abelam of New Guinea:

. . . when shown photographs of themselves in action, or of any pose other than face or full figure looking directly at the camera . . . cease to be able to 'see' the photograph at all. Even people from other villages, who came especially because they knew I had taken a photograph of a relative who had subsequently died, and were often pathetically keen to see his features, were initially unable to see him at all, turning the photograph in all directions. With colour they were happier, partly because they looked into a viewer, which itself was three-dimensional, instead of staring at a flat sheet, but they could rarely identify individuals and had a tendency to regard any brightly coloured photograph with no outstanding form as a tambaran display. Since I needed identifications from photographs of yam exchange brawls, ceremonies, and debates I wanted a few boys to see photographs; they learned to do this after a few hours of concentrated looking and discussion on both sides.

166

Alas, both the phenomenon and the training procedure are only briefly dealt with, and no mention is made of any experimental controls. (Would the subjects have recognised black and white slides in the viewer? How does the three-dimensionality of the viewer affect perception of what one presumes to have been colour transparencies?) Thus one can only regard this study as heuristic. There is on the other hand a set of observations derived from a Western culture and of sufficient methodological rigour to merit closer consideration. Hochberg and Brooks[32] tested a child brought up with as limited an exposure to pictures as was possible in the American culture and no specific instructions as to what drawings represented, up to an age of nineteen months. The child was shown pictures, and it was recorded what he called them. The correctness of the names given was later judged by two independent assessors. The results showed that the child was capable of recognizing depicted objects.

Considerations of these reports have led to a study in a very isolated area.[21] The subjects, most of whom had probably never seen a picture, were men, women and children of the lowland section of the Me'en, a remote Ethiopian tribe. It was noticed by Muldrow that members of this tribe, when given a page from a children's colouring book, would smell it, examine its texture, listen to it while flexing it, even attempt to taste it, but entirely ignore the picture. This might, however, have been due to sheer unfamiliarity with paper. It is possible that, on being confronted with what was an entirely novel material, the Me'en examined it thoroughly using all sensory modalities and ignored surface markings, thinking them to be of little consequence. To obviate this difficulty, it was decided to print pictures on coarse cloth, a material with which the Me'en are familiar. Three such pictures were prepared, all about 50 cm x 100 cm in size. Two of these showed single animals, a buck and a leopard; the third, a composite picture, showed a hunting scene. Only the first two are of interest at the moment. (The third picture was based on one of Hudson's test pictures; the test is described later.) Each subject was shown first the picture of a buck and asked, 'What do you see?' Only a small proportion of subjects responded 'Don't know'. When the second picture, illustrating a leopard, was shown and the same question was asked, there were no 'don't know' responses at all. It therefore appears that the difficulties in recognition of common objects *clearly* depicted on *familiar* material are not present in all cultures in which pictures are practically non-existent.

Fig. 4 *A buck and a leopard: the drawings used to study pictorial recognition in the Me'en.*

167

Jan B. Deregowski

It is noteworthy, however, that the recognition of depicted animals in Me'en was not instantaneous. The reports obtained, as subjects examined the pictures, show clearly how various hypotheses were tested, and how various elements were recognised and linked, in an attempt to arrive at a comprehensive whole. This gradual accumulation of information as parts of a depicted object are named is reminiscent of the observations gathered in other cultures described earlier. This way of responding is similar to that observed by Potter[10] when he presented American children with blurred photographs, and has been noted also by Abercrombie[1] in medical students learning to interpret X-ray plates. It seems, therefore, to be generally evoked by novel pictorial stimuli. The following two reports exemplify the difficulties experienced by the Me'en:

1. *Lowland man 35 years old*

Experimenter: Points to the picture: 'What do you see?'
Subject: 'I'm looking closely. That is a tail. This is a foot. That is a leg joint. Those are horns.'
E: 'What is the whole thing?'
S: 'Wait. Slowly, I am still looking. Let me look and I will tell you. In my country this is a water buck.'

2. *Lowland man 25 years old*

E: Points to the picture: 'What do you see?'
S: 'What is this? It has horns, leg ... front and back, tail, eyes. Is it a goat? A sheep? Is it a goat?'

This confirms that lowlanders have a difficulty in piecing the picture together and are unsure of the validity of their conclusion. By comparison, the more sophisticated highlanders of the same tribe on almost all occasions instantly named the animal.

There is also evidence that the Me'en find the situation stressful. Two of them, a woman of 30 and a girl of 11, tried to run away when the third picture was presented; only the older of the pair could be cajoled back to complete the test. Another woman of 20, who was anxious to participate in the experiment, appeared to the experimenter to be disturbed by the gradual perception of the picture. Yet another subject said at the end of the experiment: 'I don't know. I am tired.' It is unfortunately impossible to be sure to

168

what extent these responses were due to the testing situation as a whole, and to what extent they were the result of stresses arising when perceptual reorganization was called for. They may be similar to observations in a Western industrial setting.[65] Industrial trainees required to learn a new way of perceiving find this emotionally disturbing, especially when a new figure-ground discrimination was demanded (a task essentially the same as that required of the Me'en).

The Me'en data thus do not appear to differ radically from data obtained elsewhere and provide no convincing evidence of failure of pictorial recognition of clearly depicted objects in remote populations, but illustrate an aspect of a universal perceptual process.

However, correct recognition of a depicted object, even in pictorially rich cultures, does not mean that pictures evoke the same responses as do the objects they portray. When Klapper et al.[42] asked Western children to show by gestures how they would use a tool which they readily recognised in a picture, their responses were less vivid than when they were asked to do the same and were shown the real object. This absence of a one-to-one relationship between objects and their pictures is confirmed by observations of matching behaviour of Zambian women.[16] They were given either a model animal or a picture of such a model and asked to match it either to a corresponding model or to a corresponding picture. The task of matching two identical stimuli, either two models or two pictures, led to few errors; but when the subjects had to translate from one mode of representation into another, either by finding an appropriate picture given its model or by finding an appropriate model given its picture, the frequency of errors increased greatly. Further, it has been shown that American children coming from certain sub-cultures found it more difficult to categorise pictures than to categorise the depicted objects, although they experienced no difficulty in recognising these objects in pictures.[61] A cross-cultural experiment inspired by this finding showed that when Zambian children were asked to sort out toys and photographs of toys, which they easily recognised, and their responses were compared with those of Scottish children, the two groups did not differ on sorting of toys; but on sorting of photographs, the Zambian group performed less well.[20]

The role of pictures as symbols of reality will be considered again later; it is not the aspect which has been the main preoccupation of cross-cultural psychologists. This place of honour is occupied by 'pictorial depth': the third dimension, which by various devices the artist tries to evoke while drawing on a flat surface.

The seminal cross-cultural work on this problem was done by Hudson,[34] who designed a special pictorial depth perception test. This consists of a series of pictures on which various combinations of three pictorial depth cues occur. The three cues are:

(i) *Familiar size cue* An object 'A' (say, an elephant) which is known to be larger than object 'B' (say, an antelope) is drawn as smaller than 'B'. If this cue is understood correctly the observer should interpret the picture as showing an elephant which is further away from him than the antelope.

(ii) *Overlap cue.* When an object 'A' obscures a portion of an object 'B' the latter must be further away. Thus when an elephant stands on a hill which is partly obscured by a hill on which an antelope stands, the antelope must be nearer to the viewer than the elephant.

(iii) *Perspective cue.* A convergence of two lines known to represent two parallel lines suggests distance. An elephant drawn near such lines, representing the edges of a road, at a point where they are close together should be 'seen' as further away from the observer than an antelope drawn at a point where those lines are further apart.

Figure 5, one of seven from the original test, conveys the essential nature of two of these cues. It will be noted that a whole group of cues, known as density gradients, which have been shown[25] to be especially powerful in conveying pictorial depth, is not used in Hudson's test. These cues rely on the fact that given a set of elements which are known to be approximately uniform, be they cracks in a depicted wall, pebbles on a depicted beach, or thin air, the artist by drawing them smaller or larger, darker or lighter, can create an impression of pictorial depth. Such an omission does not invalidate the test when used cross-culturally, although, as will be shown later, it imposes certain limitations upon conclusions derived from the results it yields.

In Hudson's hunting scene the pictures are so arranged that a three-dimensional interpretation of the cues results in a response that the hunter is trying to spear the antelope, which is nearer to him than the elephant. An alternative interpretation, showing complete lack of awareness of pictorial depth, is that the elephant is nearer to the hunter and is about to be speared. Subjects are shown one picture at a time and asked to name all the depicted objects (in order to check that the elements are correctly recognised) and are then

Fig. 5 *Is the elephant or the buck nearer to the hunter? The figure contains two depth cues: familiar size and overlap.*

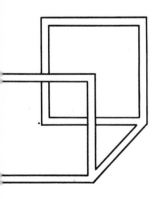

Fig. 6 *One of the figures used in the construction test, which called for making of models using sticks and Plasticine. Do you see it as a 3D representation or in a single plane?*

questioned about the relationship between these objects. 'What is closer to the man?' 'What is the man doing?' Replies to these two questions classify an observer as either a person capable of perceiving pictorial depth (a 3D-perceiver) or a person incapable of this (2D-perceiver).

This test and its derivatives have been used in many parts of Africa (see reference nos. 11, 21, 34, 36, 12, 40, 41, 15) with subjects drawn from a variety of tribal and linguistic groups. The results are unequivocal: unsophisticated African subjects find it difficult to see pictorial depth in these pictures. Furthermore this difficulty varies but appears to be present, to some extent, also at higher educational and social levels. Nor is this tendency a characteristic evoked by this particular test only. Consider fig. 6. It can be interpreted as showing two squares, one behind the other and connected by a single rod. This is a three-dimensional interpretation. A 2D perceiver should see it as showing two squares *in the same plane, the plane of the paper* and connected by a rod also *in this plane.* Hence, if Hudson's test described above is effective, the persons designated by it as two-dimensional perceivers should be capable of building only a flat model when given such and similar drawings, whereas three-dimensional perceivers should build a well-spaced frame showing unambiguous evidence of three-dimensional perception.

When this *construction task* was given to a number of people who were also tested by Hudson's method it was found that although a proportion of testees, who were, by Hudson's criteria, classified as two-dimensional perceivers, built three-dimensional constructions, very few of Hudson's three-dimensional responders made flat models.[12] Hence Hudson's test is stricter than the construction test – but its validity is not questioned by these results. A check upon the correctness of this conclusion was obtained by using a

171

Jan B. Deregowski

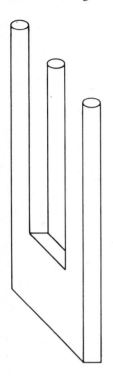

Fig. 7 *The two-pronged trident. For most observers this drawing is meaningless, yet the eye continues vainly to search for meaningful organization invoking the illusion of depth, only to be befuddled by this very illusion.*

fig. 8

'two-pronged trident'. Most of us find it strangely confusing. This confusion is a direct result of an attempt to interpret the pattern as portraying a three-dimensional object. When no such attempt is made, as in the case of two-dimensional perceivers, the pattern is seen as flat, and no confusion about the number of prongs can arise. One would expect that the 'trident' should be more difficult to recall and draw for those observers who are confused by it than for those who are not. This is indeed the case. When subjects designated as two- and three-dimensional perceivers by the *construction task* are asked to copy this figure, the former find it relatively easier to do so than the latter, when the task is so arranged that the subjects are required to retain the figure in their memories before beginning to draw. If no such requirement is imposed, the two groups do not differ.[13]

Do three-dimensional perceivers *see* depth in the pictures, as suggested by the difficulties most of us experience with the two-pronged trident, or do they merely skilfully juggle the cues available? Pandora's box can be used to obtain an answer. This apparatus is described by its designer[28] as follows:

The figure is presented back-illuminated, to avoid texture, and it is viewed through a sheet of polaroid. A second sheet of polaroid is placed over one eye crossed with the first so that no light from the figure reaches the eye. Between the eyes and the figure is a half-silvered mirror through which the figure is seen but which also reflects one or more small light sources mounted on an optical bench. These appear to lie in the figure: indeed optically they *do* lie in the figure, provided the path length of the lights to the eyes is the same as that of the figures to the eyes. But the small light sources are seen with both eyes, while the figure is seen with only *one* eye because of the crossed polaroid. By moving the lights along their optical bench, they may be placed so as to lie at the same distance as any selected part of the figure.

When a Hudson's test picture embodying both familiar size and overlap cues was made into a transparency and presented in this apparatus, African observers, drawn from a population stratum known to be largely 2D, both on Hudson's test and the construction task, did not show perception of pictorial depth. The distance at which they set the movable light was not influenced by whether they were asked to put it just above the elephant, just above the hunter or just above the antelope. In contrast with these responses, sophisti-

172

cated European observers set the light further away when setting it over the elephant than when setting it over the other two figures, showing that not merely were they interpreting conventional cues but they actually *saw* depth in the picture. On the other hand the responses of these two groups of observers did not differ when a transparency containing solely familiar size cues was used. Neither of them saw the elephant further away than the other two figures.[15] The result need not surprise us since it is known that even for sophisticated 'Western' observers familiar size cues are rather weak.[31,55] Thus while the Western observers, who would interpret both these pictures three-dimensionally, actually *see* depth only in the picture which has the overlap as well as familiar size cues, both the ability to interpret the artistic conventions and *seeing* of depth appear to be absent in the African observers in our sample.

It has been argued[73] that recognition of a depicted object itself implies a degree of perception of pictorial depth, and hence that only the *space between the objects* portrayed in the picture presents a problem to the populations which are judged two-dimensional on Hudson's test and its derivatives. No evidence is offered to sustain this contention, which is thought to be self-evident, for 'if these Africans were "entirely two-dimensional" they would not have construed lines on paper as representing solid objects'. The simplest and most convincing data in support of such a claim could be obtained by placing a simple silhouette of a clearly recognizable object, such as a cup, in Pandora's box and asking the subjects to adjust the moving light so that it coincided with the further and

Fig. 8 *Gregory's Pandora's Box, displaying one of Hudson's figures. After Hudson*

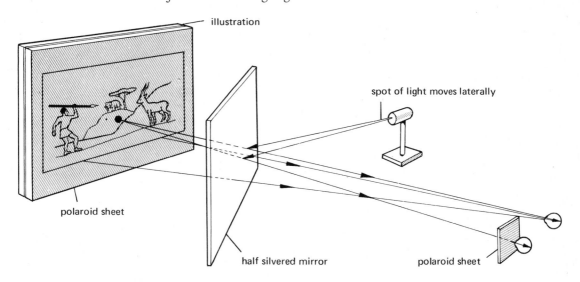

173

Jan B. Deregowski

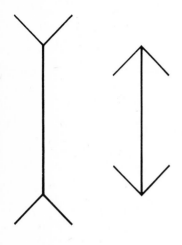

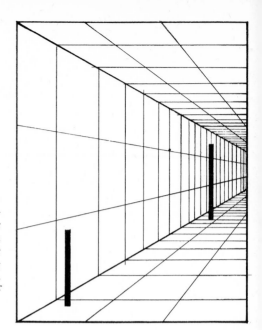

Fig. 10 *The Corridor illusion. The two vertical bars are of equal length although they do not appear to be. Even young children, unaware of perspective, see them as of different length.*

Fig. 9 *The Müller-Lyer illusion. The vertical lines are equal but the left one appears to be longer. It has been suggested that this illusion is influenced by the 'carpenteredness' of the world around us, the angled fins evoking responses similar to those evoked by rectangular objects.*

fig. 9

fig. 11

fig 10

nearer edges of the object. If these two adjustments differed consistently showing depth, the contention would be justified. Such data, however, are not at hand; but logical considerations suggest that such support would not have been obtained had an experiment been carried out. Recognition of a profile silhouette of a human head by pictorially sophisticated subjects as such does not in itself tell them anything of the width of a depicted face.

Paradoxically there are meaningless drawings which cause subjects to perceive pictorial depth. Several of the visual illusions do. Gregory[28] has shown this to be the case for the Müller-Lyer illusion. Stacey[63] did so for the Horizontal-Vertical illusion. In neither of these figures is a normal naive adult likely to see a representation of a three-dimensional object. One must also note Newman's[53] finding that the effect of the Corridor illusion is present in children, even if they do not interpret the figure as representing a three-dimensional scene.

There seems therefore to be no reason for thinking either that recognition of a drawing necessarily *implies* perception of pictorial depth, or that recognition is necessary for perception of pictorial depth.

Effect of various cues

The extent to which various pictorial cues contribute towards depth perception in populations which experience depth-perception difficulties have not hitherto been extensively investigated.

174

Illusion and culture

The Me'en study and other data described above suggest that failure to recognize the picture may be due to the more basic inability to discriminate the figure from the background. If so, this difficulty may not be an isolated aspect of the way these observers perceive the world around them. There is a widely used psychological test in which testees are asked to find a figure camouflaged by an array of spurious lines. Persons who find this task difficult are very likely to find some other tasks, which may at first sight appear unrelated, equally difficult. For example, they find it difficult not only to reconstruct a geometric pattern given a model and a set of wooden blocks, but also to judge whether a luminous line within a tilted luminous square frame, displayed in a totally dark room, is vertical or not. Only the first of these tests intuitively appears to be related to the 'search for a picture' of the Me'en. The tests, do, however, share a common element; they all call for abstraction of elements presented in a matrix of irrelevancies, and are said to measure 'field independence'. And indeed West African observations show that field independence is correlated with pictorial perception. Persons who are more field dependent tend to do worse on pictorial perception tests.[11]

One would expect drawings embodying those illusion figures which are known to evoke perception of depth to be particularly efficacious in evoking perception of pictorial depth. Of all simple illusions, the Ponzo is probably the most 'natural'. Results of American and Guamaian samples on this illusion are presented in fig. 14. It is noteworthy that data for the American sample show a steady increase of the magnitude of the illusion with an increase in the number of depth cues, and hence, presumably, an increase in perception of pictorial depth. In contrast with these results, the

Fig. 11 *The lines are equal but the vertical one seems longer. This may be because the vertical line evokes a similar response to that evoked by a horizontal line receding from the observer, and the tendency may be greater in inhabitants of open places, familiar with receding lines.*

Fig. 12 *It is more difficult for field-dependent than field-independent persons to find the figure on the left in the one on the right.*

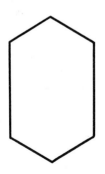

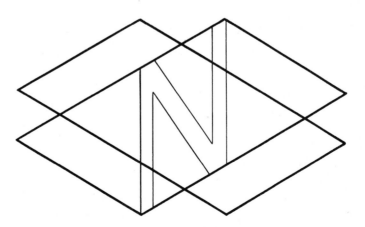

175

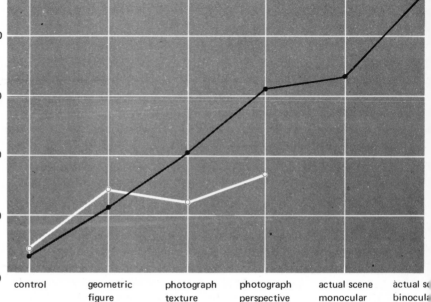

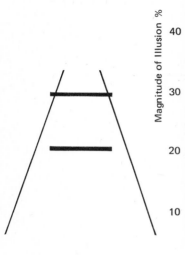

Fig. 13 *The Ponzo illusion*

Fig. 14 *The responses of American and Guamaian subjects to the Ponzo illusion, under various conditions. In control conditions two equal horizontal lines were shown. The geometric figure condition is shown in fig. 13. The photograph texture condition displayed two equal horizontal lines on a background of a richly-textured meadow. In the photographic perspective condition railway lines as well as rich grass texture served as background for the two lines.*

Guam sample shows significantly lower illusory effect and little variations between the three pictorial conditions involved. (Unfortunately no responses to monocular and binocular views of the real scene were obtained from this sample.)

The difference between the two samples is attributed by the authors[4 5] to the difference of environment in which Guamaians and American subjects live. 'There are no railroads on the island, vistas of land are short, due to hilly terrain covered by tropical plant growth, and [people] do not normally view the kind of environment typified by the study.' This is an explanation concordant with the view that our ecological and cultural experiences affect the way we see.

The relatively small effect of the density gradient in Guamaians (and they surely must have experienced density gradients) is difficult to account for and is contrary to South African observations that the density gradients are particularly efficient in evoking perception of pictorial depth.[5 7] It appears that in the case of the Guam sample the perspective and the density gradient cues, which are additive in the case of American students, do not combine to increase the illusory effect.

Consider the two possible explanations of Guamaian performance: (i) that the subjects fail to integrate two different depth cues and hence do not increase their perception of depth beyond that evoked by only one of these cues; and (ii) that the subjects reach the 'ceiling' of their performance with just one of these cues, and hence that addition of another cue cannot affect their responses. *Prima facie* the second explanation appears more plausible and is in agreement with the postulated effects of visual experience.

Other illusion figures have been shown to be concealed in 'meaningful' pictorial material, but this was done rather to demonstrate their place in general theories of perception than to investigate their role in pictorial perception. In consequence traditional forms of illusion have been used, which can perhaps be thought of as typical, although some of these forms, by virtue of their symmetry, do not present the most frequently encountered environmental characteristics which they are supposed to epitomize.

'Perception may be regarded as tending to maximize the invariance of the data presented',[69] and therefore a perspective gradient evokes perception of pictorial depth, as an alternative to the perception of a large number of different shapes and sizes. An 'economy principle' is invoked to explain why, when the number of disparate elements is small, as for example when all but two bottom rows of the figures are covered, three-dimensional perception does not occur, whereas when the number is increased a perceptual reorganization takes place and the figure is perceived as having depth. The same principle can be invoked to explain perception of depth in the *construction* task figures and the observed difference between responses to figures 6 and 16. The second of these figures is symmetrical about the observers' median plane, and symmetry, by reducing the load on the perceptual system,[17] makes it more likely that it will be perceived as flat than the first figure. In building models in response to these figures Scottish schoolboys, unlike Zambian schoolboys, tended to see fig. 6 as depicting a three-dimensional structure and fig. 16 as depicting a flat structure. Thus it would appear that the latter, taken as a group, do not invoke the economy principle as easily as the Scots and that greater perceptual load is probably required to make them do so.

In view of this effect of symmetry, it is somewhat disconcerting to observe that such a simple and symmetrical figure as the Müller-Lyer arrow evokes perception of pictorial depth. However, mechanisms involved in perception of depth are certainly more complex than they appear to be initially. This is borne out by the fact that there is no evidence of positive correlation between the Müller-Lyer and the Horizontal-Vertical illusion. Indeed these have been said to be

fig 15

Fig. 15   *A perspective gradient. Cover the figure and then uncover it slowly from the bottom, a row at a time. Only when several lines are uncovered is the 'economy principle' invoked and pictorial depth seen. After Vickers*

Jan B. Deregowski

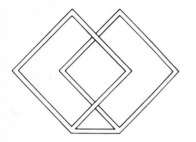

Fig. 16 *This is fig. 6 rota-ted so that it is sym-metrical about the viewer's median plane. There is a greater tendency to see this figure as flat than to see fig. 6 as flat.*

influenced by essentially different factors: by the 'carpenteredness' of the environment, i.e. the frequency of rectangular objects in the environment; and by the openness of vistas. Evidence supporting such an explanation has been found in an extensive study[59] comparing samples drawn from cultures differing in their carpen-teredness and in the openness of their environment. Observers from cultures having more rectangular artifacts (such as American urban culture) were more prone to Müller-Lyer illusion than observers from more 'circular' cultures, such as traditional Zulu culture with its contour agriculture and beehive huts. On the other hand, peoples inhabiting environments providing open vistas were, on the whole, more susceptible to the Horizontal-Vertical illusion than those coming from dense, compressed environments of tropical forests.

Some theoretical explanations

The theoretical explanations which have been advanced for the difficulties in pictorial perception fall into two categories: (i) those claiming the difficulties to be but a facet of a general cultural pattern, and therefore implying that a major cultural change would be needed to achieve Western-style perceptions; and (ii) those which attribute the effect to some specific characteristic of a culture (such as e.g. lack of pictorial art) and thus have no such global implications.

The most global explanation is probably that suggested by the studies of illusions just described. An extrapolation from these suggests that ecological and cultural factors combine and determine how pictures are seen. An extension of this work was thought to offer a startling simplification of these notions; namely[56] that people with deeper pigmented *fundus oculi* tend to be less prone to the illusory effects than people with lighter pigmentation of the *fundus*. Hence, Africans having richer pigmentation than, say, Norwegians would be less influenced by the Müller-Lyer illusion whether they did or did not come from a carpentered world. Since the same processes affect perception of geometric illusions and of meaningful pictures, pigmentation of the *fundus oculi* would qualify all pictorial perception. However, recent careful experimentation[4] on observers of the same genetic stock does not support such a conclusion.

Littlejohn's[48] suggestion that the concept of space prevalent in a culture is probably responsible for 2D perception also belongs to the global category. His view is based upon an analysis of the descriptions of space and spatial relationships used by the Temne of Sierra Leone.

178

Illusion and culture   'The Temne space is neither homogeneous nor isotropic.' It is divided into regions having different qualities. These regions, *Noru*, *Rosocki*, *Roshiron* and *Rokrifi*, have different characteristics, the first (*Noru*) 'is the "here" Temne normally walk about and live in, the everyday habitat in which people and things are open to human perception'. The second (*Rosocki*) is distinguished from the former by the fact 'that it and whatever is in it is generally invisible'. *Roshiron* is 'a sort of village witches start out from', and is likewise 'not penetrable to ordinary perception'. This attribute is also shared by *Rokrifi*, a region 'where the ancestors live'. In addition there is also a 'dream space'. This spatial heterogeneity and allied beliefs do not lead to perceptual difficulties in ordinary day-to-day life. The Temne 'must inhabit the same "objective space" as all other cultures do, but for them the "objective space" is a not-explicitly apprehended background to the space in which they are conscious of living', and it is the latter which leads to two-dimensional perception of pictures.

There are, from the psychologist's point of view, several difficulties with this explanation; but the main objection probably lies in the presence of 2D perceivers in cultures which do not share Temne beliefs. One has, therefore, to postulate a different explanation for these cultures. Such duality is hardly acceptable, especially since the validity of Littlejohn's suggestion has not been empirically investigated. In addition it is difficult to see how this theory could account for the differences between various pictorial depth-perception measures obtained from the same person, for example the 3D responses to the construction task of a fair proportion of school children classified as 2D on Hudson's test.[1][2]

Analogous objections apply to du Toit's[2][3] linguistic theory, suggesting that the specific structure of Bantu languages was responsible for Hudson's original results; the difficulties are observable with non-Bantu-speaking peoples and vary with the stimuli used.

The concept of 'field dependence' described briefly in the discussion of effectiveness of pictorial cues extends beyond the domain of visual perception. Persons who are 'field dependent' in the perceptual sense of the term tend also to be so in the social sense. They find it as difficult to see themselves as independent units within society as to isolate a diagram from a morass of lines.[71] The reverse relationship also holds: 'field independent' persons are independent in both senses of the term. Since social dependence of adults is affected by the way in which they have been brought up, this theory links social mores with perceptual skills. Extensive studies in Sierra Leone[11] offer support for such an interpretation. Two tribes, the

Temne and the Mende, differ in strictness and rigidity of child rearing, and the more rigid Temne are the more field dependent of the two tribes. Such correlation, however, is not conclusive, not only for the obvious reason that comparing only two cultures out of the great variety can scarcely be thought of as the last word, but also because these two cultures differ in more than one way. Indeed, the very study in which these results were obtained suggests that such factors as family structure and cultural experience may influence the extent of field dependence.

More specific theories (see reference nos. 11, 34, 36, 52, 12, 40, 41, 72), either implicitly or explicitly stated, all suggest lack of exposure to pictorial material as a root cause. Of these, Hudson's, which postulates that a child, if it is not to find pictures difficult in later years, must get used to them by a certain critical age, is of some interest and receives perhaps a modicum of support from a finding that Zambian domestic servants, who have probably little contact with pictures in their childhood, were more often two-dimensional perceivers than schoolchildren with about the same amount of formal schooling but probably greater pictorial experience. The effect of formal education upon pictorial perception remains obscure because, although there are studies[40,41] showing that pictorial depth perception increases in frequency as one samples higher school grades, one could not argue that such a correlation proves causation, since necessarily pupils in the higher forms tend to be older, and moreover some weaker pupils tend to leave school earlier. Further, such results as are at hand do not distinguish between a mere interpretation of pictorial cues and actual *seeing* of pictorial depth — two distinct processes demonstrable by using Pandora's box. Genetic and nutritional determinants have also been put forward and at present have about as much evidence in their favour as any of the theories above: that is to say, remarkably little.

As in the case of the consideration of various factors influencing perception of depth, so here the dearth of empirical data gives all these postulates a thin conjectural air.

Symmetry and split-type drawings

Laws, who provided such an apposite quotation for the introduction of our discussion about the difficulties in pictorial perception, has an equally apposite observation on some of the difficulties of young Malawi girls entering domestic service in western households:

180

In laying a table, there ... is ... trouble for the girl. At her home the house is round; a straight line and the right angle are things unknown to her or her parents before her. Day after day therefore she will lay the cloth with the folds anything but parallel with one edge of the table. Plates, knives and forks are set down in a corresponding manner, and it is only after lessons often repeated and much annoyance that she begins to see how things ought to be done and tries to do this.[44]

The description contains two points of interest: the suggestion that the roundness of the environment affects the girl's responses (which antecedes the 'carpentered world' hypothesis by exactly eighty years), and the observation of difficulties in orientation of objects in space. The existence of such difficulties in cultures similar to that whence Laws' servants came is sustained by the common hearsay of Western employers both industrial and domestic. The claims of the former group are best illustrated by the following quotation from a report on the abilities of an African labour force:[54]

[It] was observed in Kenya that African stonemasons who were given special training in two months' time were dressing stone quite satisfactorily, though some of them were found not to have a straight eye, an African characteristic discovered in other trades.

We have in addition some experimental evidence supporting this claim. Shapiro[60] required a group of literate and illiterate Africans to copy Kohs' type designs and measured the difference between the orientation of the drawings thus obtained and the models. The angles

Fig. 17 *Traditional Kohs' type design* above *and a modified version* below *for assessing the effect of symmetry.*

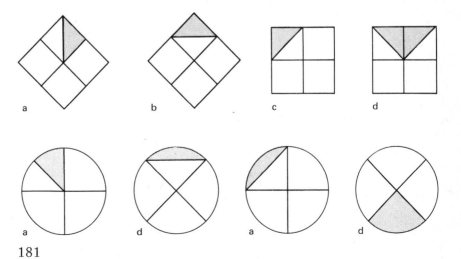

of rotation for the two groups were compared and found to differ significantly, the illiterate group rotating more. Comparisons of the illiterate group with various English control groups showed a similar difference. The responses of the illiterate group suggested that the rotations produced were a lawful outcome of two factors: (i) the orientation of the axis of the design; whether 'vertical' (items *b* and *d*, fig. 17) or 'inclined' (items *a* and *c*), and (ii) the orientation of the pattern as a whole; whether the square was presented with one of its diagonals vertical or inclined at 45° (items *a* and *b* and *c* and *d* respectively). An extension of this work[19] provided data showing that, other considerations being equal, such subjects are influenced by the symmetry of figures and tend to make reproductions symmetrical about their own median planes. This result was obtained by using a specially modified version of Kohs' stimuli, the cubes being replaced by quadrants of a circle forming flat circular patterns, in which the sole possible factor of influence left was the shape of the stimulus pattern. A group of Icelandic schoolchildren, a group of Zambian schoolchildren, and a group of Zambian workers were tested. As expected, rotations of reproductions so as to render them symmetrical about the responder's median planes occurred in both Zambian samples, but not in the Icelandic sample. It would be wrong, however, to argue on these grounds that the Western populations are less sensitive to symmetry. A comparison of Zambian and Scottish schoolboys on two orientations of the same figure described earlier showed that it was the latter group who discriminated between the two orientations in their responses, seeing the figure symmetrical about the median plane as representing a flat object significantly more often.[17] Zambians treated both figures equally, contrary to Western findings that asymmetry should lead to three-dimensional perception in diagrams.[33] Further data gathered from Zambian adults confirm a preference for symmetrical responses even to asymmetrical stimuli and a strong tendency for confusion of symmetrical patterns (mirror images). In the present context these symmetrical effects are primarily of interest because they bear upon explanation of a specific artistic style which has been variously referred to as 'split representations' or 'chain-type drawings' and which has been noted to occur in a variety of cultures. Levi-Strauss[46] has pointed out that:

This . . . collection involves the Northwest coast of America, China, Siberia, New Zealand and perhaps even India and Persia. What is more, the documents belong to entirely different periods: the eighteenth and nineteenth centuries for Alaska; the first and second millenia B.C. for China; and prehistoric era for the Amur region; and the period stretching from the fourteenth to the eighteenth century for New Zealand.

However, isolated drawings in this style, as opposed to entire schools of art, are even more widely scattered. They have been found in, for example, the Saharan culture of the Bubale era, in the central India culture of early centuries B.C., in Peruvian cave paintings, in Sumerian (2700 B.C.) silvercraft, in Byzantine art and in European heraldry. Gradual development of artistic style and transformation of split-style into orthogonal style were observed in the Azande of the Sudan:[43]

> It is only of late years that profiles have been noticed with less than two eyes; but this advance does not appear in other subjects, and, therefore, the portrayal of a deck chair, with all its legs and cross-pieces, or a motor, with four wheels, lamp and the luggage inside, is a complicated business; since nothing must be left to the imagination, but all be shown, whether visible or not.

Recently, when unsophisticated Africans and Europeans were presented with a choice of two drawings of an elephant Africans preferred the split-type drawing (with the sole exception of a man who thought that the animal was dangerously jumping about), and the Europeans preferred the orthogonal view.[35] The preference of

Fig. 18 *Hudson's elephants. The lower one was preferred by Europeans; the upper one by unsophisticated Africans.*

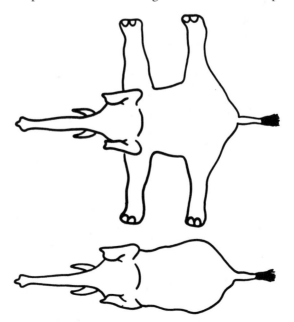

Jan B. Deregowski

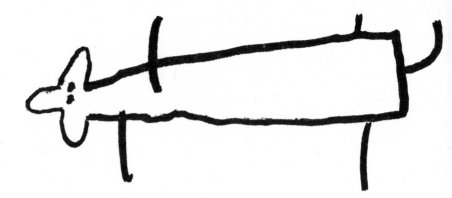

Fig. 19 *Ingela's dog; a split-type drawing by a child*

the African population was later confirmed using modified stimuli, both representational and purely geometrical.[14] The preference for split representation therefore appears to be very widespread indeed. In fact it is probably universal in children in all cultures. Young American children, for example, not only draw split-type drawings but also prefer them to other drawings.[47] It is also, paradoxically, universal in engineering design offices, where it is found to provide a better description of depicted objects; but as will be shown below better in one sense only.

fig. 19

fig. 20

Boas and Levi-Strauss have each advanced a theory explaining the prevalence of split-type representation. According to Boas,[8,9] they are a result of a slow physical transformation, 'the natural development' of the method used for decoration of solid objects, such as boxes, and adapted for the ornamentation of circular objects, such as hats or bracelets. The animal is then arranged around the opening in a solid object. Finally, when such a solid object is cut and flattened a split-type representation is created. It is possible that this represents the manner in which the Indians of the North Pacific coast arrived at this style of representation and that the aesthetic preference ensured that the style became accepted and flourished. It is noteworthy, however, that split-type drawings occur spontaneously both in children and adults, who are unlikely to have experienced the evolutionary process described by Boas, and that he offers no historical evidence to demonstrate this evolutionary sequence. Therefore the postulated genesis may perhaps be regarded as not proven.

fig. 22

According to Levi-Strauss[46] the drawings reflect psychological

184

Illusion and culture

stresses present in the societies where they prevail. 'Split presentation can be explored as a function of a sociological theory of splitting of the personality.' He maintains that this is a trait common to those 'mask cultures' in which 'a chain of privileges, emblems and degrees of prestige' is validated by means of masks. This is characteristic of *some* of the cultures in which such representations occur. However, as has been shown above, a very distinct form of split representation occurs also in cultures to which such a description cannot be applied (e.g., Black South Africans, Zambians, American schoolchildren). The explanation, therefore, is not entirely satisfactory, and a more basic psychological explanation such as is advanced below may prove better.

Neither Boas' nor Levi-Strauss' explanations take account of the probably universal prevalence of such drawings in children. Yet this very fact seems to provide the key to their origin. The purpose of

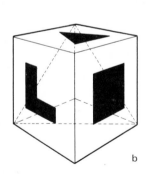

Fig. 20 *Three drawings of the same object. a: perspective drawing; b: 'transparent' drawing showing what the object really looks like; c: third-angle projection allowing direct measurement of distances in the principal planes. This view of all the faces of the unfolded cube reminds one of similar drawings found in 'primitive' cultures.*

Fig. 21 *A drawing of a cube by a Solomon Islander. After Thurnwald*

185

Fig. 22 *Drawings of North-western American tribes. a: a Tsimshian bear; b: a Haida shark; c: a Haida duck. Compare the last figure with the two-headed eagle in fig. 23.*

Fig. 23 *A two-headed eagle. Two interesting features are present: the eagle is split but the human face is shown in profile.*

drawing, other than that of eliciting emotive responses, may lay *either* in its use as an identification mark *or* as a description of the depicted object. The artist's model may be the same, but the difference in purpose makes a different style of representation more efficacious in each of these cases.

An identification mark should be easy to remember, while at the same time it should contain elements, possibly in symbolic form, which would make confusion between two identification marks unlikely. Symmetrical patterns, as has been shown, are easy to recognize[2,18] and remember, and are aesthetically pleasing. This explains why symmetry is a common ingredient of both Western armorial bearings and West Canadian art. However, heraldry generally avoids splitting the depicted objects (possible notable exceptions being two headed eagles) and merely arranges pictures so as to yield symmetrical patterns, objects generally being portrayed in orientations which make the most of their characteristics but without using perspective; in the case of animals and men, side views are often used.

Neither the armorial bearings nor the paintings in question are intended to convey to the viewer what a bear, a beaver or a sculpin looks like, in order to enable him to identify the animal, but serve primarily as means to identify objects *on* which they occur (a shield or a wigwam) and hence their owners. They are also ornamental. To make identification easier, they incorporate symbolic elements which enable the viewer to interpret the artist's intention, and to direct others to the dogfish wigwam or to the Blue Boar. Thus, for example, 'the large incisors, the tail with cross-hatching, the stick and the form of the nose are symbols of the beaver and the first two of these are sufficient characteristics of the animal'. The Scottish lion looks very much like the English lion but cannot be said to resemble the real animal.

Thus the introduction of complex symbolism to West Coast Indian art and European heraldry makes the creation of an intricate style possible, while still retaining some of the communication value, as well as facilitating verbal descriptions. Such an act, however, carries a penalty, in that the facilitation thus achieved only extends to the persons familiar with the code. Highly stylised and arbitrary symbols are not likely to be understood outside specific cultural milieux. Thus the tendency to draw split representations is in all of us in early childhood and, depending on the dominant purpose for which drawings are used in the culture in which we live, either it is allowed to flourish or it is suppressed. Split-representation drawings develop

Fig. 24 *Arms of the University of Aberdeen. Note the essential symmetry of each quartering.*

in cultures where the products of art serve as labels or marks of identification. In the cultures where drawings are intended to convey *what an object actually looks like* this style is muted and the 'perspective' style is adopted.

But even in those cultures it survives in certain ritualised forms in heraldry and in technical drawings. In engineering design offices, where detailed information is important and no apparently obvious assumptions can be made, split-type drawings offer more accurate portrayals. Hence split-type representation of objects (which in engineering would be called a development drawing) or a close approximation to such a representation (which in engineering is called a third angle projection) are used; the split-representation style of childhood has therefore to be relearned by engineering draughtsmen. But even such re-learning and subsequent long experience in its use do not make it superior to perspective when quick communication about the depicted object is required.[62] Once grasped, perspective cannot be readily shed.

Thus it would appear that Gibson[26] was right in maintaining that perspective is not a mere convention to be discarded at will but has a basis in reality, even though the evolution of perspective took considerable time. When finally evolved, it gained recognition and acclaim as 'best painter's art'.

It is not the 'best painter's art' under all conditions, however. When detailed description is required, an engineer abandons it — and sacrifices an illusion of depth for minutiae of representation. When a herald, a trade mark designer, or a Haida artist, wants to create a symbol which is likely to be remembered, they abandon it in favour of symmetrical designs — and gain a visual mnemonic.

It all depends on what one wants to say: two dimensions cannot contain three. The skill lies in the correctness of one's choice.

Frequent superiority of perspective representation as an aid to recognition must not be taken to mean that photographs are always superior to drawings. It is true that photographs present a wealth of perspective cues. Yet this very characteristic may also be their weakness. Some of these competing cues may obscure those which an observer is looking for and make photographs more difficult than drawings. A classical example of this is provided by industrial inspection. An inspector is interested in but a few characteristics of his sample, and drawings have been shown to direct his attention to these better than a photograph.[58]

So far only the representation of purely physical characteristics of objects has been considered. This, as has been shown, is very complex indeed; but an artist attempts much more. He tries to convey by 'means of light and by the way of the rectilinear propagation of light' some of the invisible but perceptible characteristics of the depicted scene or person. To do so he has to veer even further away from 'photographic' representation to use in a subtle, cunning way both colour and shape distortions sufficient to convey the mood, yet weak enough for the portrait or the scene to be recognizable. He may distort human faces or imbue inanimate objects with life, and by these and other tricks weave his net to catch an unsuspecting beholder. Or he may abandon the idea of 'recognizable' representation and create an 'abstract' of pure mood and puzzlement — and puzzlement is merely an incessant search for a meaningful organization.

References

1 Abercrombie, M.L.J. (1960), *The Anatomy of Judgement*, London.
2 Attneave, F. (1955), 'Symmetry, information and memory for patterns', *J. exp. Psychol. 68*, 209-222.
3 Bartlett, F.C., Ginsberg, M., Linden, E.J. & Thouless, R.H.(eds) (1939), *The Study of Society*, London. See especially paper by S.F. Nade.
4 Bayer, C.A. & Pressey, A.W. (1972), 'Geometric illusions as a function ot pigmentation of the fundus oculi and target size', *Psychon. Sci. 26*, 77-79.
5 Beach, H.P. (1901), *Geography and Atlas of Protestant Missions*, New York.
6 Beveridge, W.M. (1935), 'Racial differences in phenomenal regression', *Br. J. Psychol. 30*, 59-62.
7 Biesheuvel, S. (1952), 'The study of African ability: Pt.I', *African Studies 11*, 45-57.
8 Boas, F. (1897), 'The decorative art of the Indians of the North Pacific coast', *Bull. Am. Mus. nat. Hist. 9*, 123-176.
9 Boas, F. (1927), *Primitive Art*, Oslo.
10 Bruner, J.S., Olver, R. & Greenfield, P.M. (eds) (1966), *Studies in Cognitive Growth*, New York. See M.C. Potter, 'On perceptual recognition'.
11 Dawson, J.L.M. (1967), 'Cultural and physiological influences upon spatial-perceptual processes in West Africa', *Int. J. Psychol. 2*, 115-128.
12 Deregowski, J.B. (1968), Difficulties in pictorial depth perception in Africa', *Br. J. Psychol. 59*, 195-204.
13 Deregowski, J.B. (1969) 'Perception of the two-pronged trident by two- and three-dimensional perceivers', *J. exp. Psychol. 82*, 9-13.
14 Deregowski, J.B. (1970), 'A note on the possible determinants of split representation as an artistic style', *Int. J. Psychol. 5*, 21-26.
15 Deregowski, J.B. & Byth, W. (1970), 'Hudson's pictures in Pandora's box', *J. Cross-cultural Psychol. 1* 315-323.
16 Deregowski, J.B. (1971a), 'Responses mediating pictorial recognition', *J. soc. Psychol. 84*, 27-33.
17 Deregowski, J.B. (1971b), 'Orientation and perception of pictorial depth', *Int. J. Psychol. 6*, 111-114.

Jan B. Deregowski

18 Deregowski, J.B. (1971c), 'Symmetry, Gestalt and information theory', *Quart. J. exp. Psychol. 23*, 381-385.

19 Deregowski, J.B. (1972), 'Reproduction of orientation of Kohs-type figures: a cross-cultural study', *Br. J. Psychol. 63*, 283-296.

20 Deregowski, J.B. & Serpell, N. (1972), 'Performance on sorting task: a cross-cultural experiment', *Int. J. Psychol. 4*, 273-281.

21 Deregowski, J.B., Muldrow, E.S. & Muldrow, W.F. (1973), 'Pictorial recognition in a remote Ethiopian population', *Perception 1,* 417-425.

22 Doob, L.W. (1961), *Communication in Africa*, New Haven.

23 du Toit, B.M. (1966), 'Pictorial depth perception and linguistic relativity', *Psychologia Africana 11*, 51-63.

24 Fraser, A.K. (1932), *Teaching healthcraft to African women*, London.

25 Gibson, J.J. (1950), *The Perception of the Visual World*, Boston.

26 Gibson, J.J. (1960), 'Pictures, perspective and perception', *Daedalus 89*, 216-227.

27 Gombrich, E.H. (1962), *Art and Illusion*, London. p. 259.

28 Gregory, R.L. (1966), *Eye and Brain*, London.

29 Gregory, R.L. (1970), *The Intelligent Eye*, London.

30 Herskovits, M.J. (1950), *Man and His Works*, New York.

31 Hochberg, C.B. & Hochberg, J. (1952), 'Familiar size and the perception of depth', *J. Psychol. 34*, 107-114.

32 Hochberg, J. & Brooks, V. (1960), 'Psychophysics of form: Reversible perspective drawings of spatial objects,' *Am. J. Psychol. 73*, 337-354.

33 Hochberg, J. & Brooks, V.(1962), 'Pictorial recognition as an unlearned ability: a study of one child's performance', *Am. J. Psychol. 75,* 624-628.

34 Hudson, W. (1960), 'Pictorial depth perception in sub-cultural groups in Africa', *J. soc. Psychol. 52*, 183-208.

35 Hudson, W. (1962) 'Pictorial perception and educational adaptation in Africa', *Psychologia Africana 9*, 226-239.

36 Hudson, W. (1967) 'The study of the problem of pictorial perception among unacculturated groups', *Int. J. Psychol. 2*, 89-107.

37 Ivins, W.M. (1963), *Prints and Visual Communication*, London.

38 Jahoda, G. (1970), 'A cross-cultural perspective in psychology', *Advmt Sci., Br. Ass. 27*, 1-14.

39 Kidd, D. (1925), *The Essential Kaffir*, London.

40 Kilbride, P.L., Robbins, M.C. & Freeman, R.B. (1968a), 'Pictorial depth perception and education among Baganda schoolchildren', *Percept. mot. Skills 26*, 1116-1118.

41 Kilbride, P.L. & Robbins, M.C. (1968b), 'Linear perspective, pictorial depth perception and education among the Baganda', *Percept. mot. Skills 27*, 601-602.

42 Klapper, Z.S. & Birch, H.G. (1969), 'Perceptual and action equivalence of photographs in children', *Percept. mot. Skills 29*, 763-771.

43 Larken, P.M. (1927), 'Impressions of the Azande', *Sudan Notes and Records 10*, 85-134.

44 Laws, R. (1886), *Woman's Work in Heathen Lands*, Paisley.

45 Leibowitz, H., Brislin, R., Perlmutter, L. & Hennessy, R. (1969), 'Ponzo perspective as a manifestation of space perception', *Science, N.Y. 166.*

46 Lévi-Strauss, C. (1963), *Structural Anthropology*, New York.

190

47 Lewis, H.P. (1963) 'Spatial representation as a correlate of development and a basis for picture preference', *J. genet. Psychol. 102*, 95-107.

48 Littlejohn, J. (1963), 'Temne space', *Anthrop. Quart.*, 63, 1-17.

49 Lloyd, A.B. (1904) 'Acholi country: Part II', *Uganda Notes 5*, 18-22.

50 Mayer, P. (ed) (1970), *Socialization*, London. See A. Forge, 'Learning to see in New Guinea'.

51 Mead, M. (1969) *Coming of Age in Samoa*, Harmondsworth.

52 Mundy-Castle, A.C. (1966), 'Pictorial depth perception in Ghanaian children', *Int. J. Psychol. 1*, 290-300.

53 Newman, C.V. (1969), 'Children's size judgements in a picture with suggested depth', *Nature, Lond. 223*, 418-420.

54 Northcott, C.H. (ed) (1949), *African Labour Efficiency Survey*, London.

55 Ono, H. (1969), 'Apparent distance as a function of familiar size', *J. exp. Psychol. 79*, 109-115.

56 Pollack, R.H. & Silvar, S. (1967), 'Magnitude of Muller-Lyer illusion in children as a function of pigmentation of the fundus oculi', *Psychon. Sci. 8*, 83-84.

57 Poortinga, Y.U. (1971) 'Cross-cultural comparison of maximum performance tests', *Psychologia Africana, Monograph Supplement No. 6*. See report on J.M. Schepers' work.

58 Ryan, I.A. & Schwartz, C.B. (1956), 'Speed of perception as a function of mode of representation', *Am. J. Psychol. 69*, 60-69.

59 Segall, M.H., Campbell, D.T. & Herskovits, M.J. (1966), *Influence of Culture on Visual Perception*, Indianapolis.

60 Shapiro, M.S. (1960), 'Rotation of drawings by illiterate Africans', *J. soc. Psychol. 52*, 17-30.

61 Sigel, I.E. (1968), 'The distancing hypothesis: a causal hypothesis for the acquisition of representational thought', paper delivered at University of Miami symposium on the effects of early experience, 1968.

62 Spencer, J. (1965), 'Experiments in engineering drawing comprehension', *Ergonomics 8*, 93-110.

63 Stacey, B. (1969) 'Explanations of the H-V illusion and the foreshortening of receding line', *Life Sci. 8*, 1238-1246.

64 Taylor, B. (1719), *New principles of linear perspective or the art of designing on a plane the representations of all sorts of objects . . .* , London.

65 Thomas, L.F. (1962), 'Perceptual organisation in industrial inspectors', *Ergonomics 5*, 429-434.

66 Thomson, J. (1885), *Through Masai land: A journey of exploration*, London.

67 UNESCO (1963), *Simple Reading Material for Adults: Its Preparation and Use*, Paris.

68 Waburton, F.W. (1951), 'The ability of the Gurkha recruit', *Br. J. Psychol. 42*, 123-133.

69 Welford, A.T. (1970), 'Perceptual selection and integration', *Ergonomics 13.*

70 Werner, H. (1965), *Comparative psychology of mental development*, New York.

71 Witkin, H.A., Dyk, R.B., Faterson, H.F., Goodenough, D.R. & Karp, S.A. (1962), *Psychological Differentiation*. New York.

72 Wober, M. (1966), 'Sensotypes', *J. soc. Psychol. 70*, 181-189.

73 Wober, M. (1972), 'On cross-cultural psychology', *Bull. Br. psychol. Soc. 25.*

5 Illusion and Art

E. H. Gombrich

If, in Whitehead's famous words, the history of philosophy is a series of footnotes to Plato, this essay may be described as a footnote to the memorable passage in the *Republic* in which Plato prepares the ground for the banishment from the ideal State of all the arts which pander to the 'lower reaches of the soul':

'Of what are your speaking?' 'Of this: The same magnitude, I presume, viewed from near and from far does not appear equal.' 'Why, no.' 'And the same things appear bent and straight to those who view them in water and out, or concave and convex owing to similar errors of vision about colours, and there is obviously every confusion of this sort in our souls. And so scene-painting in its exploitation of this weakness of our nature falls nothing short of witchcraft, and so do jugglery and many other such contrivances.' 'True.' 'And have not measuring and numbering and weighing proved to be most gracious aids to prevent the domination in our soul of the apparently greater or less or more or heavier, and to give the control to that which has reckoned and numbered or even weighed?' 'Certainly.' 'But this surely would be the function of the part of the soul that reasons and calculates.' 'Why, yes, of that.' 'And often when this has measured and declares that certain things are larger or that some are smaller than the others or equal, there is at the same time an appearance of the contrary.' 'Yes.' 'And did we not say that it is impossible for the same thing at one time to hold contradictory opinions about the same thing?' 'And we were right in affirming that.' 'The part of the soul, then, that opines in contradiction of measurement could not be the same with that which confirms it.' 'Why, no.' 'But, further, that which puts its trust in measurement and reckoning must be the best part of the soul.' 'Necessarily.' 'This, then, was what I wished to have agreed upon when I said that poetry, and in

Fig. 1 *Rembrandt, self-portrait at the age of 63. 1669. Detail*

193

general the mimetic art . . . associates with the part of us that is remote from intelligence . . . an inferior thing cohabiting with an inferior and engendering inferior offspring.' 'It seems so.'

(*Republic* X, 602-3; Tr. Paul Shorey (Loeb).)

It is likely that Plato's diagnosis was influenced by developments in ancient art which demonstrated for the first time in human history the power of painting to deceive the eye, notably in scene painting. In ancient Greece and Rome this power continued to be the subject of countless comments and anecdotes. It is significant, in the light of Plato's assessment, that the capacity of paintings to deceive animals is so frequently singled out as a test of their excellence. Sparrows came to pick at the grapes painted by Zeuxis, a stallion attempted to mate with a mare painted by Apelles, the painted picture of a snake silenced birds and so on.[29] This emphasis on animal reactions could only be grist to the mill of those critics who spurned the claims of illusion. There is a charming little dialogue by Goethe, 'On Truth and Verisimilitude in Works of Art', in which he dismisses all the talk about deceiving the eye as 'sparrow aesthetics'. By now Platonism has been victorious all along the line and it seems that even an interest in the problems of illusion carries the taint of vulgarity. To take the problem back into the study of painting seems like discussing ventriloquism in the study of dramatic art.

I shall argue here that Plato was right in his diagnosis that illusion has something to do with 'the lower reaches of the soul', but I shall also argue – if indeed this point still has to be argued – that these lower reaches are the subject of very legitimate interest to psychologists and philosophers. Whether or not ventriloquism has anything to do with art, the compulsion to attribute the words we hear to the mouthing dummy remains intriguing and instructive. I should like to make this point at the outset because I cannot help suspecting that the new opponents of the concept of illusion in art are unconsciously influenced by the Platonic tradition. I am referring to those contemporary philosophers of art who, like R. Wollheim,[41,42] Nelson Goodman[21] and M. Polanyi,[31] have in their various ways denied what one might call paradoxically the reality of illusion in front of a painting. I cannot here enter into all the subtleties of their argumentation, but I fully agree that in looking at a seascape hanging on the wall of a museum we are never tricked into mistaking the painting for a window opening out on to the real sea. If this were the only legitimate meaning of the term 'illusion' the matter could be regarded as closed and the problem dismissed. I do not think that

Plate 14

194

Fig. 2 *Illustration from the 'Vienna Genesis'. Sixth century A.D.*

this can be done, but I must acknowledge that these philosophical opponents of illusion have been joined by one of the leading students of perception, J.J. Gibson, who has expressed his conviction that the visual perception of reality can never be mediated by painting.[5] Gibson's doubts are explained by the emphasis he places in his theory of visual perception on the effects of movement and on the importance of 'gradients' of texture for the visual information we pick up from the environment and which could never be fully simulated in a painting.[4] His objections are certainly the most weighty so far put forward, and have to be taken into account, though a more detailed response to his argument will be published elsewhere.[18]

I should perhaps confess that I feel both gratified and puzzled by the attention which my discussion of illusion has been accorded, for it had never been the central issue of *Art and Illusion*. The title of the lectures on which that book is based was 'The Visible World and the Language of Art' which approximates more nearly to a description of its topic. It so happens, however, that my publishers found this rather a mouthful, and since they also wanted to retain the word Art in the title I drew up a lengthy list of simple alternatives from which the final title was picked by a friend. We never dreamed that this title would convey to some that I considered illusion, or even deception, the main aim of art. In art-historical writing the term illusionism has no such connotations. It was introduced by Franz Wickhoff in 1895 in his famous publication of the *Vienna Genesis*, an early Christian manuscript, to characterize the deft style of brushwork which had survived from Hellenistic times. The idea that anyone should have confused the illustrations of the manuscript with reality obviously did not enter his mind. What he wanted to

fig. 2

195

convey, quite rightly, was the difference between this style and other, less illusionistic, methods. Far from being an all-or-nothing affair, illusion in these contexts is always a matter of degree. But since the issue has been raised and the debate has been joined, I must welcome the opportunity of making my views on illusion more explicit in an essay devoted to restatements and further speculations.

For this purpose the problem of the seascape on the wall appears to me too complex to tackle at once. It represents a three dimensional and changing view by flat and immobile pigments. As such it cannot be an imitation. The matter is of course different when it comes to imitating a three-dimensional object in three dimensions or a two-dimensional object in two. I always remind those who doubt this possibility of the existence of forged bank notes. Philosophically this problem of a faithful 'facsimile' is hardly very interesting. Granted that there may always be methods of distinguishing the imitation from the original, for instance under ultra violet light or by other methods of analysis, agreement should not be difficult on the point that a facsimile can be sufficiently accurate to deceive the naked eye. But whether the deceptive appearance also deceives us depends of course on a variety of extraneous circumstances. If the British Museum were to exhibit a facsimile of Shakespeare's signature as the original, most of us would be under the illusion that we had seen the real thing. The same facsimile in a book on handwriting would deceive nobody. Mediaeval worshippers of relics were certainly under the illusion that the bones they saw or touched were those of saints. We obviously must distinguish between an accurate imitation, an illusion and a false belief.

His Master's Voice

There is a branch of modern technology where these distinctions can be easily exemplified. I am referring to the reproduction of sounds rather than of sights. Without asking for the blessing of philosophers and psychologists, the gramophone industry has set out to create the perfect illusion of listening to a concert. The listener for whom it caters is not in the position to compare the original performance with the reproduction. What he wants is to have the feeling that the performance might have sounded that way. It probably did not; artists have taken to making a composite recording from various performances which are spliced together to achieve a flawless version. Theoretically it is even possible that the equipment slightly distorts

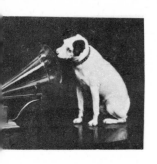

Fig. 3. *His master's voice by Francis Barraud, 1899*

the pitch by playing somewhat faster than the performers. None of this need affect the impression at which the Hi-Fi enthusiast is likely to aim, that what comes out of the loudspeaker gives him the illusion of being actually close to the musicians. In this context nobody doubts that this illusion is really a matter of degree — witness the terms in which stereo equipment and other devices are advertised as enhancing the illusion. Not that this illusion is a delusion. We do not believe that the London Philharmonic Orchestra is actually sitting in or behind the black boxes. What we say is, 'If you close your eyes you might actually believe that you are in the concert hall.' We do not have to ask here why closing the eyes is supposed to enhance the illusion. It obviously does not change the auditory impression, but it cuts out the visual impressions which tell us that we are not in a concert hall. In other words we deliberately switch off some of the means we have at our disposal to check the testimony of our ears. We do not want to employ all the resources of critical reasoning because we wish to surrender to our imagination and fancy ourselves in the presence of the great performer. This is what Coleridge so beautifully described as 'the willing suspension of disbelief' — and what Plato despised as a sacrifice of the higher faculties in favour of the lower reaches of the soul. Perhaps the illusion merchants actually agree with him — for is not the most famous trademark of any gramophone firm the picture of the dog listening to 'His Master's Voice'? The picture makes the same claim for illusion by appealing to the reaction of an animal that the ancients made for masterpieces of painting. It so happens that neither of these claims is as unbelievable as they were both once thought to be. Animals certainly can be deceived by recorded voices, and they also react to representations. There is experimental material demonstrating that pigeons can be taught to respond to the presence or absence of human beings in photographs. 'They were trained to peck one disc if there was any sign of a human being in the photograph, and another if there was no sign. It was found that the most fragmentary, and presumably unfamiliar, aspects of the human being . . . were sufficient to cause the birds to give a positive response'.[35] Similar results have been achieved with monkeys.

Professor W.H. Thorpe who drew attention to these facts in a recent paper has been kind enough to place the following more personal observation at my disposal. It suggests that the stories of animals responding to paintings need not be mythical:

'On 1 September 1952 my family and I were staying at the

197

E.H. Gombrich

Moorings Hotel, Burnham Overy Staithe, Norfolk. We had with us a Shetland Sheep Dog bitch named 'Tessa', then three years old. On this day she apparently saw for the first time an oil painting of Mr Phillips senior, hanging on the dining room wall. She was sitting on the floor about 10 or 12 feet from the picture when she looked up at it with ears cocked and growled several times. There was no one at that end of the room at all except myself and my daughter Margaret. We were sitting at a table by her side. It was perfectly evident that she was growling at the picture, as she stopped directly I distracted her attention but started again as soon as she looked at it again. Margaret picked her up and carried her towards the picture and she growled again in Margaret's arms a number of times. She also growled again several times when she was put back on the floor. We then left the room. There was no reaction at dinner time that evening but the room was then crowded and noisy. The picture is an oil painting (half-length figure portrait). The sitter is leaning slightly forward, on folded arms, looking straight out into the room in a rather striking manner. It measures approximately two-and-a-half by one-and-a-half feet and the head itself is about 9 ins. by 5 ins. Tessa had been in the room many times during the previous two weeks but until two days before we had always sat at a table the other end of the room and she would probably not have seen it at all easily or clearly. Moreover she normally sat right under the table at meals. This also probably explains why she had not responded the previous day. As we have no large-scale portraits in our house she had perhaps never seen a portrait before; though she might have had a chance to see portraits life, or near life, size at Icomb Manor, near Stow-on-the-Wold, Gloucestershire, on 29-31 July previously. I do not think she has had any other chance during her life as I know all the houses she has ever been in. In any case she would probably not react in a strange house where she feels somewhat intimidated; not until she has got sufficiently used to a place to treat it as home does she feel secure enough to express her rather unusual and particular dislike of strange men. By the time she responded to this picture she had been at the 'Moorings' long enough to show most of the usual signs of treating it as her home. There was no question of personal recognition of the portrait as Mr Phillips had died many years previously.'

It is not very likely that the painter of the portrait of Mr Phillips senior deserves to be hailed as another Apelles, and this, perhaps, justifies the disdain with which aestheticians have regarded the stories of animal reactions. But the student of illusion cannot afford this unconcern; the interest of these reactions lies in the light they may throw on the relation between illusion and awareness. We do not generally attribute awareness to animals; in any case we would not think that the dog was conscious of a deceptive appearance. She simply reacted to a configuration that aroused in her the same response as strangers generally did. We may call it an inappropriate reaction, but some would call it an illusion only if it could be accessible to conscious probing. I believe indeed that this is the basic problem of illusion. The responses that motivated the dog to react to the painting as if it were a real person may also be potentially present in us.[16] True, they are overlaid by that critical reason that Plato located in the higher reaches of the soul, but Plato, if anyone, knew that the dominance of these higher reaches is insecure. Reason is also slower than are automatic responses. Hence we can observe ourselves reacting to an imitation as if it were the real thing. It is this experience of discrepancy between the various systems of response, the various 'reaches of the soul' to which the student of illusion must turn his attention.

Simulation and stimulation

It may be useful to follow Plato and to start a discussion of illusion by considering the lowest layers, what he would have called the vegetative soul. Clearly any organism must be 'programmed' to react to internal and external stimuli in a specific way which allows it to adapt to diverse conditions. Science has been hard at work decoding these 'messages' which cause the organism to 'take action' and even to achieve certain effects by the simulation of false reports. Thus the 'pill' may be said to act by sending out a false chemical message to the effect that pregnancy has occurred after which ovulation is inhibited. While these and many similar effects are not directly 'monitored' by the conscious mind, other forms of simulation notoriously carry over into mental states. Not that these stages should be confused with a veridical perception of the trigger action. Black coffee after a heavy meal – to mention no more noxious drugs – gives us the illusion of easing the digestion by numbing the vegetative nerves which are labouring with this task and preventing them from sending groans to our brain. We feel relieved, but are not.

E.H. Gombrich

Plato would certainly not have objected to discussing drugs in conjunction with the illusion of art. It was a commonplace of ancient critisicm that what mattered in art were the 'effects' and these were as close to the action of drugs as they were to that of magic.[13] Orators and poets, musicians and even painters were celebrated as 'spell binders' who were able to arouse or to calm the emotions. Here, too, the 'animal experiment' was never far from the critic's mind. Orpheus who could attract and charm the wild beasts was the model artist.

What must interest us in this time-honoured approach is precisely the insight that stimulation can, but need not, rely on the imitation of the trigger. There are plants and animals which are found to have an 'internal clock' regulating growth and behaviour to the length of daylight throughout the seasons.[38] These can certainly be 'deceived' by simulating the identical effect with artificial light, that is to say by *mimesis*, but there are other biological reactions which yield to a much wider spectrum of stimulations. We know that Nature herself — that is evolutionary pressure — has evolved such dummy keys by which one species ensures its survival at the expense of another and it is much to be welcomed that this important aspect of illusion is discussed in this book by Professor Hinton. What these astounding phenomena teach the student of art is precisely that there is a limit to perceptual relativism. What looks like a leaf to modern European must also have looked likè a leaf to predators in fairly distant geological epochs.[10] Likeness is not only in the beholder's eye. But sometimes it can be. Following the lead of Konrad Lorenz, ethologists have systematically varied their dummies to find out what minimum features are needed to stimulate or 'release' a particular reaction. It appears that there are two variables here to be considered — the internal state of the organism, its disposition to respond in a particular way, and the character of the trigger. The strange experiment of 'imprinting' shows how far objective likeness can be dispensed with in certain situations. The duckling that is 'set' to follow its mother will also follow any other moving object, such as a brown cardboard box, and once it has been made to react in this way it will apparently remain under the illusion for the rest of its existence that the cardboard box is its mother. There are situations, it seems, where such triumphs as that of Apelles can easily be achieved.

Readers of *Art and Illusion*[7] will not be surprised to find me appealing to these observations for I have emphasized their importance in summing up some of its results:

200

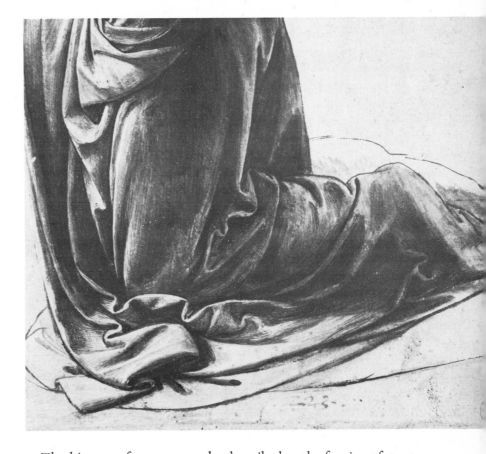

Figs 4, 5 and 6 *The mastery of representational devices, foreshortening, modelling, texture and caricature, in drawings by Leonardo.*

The history of art . . . may be described as the forging of master keys for opening the mysterious locks of our senses to which only nature herself originally held the key. They are complex locks which respond only when various screws are first set in readiness and when a number of bolts are shifted at the same time. Like the burglar who tries to break a safe, the artist has no direct access to the inner mechanism. He can only feel his way with sensitive fingers, probing and adjusting his hook or wire when something gives way. Of course, once the door springs open, once the key is shaped, it is easy to repeat the performance. The next person needs no special insight – no more, that is, than is needed to copy his predecessor's master key.

There are inventions in the history of art that have something of the character of such an open-sesame. Foreshortening may be one of them in the way it produces the impression of depth; others are the tonal system of modelling, highlights for texture, or the clues to expression discovered by humorous art. The question is not whether nature 'really looks' like these pictorial devices but whether pictures with such features suggest a reading in terms of natural objects. Admittedly the degree to which they do depends to some extent on what we called 'mental set'. We respond differently when we are 'keyed up' by expectation, by need, and by cultural habituation. All these factors may affect the preliminary setting of the lock but not its opening, which still depends on turning the right key.

Response to meaning: the magic of eyes

It will be noticed that this argument makes no sharp distinction between emotional arousal and perceptual reactions. The 'clues to expression' discovered by humorous art are treated on a par with the suggestion of texture by means of highlights. I believe that this approach can be justified, but it may still be in need of explanation and elaboration. I should like therefore to take an example in which the two types of reaction are particularly closely allied, the perception and representation of eyes.

It is clear from the outset that real eyes cannot be simulated in images. Seeing eyes are in constant motion, pupils expand and contract, their colour tends to change with the light, their moisture varies, not to speak of the lids and surrounds that will incessantly transform the 'look' of the eye.

Without this influence the 'art' of make-up would never have developed.[15] The setting transforms the appearance of the eye, though exactly how it will transform it is impossible to predict in advance. It is experience, tradition and trial and error which show the make-up expert how to create 'the gentle look'. We know it when we see it, because the springs of our response have been touched in the right way, but it is the meaning we perceive, not the means.

So dominant is this immediate reaction, that it comes as a mortifying discovery how hard it is to answer specific questions about the shape and appearance of the human eye. Of course this difficulty will not be experienced by ophthalmologists or by artists who were trained in the traditional way, but most of us will hesitate when we are asked to draw a horizontal section through the head, across the root of the nose, and indicating the exact shape of the eye sockets. It then turns out that we have a schematic image in our mind of their position when seen from *en face* and another, less accurate one, of the profile, but it is difficult for most people to visualize exactly the transition from one view to another, though

Figs 7 and 8 The spatial relationship between eyes and the surface of the face is shown in the cross section. The drawing below, from an artist's instruction manual by Louis Corinth, shows the eyes lying on a curve.

they see it continually. I confess that I have to touch the two corners of my eyes to become fully aware of their relation in space.

This tendency of ours to look for meaning rather than to take in the real appearance of the world has been a constant theme of art educators who want to change our attitude. I would not deny for a moment that it can be an exciting and liberating experience to discover the true look of things by learning to draw or by studying art, but what I am disposed to question is the assumption that scanning for meaning is just a form of mental laziness. We could not function without this vital principle which Bartlett called 'the effort after meaning'.

I believe this principle to be part of our biological inheritance. Whether or not our response to eyes is inborn – as I would suspect – or learned through something like early 'imprinting', there is an obvious survival value in recognizing the eyes, and even the direction of the gaze, of our fellow creatures. It is useful to know

Fig. 9 The gentle look and how you achieve it.

203

Fig. 10 *The eye spot on the wing of an Emperor moth even has a highlight in the 'pupil'*

when and how we are being looked at if we want to respond adequately to the threat or invitation of another creature. Professor Hinton's chapter shows that this advantage has also led other organisms to react to the standard configuration of two eyes which may act as a warning signal of the presence of a lurking predator.[28] This, at least, would explain the frequency with which certain moths have become marked with 'eyes' on the wings, a marking that appears to deter birds from approaching them. When the markings are artificially obliterated the moths are more frequently eaten by predators.[10],[37]

Not even those of us who are not behaviourists would ever want to say that the markings of the wings have produced an illusion in the birds, if by illusion we mean a state of consciousness, a false belief. Very likely the bird is stimulated to react without the possibility of conscious reflection. But the point is just that reaction precedes reflection, both phylogenetically as psychologically. What distinguishes us from the animal is not the absence of automatic responses, but the capacity to probe them and to experiment with them.

I have appealed to this method in my book *The Story of Art*[6] where I asked the reader to scrawl an eyeless face on a piece of paper and to watch the experience of relief when two dots at last enable it to look at us. When I wrote the book I did not yet know the full weight of anthropological evidence which shows the strength and immediacy of this type of reaction. In Ceylon the act of endowing a Buddha statue with eyes is surrounded by strict taboos, because in painting in the eyes the craftsman brings the image to life. The effect is regarded with such awe that not even the craftsman himself is allowed to look while this miraculous transformation takes place. He paints them over his shoulder while looking into a mirror, and nobody else is allowed to watch the ceremony. On his return from the sacred act the craftsman must be purged, and if he omits these precautions he will be exposed to supernatural sanctions. Richard F. Gombrich, to whom I owe this account,[19] stresses the paradox inherent in the situation. Any Buddhist knows that the Buddha has entered the Nirvana and has been thus liberated from the wheel of existence. Rationally, therefore, the Buddha image can be no more than a mere reminder of the great teacher. But man is not merely rational, and so he will react affectively to the image as if it could look through its eyes. The ritual testifies to the strength of an illusion that is explicitly ruled out by the cognitive doctrine which it serves.[20]

Yet, the illusion is not one of visual reality, it is one of meaning:

204

Fig. 11 *A modern Buddha image from a monastery in central Ceylon*

the eyes appear to give the image sight. But is not this exactly the same reaction we have when looking at our fellow humans? We see them looking. Though we may know rationally that there is no difference in outward appearance between a seeing eye and a blind one and that even a glass eye can reasonably simulate this appearance, I contend it would be false to experience to say that any eye looks like a vitreous sphere. The task of the artist therefore is not necessarily to fashion a facsimile eye. It is to find a way of stimulating the response to a living gaze.

Different styles have adopted very different means of coping with this problem, which may be compounded by the very taboos I have mentioned. It would not be without interest to investigate in the light of this problem the variety of ways the human eye has been rendered in the history of art.

There is ample evidence in the history of sculpture for the difficulties craftsmen experienced in correctly shaping a face in the round. The eye sockets are frequently set into a flattened face, though squeezed profiles also occur. As far as the shape of the eye is concerned, there is a whole spectrum of possibilities, from the schematic dot to the artificial eye of a wax dummy. What may strike the historian of art as odd is how far some of the conventions

Figs 12 and 13 *A. Gaddi, Madonna of Humility* top and Renoir, *La Loge. For details showing the painting of the eyes see plates 12 and 13, page 233*

adopted in certain periods or by various artist were at variance with real appearance. The Giottesque tradition favoured slanted eyes which almost look mongoloid; Poussin so emphasised the rim round the eyes that his figures often acquire the stony stare of the classical statues he so admired. It is impossible for us to tell how such deviations affected the artist's contemporaries who were not used to alternative solutions. Using the formulation I have quoted above, it might be said that we have acquired a different 'mental set' through 'cultural habituation' and no longer respond spontaneously to these renderings. It is because we do not so respond that we see these eyes less as eyes than as slightly odd shapes on the canvas.

But here, as always, there is no need to draw a relativistic conclusion from this variety. There is little doubt in this case that the discovery that a glint can be given to the eye and make it shine enhanced the appeal of the image. Not that a great painter, a Rembrandt, a Renoir, needed to make an exact copy of the eye to achieve this effect. On the contrary, the true masters of illusionism knew of ever fresh ways to trigger our responses, precisely in the way I tried to describe in the simile of the lock and key. The most astounding of these devices is the one employed by the eighteenth-century sculptor Houdon. Marble, of course, is even less capable of imitating the appearance of a real eye than are pigments, and so he had recourse to the daring trick of making a protruding piece of stone stand for the light in the eye. Much as I have always admired Houdon's splendidly lifelike heads, I did not see this device till it was pointed out to me. The more a master succeeds in convincing us that the image looks at us, the less likely we are to realise what is actually there. He has transformed the image into a living presence.

·We might say that the eyes look like real eyes, though real eyes do not look at all like his representation. I am aware of the fact that logically this proposition is absurd. If *a* equals *b*, *b* must also equal *a* But I have argued elsewhere that this symmetrical relationship does not describe what we experience as likeness in art. I have trailed my coat and proposed the formulation that the world does not look like a picture, but a picture can look like the world.[7,14] The catch, of course, is the word 'look'. I have argued that we are less aware of the look of things than of our response. If it is really part of our biological heritage that certain perceptual configurations can 'trigger' specific reactions, it is clear that these reactions are adjusted to our survival in the real world, not to our contemplation of pictures. If I am right that in this respect, too, we are closer to the animal than our

Fig. 14 *Bust of Voltaire by Houdon, 1781*

pride would want us to be, this might suggest that like the animals we do not know and do not have to be aware of what the world looks like. The person who has to be — so it would seem at first — is the artist who wants to contrive a configuration to which we react as if it were an aspect of the world. I have argued in *Art and Illusion* that even this conclusion need not hold; that even the artist has to grope his way by trial and error till he discovers the configuration that produces the desired response.

This response need not be visual — but clearly it can be. We may easily believe that we see more of the eye on the canvas than is present in the artist's brushstrokes. In other words the response to meaning guides our projection, and we think we see shapes and colours which are not actually there.

207

E.H. Gombrich   *The emergence of prediction*

We come here to the nub of the problem, the real point at issue in the discussion about illusion to which I have referred at the outset. When and how can artifice trigger not only response of the kind I have discussed at some length, but something akin to a visual hallucination? I do not claim any particular aesthetic merit for this capacity as such, for as I have also stressed in *Art and Illusion* phantom percepts are frequently set up by such conjuring tricks as the act of pretending to thread a needle and to sew with it, which may induce in the suggestible the appearance of a phantom thread. Descending lower still, there was a trick of 'strip tease' in which the taboo against nudity on the stage was apparently circumvented by switching off the light at the last moment and letting the imagination take over. The sight which is conjured up is best described as a shape we see because we have every reason to believe it is there. It would be a mistake to believe that this reaction is confined to special states of excitement or hallucination. The paradigm for such a phantom percept is in fact the appearance of shadow lettering which makes us complete the whole letters from the strong indications which start us off. I can here refer to Professor Gregory's chapter which explores the role which hypotheses play in our perception. Like myself, Gregory links illusion with the hypotheses formed by the organism; they may be described as the consequence of unrefuted perceptual hypotheses.

IMAGE

I am not sure that I succeeded in *Art and Illusion* in explaining the way I see the connection between the automatisms that can be described in terms of trigger actions and the explanation of certain illusions in terms of perceptual hypotheses. Welcome as is this opportunity to spell out what was perhaps only implied in my previous account, it must inevitably involve me in further speculations of a rather sweeping nature. They have to concern no more and no less than the problem of freedom and necessity. Not that I need depart much from tradition. The ladder of evolution has always been seen as a ladder towards freedom, or at least flexibility. Not even the convinced determinist doubts that the plant is more rigid in its responses than human beings. The higher organisms can learn more readily from experience than the lower animals. A fly will buzz against a window pane and never accept its mistake. Birds will posture

fig. 16   in front of a mirror, and so will kittens, but the latter will soon lose interest as if they had learned to discount the illusion. Bruner[3] has recently used this reaction as a gauge of evolutionary advance. The

208

Fig. 16 *A Ringed Plover threatens its mirror image*

Fig. 17 *Groucho Marx puts his foot through the looking glass to test his 'mirror image' in 'Duck Soup'*

macaque seems only able to attack or threaten its mirror image or to ignore it. Chimpanzees can recognize their mirror image and guide self-directed behaviour by it (e.g. by touching a spot on the forehead seen in the mirror). We are not exempt from being deceived by mirrors, but we can also systematically test a mirror image for its reality – witness the marvellous sequence in a Marx brothers film where Groucho applies such tests to his double on the other side of the door. What is more surprising still, perhaps, than this ability to test for reality is the variety of ways we can learn to control and to utilize the illusion. The actor who postures before the mirror can try out the effect of his expressions as if he were watching another person. Engravers, dentists, and even car drivers must be able to switch their innervations and movements, the whole feedback mechanism in relation to the reversed image, without thereby losing the capacity to react to impressions outside the mirror in the appropriate way. They learn a willing suspension of disbelief that may still not be fully understood.

Strict behaviourism has linked any capacity to learn with the models of automatic trigger actions, by introducing the idea of the 'conditioned reflex', the notorious dinner bell that made Pavlov's dog salivate because it had frequently heard it before being fed. There is

209

E.H. Gombrich   plenty of experimental evidence testifying to the possibility of such conditioning, but we are still entitled to ask how and why organisms became amenable to conditioning. The answer must be in terms of survival chances. The inborn response to specified stimuli will reduce the danger of mistakes by making it most unlikely that the response will be released by accident. (Elaborate simulation of stimuli by nature or by human cunning is not a contingency that evolution can guard against.) But the same rigidity will also prevent an organism from ever learning from experience. To do so it must become flexible, more flexible indeed than is postulated by the idea of conditioning. Pavlov's dog was confined in an apparatus, but had it not been, hunger would clearly have made it search its environment for food. Who is to draw the line in such a situation between the scents and sights that would have triggered an inborn reaction of pursuit and others that have been learned? Should we not rather picture the organism as scanning the world for meaningful configurations — meaningful, that is, in relation to its chances of survival? Danger has to be avoided, food and mates have to be found, the brood has to be protected, and each of these needs in its turn necessitates complex responses to an infinite variety of situations. When the organism is 'keyed up', not only the goal itself elicits strong reactions, but anything that may be said to point to the presence of the goal. It should be clear that this widening of the waveband to which the organism can respond has both advantages and disadvantages for its survival chances. Being hyper-alerted, it is more likely to detect the goal, but it is also more prone to jump to false conclusions. Scanning the world for meaning, it is confronted with the necessity to interpret the evidence. I know that some philosophers and psychologists are suspicious of the terms 'conclusion' and 'interpretation' in relation to reaction below the threshold of awareness. But unless we concede the possibility of the animal making some kind of inference from evidence, we cannot envisage evolution ever getting on to the ladder that leads from the lower reaches of the soul to critical reason. An organism that lacks the flexibility of making mistakes through misjudging the evidence must also lack the potentiality of learning. It is clear that in the condition of search the possibility of anticipating events must sometimes make the difference between life and death. A capacity for anticipatory reactions must therefore be one of the greatest assets evolution can bestow on an organism. The best type of anticipation would be conscious prophecy, genuine prediction of coming events, but since this desirable gift is not to be had on this earth, the

210

organism has to be content with the next best endowment, the gift of guessing or gambling. Granted that a false guess may be lethal, in the absence of any guessing there could be no lucky hits either. The situation has rightly been compared with that of the scientist who must test and probe nature and can only do so in the light of a hypothesis. It is true that Francis Bacon specifically condemned what he called the *anticipatio mentis*, the prejudice that, as he thought, would cloud the scientist's capacity for unbiased observation. I have referred in *Art and Illusion* to the opposite point of view, K.R. Popper's conviction that all acquisition of knowledge 'from the amoeba to Einstein' demands a process of trial and error, which proceeds through 'conjectures and refutations'.[32],[33] The elimination of false guesses does not, by itself, stand in need of conscious thought. All higher animals can learn from their mistakes.

If it thus turns out that the readiness to gamble, to anticipate on insufficient evidence, is a precious asset rather than a liability in any search or quest, we can attribute to the lower reaches of the soul something of the qualities of a detective. Once the hunt is on, the slightest clue can become important for a tentative anticipation, a hypothesis which could lead to the desired goal. We do not know how these anticipations are represented to the organism — very likely in terms of innervations and other nervous states of readiness, which would include the salivation of Pavlov's dog. Could they also lead to perceptual anticipations? Does a dog to whom we throw a stick not only tense its muscles but actually see it leave our hands for a fraction of a second even if we trick him and do not throw? It may be difficult to establish the existence of such phantom images among the percepts of animals, though Gregory has told me that there is some evidence that they may indeed exist. One thing is certain — any 'prognostic' mechanism of perception would be of immense survival value. This value, alas, can best be illustrated by the 'predictors' which have been built into anti-aircraft guns and other weapons to compute the likely position of a moving target at the moment of impact. One could easily imagine such an aiming device being equipped with a predictive image towards which a pointer had to be moved. Be that as it may, it is obvious that such a pre-image would be the easiest way for the anticipation to be represented to the organism. A perceptual system that is capable of showing both the present and the predicted state in a changing situation could be said to achieve for events in time what binocular vision achieves for objects in space. Nor would the tracking of a moving target be the only function that would benefit from such a perceptual predictor.

211

E.H. Gombrich

Self-movement always produces changes in the environment which demand predictive assessment, and so do eye movements. Any shift in focus entails a situation in which we can and must confirm or refute an expectation – however fleeting. The stimulus that reaches us from the margin of the field of vision may lead to an anticipation of what we shall find on inspection. It is true that confirmation never enters our awareness, and even refutation but rarely. We have no need to remind ourselves of the expectations that were fulfilled. Prediction and actuality merge in our awareness, just as the two retinal images fuse in binocular vision. Where our anticipation is belied by events we may suffer a shock of surprise, but we have other things to attend to than our disappointed expectations. More often than not they are blotted out by the quantities of incoming information which set up fresh expectations in their turn. The existence of prognostic perception would thus be impossible to prove, were it not for situations where the predictive phantom does become available to introspection. They occur, as we have seen, when the erasure mechanism fails in the absence of contradictory percepts or when the phantom becomes too strong to yield to the pressures of refutation.

The most dramatic instance of this kind I know is the gruesome account given to me by a former soldier who was hit on the head by a shrapnel during the war: he saw his own head rolling on the ground, before he passed out. It is only his critical reason that tells him that he hallucinated.

It may seem a harsh transition to turn from such extremes to our normal experience of art, but our problem is precisely to what extent art may elicit phantom perceptions. A recent paper on the great mime Marcel Marceau[34] is significantly called 'Notes on the Creation of the Perceptual Object'. Pretending to interact with things of the physical world – the bars of a cage in which he is imprisoned, the mantlepiece on which he is leaning with his elbows or the ball he is bouncing – Marcel Marceau creates, in the author's words, 'for the spectator percepts, and does this in the absence of the physical supports that we normally regard as the sources of, or distal stimuli for, such percepts. He makes us see objects on the empty stage'. This is the type of illusion I exemplified by the trick of the needle and thread, but a thread is an elusive percept at the best of times, and so we more easily believe that we see what is not there. Do we really 'see' the objects Marcel Marceau appears to manipulate, or do we only 'imagine' them? A philosophical critic would certainly ask this question, but can it ever be completely answered? People may differ

Fig. 18 *The mime Marcel Marceau on an empty stage interacts with imaginary objects*

212

in the intensity of their response and in their willingness to go along with the illusion. As far as I can judge my own reactions, it seems to me that the phantoms I see on the stage during a performance of this kind resemble marginally perceived objects. These are the objects on the fringe of our visual field which we expect to come into focus if we turned towards them. Introspection suggests to me that I focus on the body of the mime, but I experience the fleeting expectation that, were I to focus elsewhere, the objects with which he pretends to interact would come into view.

If this account could be substantiated it would also explain the reason why this experience can so easily be strengthened by offering some rudimentary support to the expectation. It is impossible to be sure whether an object on the margin of vision is a stick or a gun. It may even be impossible to specify the exact moment when we stop projecting our expectation of what it is, and really see it. Our reaction, as we have seen, does not wait for such a cool examination. We start projecting as soon as we are aroused by context and anticipation, though we may subsequently revise our reaction when we have had time to sort out the illusion from the perception.

I hope there was some justification, therefore, in my comparing our response to painted highlights to trigger actions, while yet insisting that the pigment must be correctly interpreted if it is to have this effect of causing an illusion. It is this interpretation which will be affected by what I described as expectation, need, or cultural habituation. We search for the meaning and take the hint; in other words, we correctly interpret the white patch as a gleam in the eye because it is found to fit the hypothetical meaning. It reinforces rather than erases the anticipatory phantom.

I believe this account to be well in line with Gregory's theories, though his chapter shows how much more complex the situation must look to the psychologist who studies the variety of mechanisms involved in the generation of illusion. It remains a matter of speculation and debate which of these various mechanisms might be subsumed under such a more general biological hypothesis. Some of them might be interpreted as functions or malfunctions of reactions serving the same aim on different levels. Thus the 'waterfall illusion', which makes us see our visual impressions streak upwards after we have stared at downward movement for too long, can be described as the consequence of an assumption that the frame of reference is constantly shifting downwards, though this type of 'assumption' is certainly lodged in a different part of the brain from the type of expectation that causes the phantom contours of letters.

Association and the power of words

Any trespasser into an intellectual field not his own may find to his cost that his retreat is barred. Once he has committed himself to certain surmises or speculations, he must be prepared to explain how these might be squared with the observations or assumptions of others, and soon he finds himself in the uneasy position of the heretic tilting at orthodoxy. True, the orthodoxy with which my account is in danger of colliding is a rather superannuated and battered one – I mean the empiricist theory of the association of ideas. For those who accept this theory wholesale, the problems of illusions are deceptively simple. Whether we read a book or look at a picture, we will have associations which will arise in our 'imagination'. The theory would not have enjoyed so long a run if it had not been found to offer a superficial explanation of our whole mental life, but some of its weaknesses have long been pointed out, most emphatically perhaps by Bradley, who called it 'mere nonsense'.[40] There is indeed a hidden assumption here which creates serious difficulties: if there are to be associations of ideas there must be 'ideas', simple entities that can form into chains or complexes. In the original version of the theory, these entities were the residues of 'sensations', the simplest traces of sensory stimuli. It was these which combined into percepts of objects and further into the associated images that floated into our consciousness. To see an orange, as we have been told in countless variations, is first to have the sensations of colour and shape, which are associated with the memories of tactile sensations forming the percept of the orange, which evokes associations of its smell and taste. Maybe these will drag further images out of our memory into consciousness – the sight of a garden in Sicily or the name of Nell Gwyn. The word 'orange' in its turn is also associated with the fruit – its meaning being merely a form of association which brings up the image into the mind. But the very distinction between sensation and perception which belongs to this simple picture of the mind has been challenged, most recently by J.J. Gibson.[4] Whatever may be going on when we see an orange, we are not simply putting together a number of elementary sensations.

I believe the main philosophical weakness of the theory of sensations and associations sprang from the belief in the efficacy of introspection. Unlike the animal, man was supposed to have privileged access to his own mental experiences. If I have stressed the link of both perception and illusion with the 'lower reaches of the soul', it is precisely because I have come to doubt the validity of

214

introspection. But in concentrating on the biological point of view I was not out to 'debunk' what is specifically human, the use of language and other systems of symbols. In common with other students of language I do not think that a purely associationist theory of language can ever be successful, but the functions of language that warrant this conclusion are largely outside the purview of this chapter. Language can certainly be used to evoke expectations, and therefore illusions. We do not know whether the dog may experience a phantom image when the stick is thrown, or when the word of command is uttered, but we do know that humans can so succumb to the suggestion of words. It is my feeling that the images which may ordinarily accompany the perception of speech are more effortlessly described as expectations or anticipations than as residual memories. When we were children we were unlikely to discuss oranges in the abstract. If one was mentioned, it was probably in a context in which the fruit would also be produced. It is true that as grown-ups we live in a rich web of possible contexts which are far removed from action and actuality. The orange may really be a signal for me to reminisce about Sicily or to talk about Nell Gwyn. True this sounds a strained interpretation, but only because word association tests are so often conducted in artificial isolation. Normally our associations are not random; they are guided by our aims and momentary interests. They are the signs that we are approaching our goal, whether in thought or in action; in other words they are meaningful. The main advantage of such a shift of emphasis from the past to the future, from casual traces to purposeful aids, would lie precisely in the possibility of discarding the elusive notions of 'ideas' and 'sensations' that form into chains. What emerge into consciousness are aspects of the vaguely anticipated context.

Extreme situations such as suggestion under hypnosis may best exemplify the power of words to mediate an illusion through anticipation. There is an unforgettable episode of this kind in the ninth chapter of Rudyard Kipling's *Kim*, when Lurgan Sahib, the member of the Secret Service, is testing the young hero of the story for his ability to resist suggestion by first impressing him with a conjuring trick and then predicting a miracle. He had spirited a water jug across the table and asked Kim to throw it back. The jar breaks.

Lurgan Sahib laid one hand gently on the nape of his neck, stroked it twice or thrice, and whispered: 'Look! It shall come to life again, piece by piece. First the big piece shall join itself to two others on the right and the left — on the right and the left. Look!'

To save his life Kim could not have turned his head. The light touch held him as in a vice, and his blood tingled pleasantly through him. There was one large piece of the jar where there had been three, and above them the shadowy outline of the entire vessel. He could see the veranda through it, but it was thickening and darkening with each beat of his pulse . . .

'Look! It is coming into shape,' said Lurgan Sahib.

So far Kim had been thinking in Hindi but a tremor came on him, and with an effort like that of a swimmer before sharks, who hurls himself half out of the water, his mind leaped up from the darkness that was swallowing it and took refuge in — the multiplication-table in English!

'Look! It is coming into shape,' whispered Lurgan Sahib.

The jar has been smashed — yess, smashed — not the native word, he would not think of that — but smashed — into fifty pieces, and twice three was six, and thrice three was nine, and four times three was twelve. He clung desperately to the repetition. The shadow-outline of the jar cleared like a mist after rubbing eyes. There were the broken shards; there was the spilt water drying in the sun, and through the cracks of the veranda showed, all ribbed, the white house — well below — and thrice twelve was thirty-six.

What Plato called the part of the soul which 'puts its trust in measurement and reckoning' had triumphed over the 'lower reaches'. Did Kipling remember the passage from the *Republic*?

The shadowy outline of the vessel exactly corresponds to the phantom percepts which were the subject of the previous section. There they were evoked by actions, expectations and images. Here they are aroused by words. It is easy to understand how the child could be tempted to surrender to their suggestion, but what of the reader of Kipling's story? Will he also visualize the jug and the veranda? People differ in these matters. But one thing is sure — once we are absorbed in a story we shut out other impressions, much as the Hi-fi enthusiast who closes his eyes. Only when we want to resist the pull of the illusion, when what we read becomes too unpleasant, we take recourse to the equivalent of Kim's multiplication-table and tell ourselves that after all we need not submit to words on paper.

There is a theory of the mind which links its capacity to produce illusions — artistic or otherwise — with the quest for satisfactions which real life too often denies us. According to Freud our whole psychic life might be described in terms of a conflict between what he calls the pleasure principle and the reality principle. The first rules the 'lower reaches of the soul', the latter the higher ones. The pleasures of illusion are generally bought at the expense of reality testing. Freud, of course, operated with an associationist psychology which strongly influenced his model of the mind. In other respects our interpretation would not clash with his account of the dream.

During sleep the search that goes on in the 'lower reaches of the soul' is not restrained by critical reason, and almost any internal or external stimuli can trigger anticipatory phantoms. It is different when we are awake and are compelled to erase those phantoms that do not square with our critical tests. Not that there is an absolutely strict borderline here between the delusion of dreaming and the veridical perceptions of our active life. Sometimes a phantom of critical reason sneaks into our dreams to perplex us. I remember being puzzled in a dream by the discovery that I could walk in the air, and deciding to test whether I was dreaming. I reasoned that I should focus on the facades of the houses past which I was flying to see whether their details would come into prominence. They did. I clearly saw the actual brickwork and was convinced that my experience must therefore be real. Whether or not this dream was prompted by my interest in the very problems to which this essay is directed is a different matter. At any rate it is not surprising that the idea of life being a dream has always been popular with introspective people. It is notorious that this belief can never be disproved.

Illusion and the hierarchy of beliefs

It is clear from what has been said, that the study of illusion would always have to be supplemented by an investigation of the resources we employ for spotting our own illusions. Such an investigation would take us far beyond the scope of this chapter. What is relevant here is mainly that we can no longer equate illusion with mistaken beliefs. It is at this point, perhaps, that our footnotes to Plato would have to become critical, because it is the tradition stemming from him that is responsible for this equation. Plato saw the distinction between truth and error largely as a moral problem. In his most famous image, in the *Phaedrus* (246B and 253D, E), he likened the parts of the soul to two unequal horses, one heavy, insolent and recalcitrant, the other noble, good and obedient, which must both be kept in step by the skilled charioteer. It is the distinction between reason and instinct, imperfectly controlled by man that survives in

Freud's concept of the 'id', the 'ego' and the 'superego'. But it is clear from the biological point of view that— if we want to stay with Plato's image — the good horse alone could not pull the chariot at all. *Mutatis mutandis* this criticism applies also to Plato's verdict on the senses. Basic for his whole theory of knowledge is the polarity between mere opinion (*doxa*), which is due to the fallible senses, and knowledge (*epistêmê*), the product of reason. He was certainly right in stressing the fallibility of our senses, but we have seen that it is not really the senses which matter here. Imagine if the demiurge had endowed us instead with a perfect registration apparatus of infinite capacity, instantly producing an internal representation of our whole environment down to the finest detail. Imagine even for arguments sake that such a complete inventory of the environment could be drawn up every second or so, to give us unimpeachable knowledge of every object in our world. But imagine also that he had failed to equip us with the power of extrapolation, the power of framing hypotheses about the future so that, *per impossibile*, we would know in crossing a road where every car is, but not its direction or speed. We would obviously not survive long. We have seen indeed that what the organism needs is something very different, an adjustment to future situations — events, that is, which are not yet presented but must be anticipated.

I believe that not only the doctrine of association but also the schema of stimulus and response has somewhat obscured the prognostic character of perception. The response is not so much to the stimulus as such — any stimulus — but to its meaning as a warning signal or a promise. We blink when there is a danger of something getting into our eyes, and this reflex serves us in good stead even if it is sometimes triggered by a false warning. The response of salivation prepares the dog for digesting food, just as the fear reaction increases the adrenalin content of our blood and provides extra energy for flight. Whether the senses convey to us signals for arousal or for reassurance, the messages from the environment are related to the organism's need. It must get into a state of readiness to cope with coming situations rather than with the passing present. True, we could not survive if we misinterpreted the signs and portents too often, but the truth we seek with our senses is not the static and eternal truth that interested Plato, but the correct assessment of the developing situation with which we interact.

I believe with Popper[33] that epistemology can teach us much about psychology. He has shown that there is a continuity between the procedures of science in framing and testing hypotheses and the methods used by organisms in finding their way through the world. Plato's dichotomy between opinion and knowledge is untenable. The lower reaches of the soul are not to be regarded as the sources of noxious disturbances. Whether we compare them to a wild horse, or to a rash gambler, the fact remains that life goes on into an unknowable future. There is no antithesis between reflex and reflection, but a continuous spectrum extending from the one to the other, or rather a hierarchy of systems which interact on many levels. The lower system of impulse and anticipation offers material for the higher centres in a chain of processes that extends from unconscious reaction to conscious scrutiny and beyond to the refined methods of testing developed by science. Let us grant again that Plato was right in his diagnosis that art exploits our first, our uncritical reactions. It is precisely because we are less concerned with what is than with what might be, that we find it easy to enter into the illusion of a painted scenery or of the action of the play. We allow ourselves to be aroused by martial music and to be soothed by a lullaby because these affect us in any case. And much to Plato's concern we have set aside a domain, even an institution, called 'art' in which we seek such arousal — of 'fear and pity', of thrills and 'kicks — in the safe knowledge that these are mere exercises, without 'consequence'.

We have developed another institution, called 'science' in which we systematically submit our reactions and responses to the scrutiny of reason. It is reason that tells us in Plato's words that 'it is impossible . . . at one time to hold contradictory opinions about the same thing'. Contrasting the fallible report of our eyes with the results of measurements, Plato rightly concluded that if the two prove inconsistent one of them must be due for revision. The illustration remains instructive because we have meanwhile learned that these measurements themselves do not result in the final certainty of *epistêmê*. Spurred by the inconsistencies obtained in the measurement of the speed of light, Einstein proposed that our measuring rods cannot be considered stable in relation to an 'absolute space'. Their rigidity is an illusion.

Scientists know this, and yet they continue to use measuring rods 'as if' they were stable in contexts where relativity theory makes no difference. They decide to ignore the further level of the hierarchy of hypotheses while they get on with the job. In other words even scientists sometimes act as if they could hold 'contradictory opinions about the same thing'. For those of us who study the problem of illusion in its wider context this is a salutary reminder.

For here we can again apply Popper's principle of continuity between all processes of cognition, and recognise that life would be impossible if we always wanted to test our perceptions against all levels of belief. Even where such tests are possible, they take time and energy away from more urgent tasks, that is from the task of adjusting to the future. I happen to have little sympathy with the champions of instinct and intuition who decry reason as the enemy of life, but so much is true in their contention that an extreme of critical awareness would ultimately paralyse our actions. We must always 'run ahead of the evidence', as Gregory puts it; we always fill in from our imagination what we anticipate to be there. The 'effort after meaning' must always be selective. We must learn to ignore as well as to supplement. It is this dual activity that makes discussions about the relation between perception and illusion so tricky.

One thing is sure. It no longer makes sense to start this discussion from a separation between what is 'given' — the so-called sense data — and what is merely imagined. 'Hoeffding long ago demonstrated logically that memory is involved in almost all perception, for except under highly unusual conditions, we do not simply see but recognize what we see'.[25] But neither this nor any other perceptual process is inherently infallible. We should not speak of re-cognition, but of classification in terms influenced by previous experience, in other words of interpretation.

It may be useful here to distinguish between errors which can only be found out in the course of events, and others which we recognise as false perceptions. There are many 'sense data' which contradict our firmly held convictions and which we therefore classify as illusions without much attending to them. This applies to after-images, the double vision of objects close by when we focus on the distance, and all the major and minor pathologies that may afflict our eyesight without influencing our hypotheses about the world. They may be compared to irrelevant reports from the front which the intelligence officer discards without even passing them on to higher quarters. What is more interesting and more intriguing is the propensity of these higher quarters to ask the senses to re-write their reports if they happen not to fit in with their expectations. Gregory here speaks of 'scaling downwards from perceptual hypotheses'. It is the range of phenomena we mean when we say that 'seeing depends on knowledge'. What we should say is that seeing often varies with belief. Like so many perceptual mechanisms, this mutual adjustment is not normally open to introspection, but it is not in conflict with the prognostic purpose of perception that must interest the student of illusion. The situation-report, on which the higher quarters intend to base their decision, may be pictured like a map, onto which certain assumptions are entered. There may be arrows indicating the expected movement of regiments, and these arrows should not and could not be redrawn on the report that one individual soldier was seen walking in another direction. The point at which the whole picture must be revised is hard to establish *a priori*, but clearly a certain amount of dogmatism is as useful to the commander as an excess may be fatal.

If we put on pink spectacles, the report of our eyes will clash with our hypotheses of the world, and if I am in the right mood, I may enjoy the sight of a rose-coloured world, without falling into any errors. But for practical purposes I learn to disregard the biased evidence, and achieve an alteration of the messages to the extent that the normal colours may be restored and the cognitive map is perfectly re-established. If I take off the glasses, the contrary bias will appear and the world will take on the complementary hue of green — at least for a short while. Which of these three experiences should be called an 'illusion'? Frankly, I cannot attach much importance to this question. The phenomenon which Gregory discusses under the heading of 'perceptual calibration' seems to me much more interesting than the mere question of linguistic usage.

There certainly are situations in which usage equates perceptual errors with illusion. The question then remains, to what extent the illusion depends on the error. Imagine a car driver who takes some shadows on the road for an obstacle and swerves into a ditch. Clambering out and investigating the spot, he recognises his mistake, but he may still be able to recapture his illusion. Nor need this be due simply to memory. His companion may say, 'I can imagine how you could make this mistake'. In other words he can make himself 'see' the shadows as a potential obstacle. To what extent he will succeed may depend on a large number of variables, the degree to which he is a visualiser, his willingness to identify with the driver and his ability to 'suspend his disbelief'. Much has been written since Wittgenstein on what we mean by 'seeing as', but it is likely that there are any number of degrees in this elusive experience.

It is certainly important here not to equate the experience in front of pictorial representations uncritically with that of a three-dimensional sight. It is easier to see the notorious ambiguous inkblot either 'as' a rabbit or duck[7] than it would be to make such a voluntary switch between real rabbits and ducks. The element of 'interpretation' is more to the fore in relation to symbolic material than it is in a life situation, but even in this latter case we can observe

221

how our involuntary or assumed beliefs will influence our perception. In an earlier paper[1][2] I have quoted a vivid account by Professor N. Tinbergen of the way he was influenced by his expectations to misperceive rigid pack ice as a turbulent sea.

Both the degree and the limits of this effect present fascinating problems for study. Here the development of the scientific world-picture offers an interesting test case. We now 'know' that the stars are scattered over immense distances in outer space, but how far does this knowledge affect the illusion of the night sky as a starry vault?[18] It still persists, though very likely our visual experience is no longer quite the same as that of an ancient Greek, who believed in the reality of the enveloping sphere. Does even the moon look quite the same to us as it did to the poets of yore since we have seen the astronauts cavorting on its surface on our television screens?

It may not be quite too late to try to answer some of these questions through anthropological field-work, along some of the lines discussed in Deregowski's chapter, though it is certainly far from easy to formulate the right questions. Perhaps a preliminary question may be suggested. Do all cultures make the same radical distinction between 'appearance' and 'reality' which ours has inherited from Plato? Are their hierarchies the same? In other words, do they necessarily accept the demand that contradictions must be ironed out and that all perceptions that clash with beliefs must force us either to change our views of the 'objective world' or declare the perception to have been a subjective experience — an illusion? Even in our rationalist culture we don't often live up to this logical precept. We try to evade it, especially when our emotions are involved.

It is not surprising that this should be so, because most of the beliefs which may here come into play concern probabilities, and all of them are based on hearsay rather than first-hand experience. Take the true story told to me by an elderly friend who drove one morning through the peaceful lanes of Wiltshire when he suddenly saw the shape of an elephant lumbering through the morning mists. He certainly 'rubbed his eyes' to be sure he was not asleep (a doubtful test, as we know), because elephants are sufficiently rare in Wiltshire to make this sight surprising. The observation of a circus tent parked on the meadows restored consistency to the scene and made my friend rightly adopt the hypothesis that the elephant was not a subjective but an objective experience. What if he had seen a ghost or a dragon? Here the reaction will obviously depend on the tradition of the perceiver's culture. When we cried as children and complained that there was a terrible dragon under the bed we were

222

probably reassured: 'Nonsense, darling! You must have had a bad dream. There are no dragons.' 'Promise?' 'Promise!' But, strictly speaking, it was rash to make this promise, for the non-existence of dragons cannot be proved. Small wonder that our assurance may break down when we find ourselves in a dark forest at night and see what looks like a dragon. Take no chances. Act first, think later. Reaction precedes reflection. Whether or not we may have to revise our beliefs is after all *cura posterior*. Better pray and run.

I do not want to insinuate that every reader of this chapter would necessarily react in this way. It is sufficient to acknowledge that the 'cognitive systems' of a culture frequently clash with the actions its members are seen to perform.[20] An example of this kind was discussed in the previous section. Cognitively the Buddha is believed to have entered Nirvana, but affectively he is still invoked, and his image is treated as a numinous object that can be given eyes to see.

Not that our own culture is less productive of similar contradictions. There can be few people who would formulate it as their belief that the touching of wood after certain utterances will prevent unseen powers from manifesting their envy. But they do say 'touch wood' all the same. The Italian idiom *Non è vero, ma ci credo* (It is not true, but I believe it) sums up the situation.

Here we must certainly agree with Freud that we are born with emotional needs that demand an outlet even at the price of intellectual consistency. It is the assumption of such consistency that has vitiated the discussions about illusion in art. But art is not the only type of experience which demonstrates our willingness to embrace illusions. How, for instance, should we describe the relation of people in our culture to their pets? We all know the old spinster who is convinced her dog understands her every word. We can also guess at the emotional need that underlies her actions. It is easy for her to refrain from critical tests, because they are in any case hard to come by. Undoubtedly the dog does understand some of her utterances and will respond to her voice and her signs of affection. Where is the line between objective truth and subjective illusion? Are we even right in characterizing her fond illusion as a delusion? She is not mental. 'Somewhere' she knows perfectly well that there are limits to what she can tell the dog, but do we not even talk to ourselves at times?

One of the most searching books on this elusive borderline between belief and 'make-belief' takes its starting point not from art but from that 'willing suspension of disbelief' we call play. I am referring to Johan Huizinga's *Homo Ludens*,[26] which I have discussed elsewhere.[17] What characterizes play is the element of social compact, the exclusion of the 'spoilsport' whose uttered disbelief will 'break the illusion'. In the game the consistency test with the outside world is deliberately dispensed with, it creates an enclosure in which the 'hypothesis' that we are cops and robbers is applied to the best of our ability. There is no delusion, but plenty of illusion, for in the heat of the game the outside world may sink beyond our awareness. Maybe the robbers will even begin to look different from the cops, once we have entered into the spirit of the thing.

What links play with art is precisely the way in which external consistency is traded against internal coherence. It is this 'inner logic' that distinguishes the world of 'make believe' in games and fantasies from the dream. W.H. Auden[2] has described how he submitted his daydreams of a mining enterprise to the most rigorous tests of technical consistency. He has shown that for him this creation of a self-consistent enclave was the way to poetry.

The demand for internal cohesion, for freedom from contradictions is of course a commonplace of criticism. I believe that those who are interested in the illusions of art might do worse than study the opposite effect and ask what happens when the illusion is broken? What kind of experience is likely to disrupt it?

Clearly, here as always, much depends on our expectations, our knowledge of the convention of a given genre that permits us to enter into the game and to *concentrate* on it — an excellent word for the mental operation we have to perform. Watching a Japanese Kabuki play where the under-life-size puppets are operated by hooded players on the stage, we soon submit to the 'illusion' and adjust to the extent that the irruption of the puppet master's hand may cause a shock because of its gigantic scale.

It is well known that it is not always easy in the theatre to prevent the public from taking any event as part of the show, and Pirandello and his followers have exploited these uncertainties to unsettle our hierarchies of beliefs. We obviously must distinguish between the consistency of the work of art and the consistency of the illusion: entering into a story — whether on the stage or in a book — we do not mind being presented with a world that does not answer our normal reality tests. But we want to know the confines of that world. We are mildly disturbed if the author of a novel breaks in to ask us whether he should let his hero live or die. But when we read a narrative such as Agatha Christie's thriller *The Murder of Roger Akroyd* and discover that the story into which we entered in good faith was really concocted by the criminal to deceive us, our head begins to spin round. Only after the silent compact with the narrator has thus been broken do we discover the existence of this compact, the frame within which we accept the illusion.

Illusionistic painting

Maybe we are now at last equipped to return to the starting point of this debate, the degree of illusion evoked by a seascape on the museum wall. Those philosophers who claim that there is no difference in principle between the shapes we see on an illusionistic canvas and other conventional forms of notation may be granted the fact that any symbolic system could appeal to our imagination and transport us into an illusionary world.

It is quite true that if I am shown a map of my native city and asked to trace my daily way to school the shape and names of the streets may affect me emotionally. I may even find that my imagination is stirred and that sights I had almost forgotten arise

Fig. 19 *Vienna: a map of the inner city and* overleaf *a view of part of Vienna.*

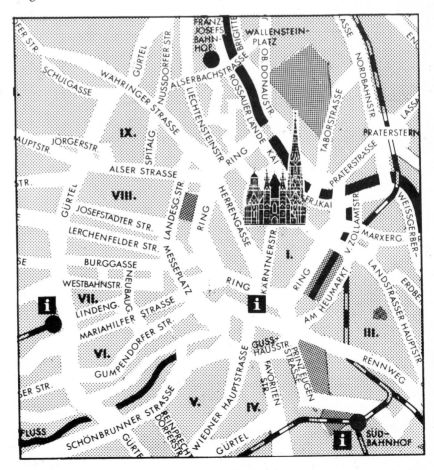

E.H. Gombrich

before the eyes of my mind. But of my mind only. My daydreaming would not interfere with my perception of the map or cause me to imagine shapes which on examination would prove to be illusory.

There are styles in art which are essentially map-like. They offer us an enumeration of what — for want of a better word — I still would like to call 'conceptual images', pictographs which tell a story or give an inventory of stage props. Many a mediaeval picture of the sea would fall into this category. To read it may not differ much from reading a poem about the sea. But the historian of art also knows that at a given moment such diagrammatic pictures were rejected as inadequate, precisely because they fell so far short of the claims that had been made for the power of painting to create an illusion.[10],[11] Slowly but surely those devices were developed which I have described as keys to the lock of our perception. Not that this fresh dimension would stunt the appeal to the imagination. A Dutch seascape may also cause me to dream and to imagine in a fleeting reverie that I hear the rush of the wind or sense the breeze. Why else should Fuseli have quipped that the sight of Constable's landscapes made him open his umberella? Needless to say, however, he was not acting under the influence of an illusion. The visual illusion can only be said to take over where the beholder's reaction fuses with the picture and so transforms it that it becomes increasingly hard to specify exactly what is really there on the canvas.

Once more it seems to me a mistake to start this examination by asking whether I see painted distance as distant. It is more prudent to begin with the question as to whether certain tones or lines are actually given or merely imagined. For here, as always, perception will tend to 'run ahead of the evidence'. The problem, then, is in what direction it will run. It is here that the perception of meaning plays such a vital part. Take what we call the illusion of movement in a painting. Nobody thinks that the sailing boat is actually racing out of the frame, but there are experiments to suggest that if we understand its direction and speed we will anticipate its shift to some extent [27],[9]. The configuration will be tense with a directional thrust which can be measured in the tachystoscope.

Gestalt psychologists have investigated the phenomenon of 'closure', the tendency to ignore the gap in the circle exposed to the view for a moment. Here, too, similar experiments might be devised for representational pictures. My hypothesis would be that the 'filling in' would again be determined by the interpretation of what is represented. Everyday experience, even in looking at a blurred photograph, supports this assumption. In my submission we can even

228

tremor adprehendit eol
| bidolorel ut parturienta!
inspu uehementa conteref nauesthariil:

Fig. 21 *The raging sea as pictured in the Stuttgart Psalter, tenth century*

go further here. For I would contend that the filling in, the phantom percept, if we so want to call it, will not follow the lines on the surface as it does in the phenomenon of closure, but will obey the laws of three dimensional representation. If I look at a painting of the calm sea convincingly showing the ripples of the waves, the reflections of boats and the sheen of light, I will fill in the surface of the water that is not actually represented in paint and will fill it in as a horizontal expanse, not as a vertical patch of pigment on the panel. The question of 'depth' or 'space', in other words, is bound up with that imagined orientation. To say that I have no illusion of depth is really to say that I only know intellectually that the ripples are not meant to be on top of each other but signify an extension into the distance.

Plate 14

Now this contention has in fact been experimentally tested and refuted. It has been refuted precisely because the 'tendency to run ahead of the evidence' can be shown to have the same kind of effect on the appearance of objects represented in pictures as it has on those in three-dimensional space. Our 'expectation' that a small object in the distance would prove to be larger than it appears to be

229

Plate 14

at the moment, once we approach it, notoriously makes us see distant objects as larger than their retinal size would allow us to infer. This is the so-called 'constancy' phenomenon. The term has been criticized because, as Dr Thouless has stressed[36] phenomenal size appears to be a compromise between retinal size and inferred size. Personally I am not very happy with the concept of phenomenal size altogether, because in real life situations it proves to be a very elusive entity.[7,18] It is different with paintings.[7,10,14,22] We can measure the represented size and the apparent size by a variety of methods[1] and see that patches of paint which are objectively equal in extension 'appear' to be very different in size if they stand for a distant sail or for a pebble on the beach in the foreground. More evidence for the illusion of depth comes from the shift in apparent

230

Figs 22-24 *Seen from any angle the road in the picture appears to lead towards us. The illusion is due to the transformations of the picture plane.*

orientation following a change of viewing point.[14] The 'constancies' mask the perspectival distortions of the picture plane and make us read them as movement in space.

If illusion was not a dirty word in visual research, we would by now know as much of these effects as Hi-Fi engineers presumably know about auditory perception. What, for instance, is the exact effect of stereoscopic devices on these illusory transformations? What is the relative importance of facsimile fidelity and of context? There is obviously a spectrum in the 'imitation of reality'. At one extreme we would find the panoramas beloved of the nineteenth century, in which real bushes and pebbles were placed in front of the curving canvas to give the visitor as complete an illusion as possible of being transported to an imaginary scene, be it a battle (as in the

231

fig. 25

panorama of the Berg Isel still shown in Innsbruck) or a seascape (as in the Mesdag Museum in The Hague). Here the visitor can look around on all sides without encountering blatant contradictions, but it is well known that the very fidelity of detail may enhance the clash with the absence of movement and life. At the other end of the spectrum we would have to place those media which exclude surface fidelity, be they monochrome sculptures or line drawings. What happens here to the observed effects on the constancies of size and orientations?

To some extent these phenomena are independent of the medium: they occur in line drawings as well as in naturalistic paintings. The question would be to what extent. Gibson, of course, is quite right in stressing the relative character of naturalism when it comes to representing an open air scene.[5] Pigments can never fully simulate those textural gradients which he has shown to be of such importance to our perception of depth, nor can painting offer us the resources of binocular vision. The field is wide open for experiments to probe and explain the degree to which these apparent handicaps can be overcome in mobilising our response and projection. One of these experiments is easy to perform. We need only look at our seascape through a tube, thus cutting out the frame and any surrounding features. The result can be dramatic, so much so that I know of a medical student who, having discovered this effect for himself, wanted tubes to be on sale or loan at picture galleries to facilitate the enjoyment of paintings. Artists and critics are unlikely to adopt this device, but psychologists should not ignore its heuristic value. Obviously the tube masks the contradictory percepts of the frame and the wall and obviates in this respect the need for the all-round panorama. Even more important, it cuts out binocular disparity which normally enables us to perceive the orientation and location of the canvas, and this alone eliminates more contradictory percepts. It becomes genuinely difficult in this situation to estimate our distance from the painting. True, it may not always be easy to estimate our distance from a blank wall either, when we look at it through a tube, but the point is precisely that where our perception is unsettled, as it is in this case, illusion more easily takes over. We fill the void of our uncertainty with the information we are fed by the pictures, and since it coheres in our field of vision we begin to enter into the game.

Here, moreover, is the moment to recall the fact mentioned at the outset, that the production of a perfect facsimile of a flat object is not, by itself, beyond the resources of art. There are passages in many naturalistic paintings which come close to such a facsimile, be

Fig. 24a *The Tiber above Rome by Claude Lorrain shows his mastery of the use of gradients.*

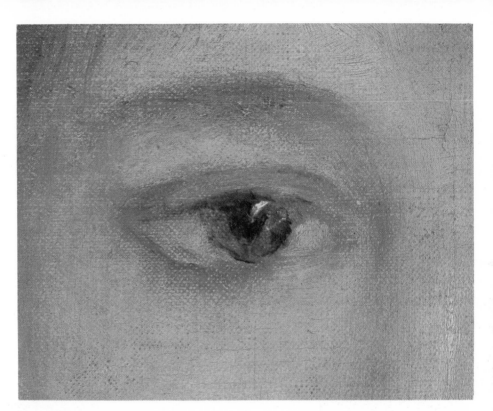

Plate 12 *The right eye of Renoir's La Loge.*

Plate 13 *The left eye of Gaddi's Madonna of Humility.*

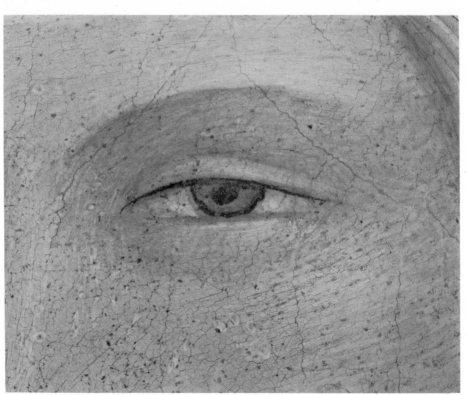

233

Plate 14, above *Van der Velde, Shore at Scheveningen.*

Plate 15, left *A detail of La Madone et la Chanoine Georges Van der Paele, by Jan van Eyck.*

Fig. 25 *Two Men of War at Anchor with Three Small Boats, by Willem Van der Velde the Younger*

it of a curtain, a book cover or a leaf. Isolating such passages will naturally enhance their *trompe l'oeil* effect, but it will also make us more ready to give credit to the surround – the same effect that is served by the real foreground features of the panorama. The smaller the visual field the more likely will this effect obtain, though here again we would need controlled experiments to examine the variables that come into play.

One thing might be predicted. In low-fidelity media the tube experiment would reveal more complex relationships. Looking at a painting as meticulously detailed as a Van Eyck even the smallest area of a painted damask, or even of a lawn, would mobilise our projection. Looking at a line drawing we would obviously have to see enough to be able to make sense of the configuration before the effects of illusion could take over. It is precisely in this way that we

Plate 15

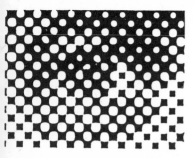

Fig. 26 *Has the medium – dots of varying size – to be suppressed if we are to see the message? Hold the book at a distance and the image becomes an eye. What happens when you return to the close-up?*

figs. 19, 20

could therefore study the devices evolved by art to suggest convincing readings without any recourse to facsimile. We would find that it is in the exploitation of our response to gradients that the graphic arts have found such a compelling trick. The invention of hatching enables the draughtsman or engraver to indicate form and depth by variations of density. If we narrow our tube, the moment will surely come when we see the medium rather than the message. There will be senseless lines rather than a representation. What happens when we then return to the unimpeded view? To what extent can we retain our awareness of the means and see the representation at the same time? Perhaps the word 'seeing' is too imprecise here to settle this much-discussed question.[29] What can be investigated is the tendency so to ignore contradictory clues that the percept in fromt of us is transformed. I contend (to repeat) that there is a difference between the appearance of a piece of paper showing the map of a city and one showing a view of a city. In the first case there is 'ground', in the other 'background'. The degree of this transformation must depend on many variables – cultural conditioning, emotional involvement and therefore the nature of the subject matter. Some of these variables I discussed in the section dealing with the rendering of eyes. It is probably less easy to see an eye in a drawing as a mere scrawl on the surface of the paper than it is to see a fold in a sleeve in this way. But as soon as the representation clicks and we obey its instruction the object that we recognise will also be felt to be potentially mobile. It will tend to be surrounded by a fluctuating halo of imaginary space. Unless my introspection deceives me, the extent of this halo on a plain background will roughly coincide with the area of focussed vision. We can fix it more firmly by drawing a frame round the object. Provided we take in the framing line and the image at one glance the drawing surface is likely to recede from our awareness.

It is for this reason that I am not quite happy with the suggestion made by Gregory[23] that representations should be classified as 'impossible objects' – objects, that is which give us contradictory impressions at the same time. Once more it may be worth reverting to our tube. Viewing a drawing of an 'impossible object', such as the notorious tuning-fork through a narrow opening, we see indeed a coherent configuration which suggests a hypothesis of what might come into view when we move the tube elsewhere.[12] These assumptions will be belied by another view, which will suggest a different reading, inconsistent with the first. But here there is no uncertainty, no way of ironing out these disturbing contradictions

236

except by adopting the correct hypothesis that what we see is not a turning-fork of impossible shape but a very possible drawing on paper.

The situation may be a little more complex in the case of a real object, such as the barber-pole illusion. Looking at the turning pole through our tube, we have no means of knowing that there is not a real ribbon rising and rising. Seeing the whole we must revise our interpretation, but since the correct hypothesis is a little harder to grasp, the illusion of the rising ribbon may persist against our better knowledge.

One may grant that there is something of this experience in the viewing of certain representations when our attention becomes divided. The Victorian literature on decoration is full of warnings against the use of illusionistic three dimensional pictures on fabrics or china, lest the conflict of looking at the jug and at the landscape may be felt to be disturbing. But I do not believe that such a conflict is frequently experienced. Few of us find it troublesome to look at a

fig. 29

G. Perrelle fecit   *P. Mariette ex auec priuil du Roy*

Figs 27, left, and 28 *The meaningless cross hatching, has to be put into context to become a wall in front of a flight of steps at the centre of the etching by Mariette on the right.*

237

Fig. 29 *Vase decorated with a landscape picture. Is there a conflict between landscape and vase?*

Chap. 6, figs 4–7

cereal package with lettering and pictures. There is nothing paradoxical about them, and neither is there, I would suggest, in a painting on the wall.

It is here that we may concede a point to the 'conventionalists' who compare the inspection of paintings with the reading of any other notation. What the two activities have in common is surely the effort after meaning to which I have devoted so much space in this essay. This effort involves the 'mental set' of readiness for anticipation; it implies fitting the percept at least provisionally into an imaginary sequence to which we become keyed to attend.[24,8]

All looking – not only looking at pictures – involves a sequential process that has something in common with reading. True, we can sweep our focus more readily round the room than we can pick up the letters, words and meanings of this page, but both activities are essentially constructive processes that happen over time.[30]

Photographs of eye movements in inspecting paintings confirm that trying to understand a representation involves a test of consistency. As such, it is a sequential process with a logic of its own. The focus of attention shifts from points of high information content to those areas where the postulated interpretation is likely to be confirmed or refuted. The road towards illusionism is the road towards visual consistency, the non-refutation of any assumption the representation evokes. The road away from illusion in twentieth-century art led through the cunning inconsistencies and ambiguities of Cubism which deny us the resolution of a coherent reading – except that of the canvas.[7]

A number of experiments might be devised to test the sequential nature of these activities and its influence on our perceptions. They might make use of ambiguous figures, new and old, but put them into a slightly novel context. Take the example of eyes for a last time. There are humorous drawings which show an eye that is common to two faces. We can make the one a happy and the other a melancholy face. Clearly, in focussing on the alternate faces the double eye changes its character and mood, reinforced by the fact that once it is a left eye with eyebrows raised to the centre, and then a right eye with the eyebrows drooping in the other direction. It is the direction through which we come at these drawings that may determine our reading.

It might be worth while to investigate some of the familiar ambiguous figures and other illusions known to psychologists to see how a given reading can be suggested or enforced. Rubin's vase easily becomes a vase when we add flowers and just as easily two faces

238

Fig. 31 *Indian or Eskimo? The Winson figure.*

Fig. 32 *Rubin's vase.*

when we give them ears outside the frame. Mask either, and the other reading is ensured. Put the 'Indian or Eskimo' figure into appropriate contexts, and you may also eliminate the other reading.

It is from here that I should like to return to our central problem, the double perception of paintings, the one demanding concentration within the frame, the other a different sequence that takes in the wall and the surround. The effect of these sequences could also be tested by making use of those constancy illusions that occur within paintings. Take the shapes of objectively equal size which appear to grow as they are placed farther back in a perspective schema. How far would the phenomenon persist if we repeated the shapes outside the frame and turned it into a motif of the wall-paper? In that case, I suggest, the effect would be influenced by the sequence of fixation

239

E.H. Gombrich

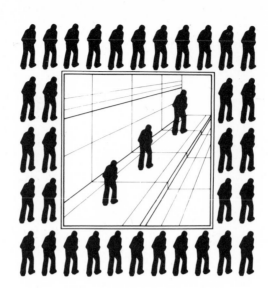

Fig. 33 *When we isolate the perspectival picture (by covering up the rest of the illustration) the three figures within the frame appear to take up a different amount of room on the page. What happens when we see them in conjunction with the identical silhouettes arranged in a pattern?*

points. The illusion should diminish if we read the shapes across the picture and concentrated on the repeat pattern.

Those who ask about our 'beliefs' in front of paintings are certainly asking the wrong question. Illusions are not false beliefs, though false beliefs may be caused by illusions. What may make a painting like a distant view through a window is not the fact that the two can be as indistinguishable as is a facsimile from the original: it is the similarity between the mental activities both can arouse, the search for meaning, the testing for consistency, expressed in the movements of the eye and, more important, in the movements of the mind.

This result does not seem to square too badly with the main findings of Deregowski's chapter about the reactions of naive subjects to representations, though the interpretation of these findings may well be in need of further refinement. For anyone who has never seen a snapshot, an illustration or a painting it cannot be obvious how to deal with this unfamiliar object. But if the picture coheres in the manner described above so as to confirm and refute predictions it should not be hard to transfer the skill of perceiving a scene to the reading of the representation.

This hypothesis seems to me strengthened by the effect of moving pictures. Where there is a sequence imposed upon us within the frame which carries the confirmation and refutations we employ in real-life situations, it becomes indeed almost impossible to read the picture and attend to the alternative system in which the screen is an object like any other in the room. The cinema, of course, enhances

240

the illusion by darkening the room, and television viewers may do the same, but even without this additional aid to illusion it seems to me very hard to remain aware of the projecting surface. Even if the show will not involve us emotionally, it is next to impossible to 'concentrate' on the screen to the extent that we merely see expanding and contracting shapes rather than people and objects approaching and receding. I, for one, have never succeeded in so suppressing my responses and anticipations. Not, to repeat, that this compels me to say that the cinema or television so overwhelms my critical faculty that I become deluded; but my experience is shot through with illusions which remain uncorrected. One of them – as Gregory has reminded me – is actually the same as the despised ventriloquist illusion. I hear the voice of people coming out of their moving mouths and shift direction as they change their place on the screen, but this is merely due to the unrefuted expectation that speech and lip movements are connected.

It would be interesting to investigate further the hypothesis here presented, that the illusion of representations rest on the degree to which they arouse our mental and physical activity, much of which lies outside the reach of introspection. Perhaps we could take our doubting Thomases to one of the simulators used for training drivers and pilots, where the screen shows a moving picture of the road or landscape through which they are supposed to be moving while they have to make such predictions and take such actions as the situation would demand, steering clear of sudden obstacles or correcting the tilt of the plane by pressing levers and reading instruments. Not that even this creation of a highly consistent interlocking system would necessarily blot out their knowledge of where they are and what they are doing, but they would have less and less time to spare for the confirmation of their disbelief.

I should like to make it clear that I do not propose to subject my philosophical critics to this ordeal in order to demonstrate to them that all art aspires to the condition of simulators. It does not. My point is rather that they might be hard put to if they wanted to describe their reactions in what is called 'ordinary language'. Language, I believe, developed as a social tool to communicate ordinary experiences, hypotheses about the world out there and our normal reaction to typical events. It fails notoriously when we want to convey the elusive states of subjective reactions and automatic responses. Art, I have tried to show, plays on these responses, which lie largely outside our awareness. Plato, indeed, wanted to see it banished from the state precisely because it strengthened those responses of the 'lower reaches of the soul' which he wanted to submit to the dominance of reason. To him illusion was tantamount to delusion. He saw art in terms of a drug that enslaved the mind by numbing our critical sense. No wonder the tradition of classical aesthetics has tried to rescue art from this charge by insisting on the 'aesthetic distance' that keeps the mind in control. There is much value in this tradition, but I believe that no verbal formula can do justice to the complex interplay between reflex and reflection, involvement and detachment that we so inadequately sum up in he term 'illusion'.

References

1 Adams, K.R. (1972), 'Perspective and the viewpoint', *Leonardo 5*, 214 f.

2 Auden, W.H. (1970), 'Freedom and necessity in poetry', in Tiselius, A. and Nilsson, S. (eds), *The Place of Value in a World of Fact*, Fourteenth Nobel Symposium, Stockholm.

3 Bruner, J.S. (1972), 'Nature and uses of immaturity', *Amer. Psychol. 8*, 1-22.

4 Gibson, J.J. (1966), *The Senses Considered as Perceptual Systems*, Boston.

5 Gibson, J.J. (1971), 'The information available in pictures', *Leonardo 4*, 27-35 and 195-199.

6 Gombrich, E.H. (1950), *The Story of Art*, London. The reference is to p.24.

7 Gombrich, E.H. (1960), *Art and Illusion: A Study in the Psychology of Pictorial Representation*, London. The quotation is from p.304, and the reference to p.4.

8 Gombrich, E.H. (1961), 'How to read a painting', *Saturday Evening Post*, 234, reprinted as 'Perception and visual deadlock' in *Meditations on a Hobby Horse*, London 1963.

9 Gombrich, E.H. (1964), 'Moment and movement in art', *Journal of the Warburg and Courtauld Institutes* 27, 293-306.

10 Gombrich, E.H. (1965), 'Visual discovery through art', *Arts Magazine*, November, reprinted in Hogg, J. (ed.), *Pyschology and the Visual Arts*, Harmondsworth 1969.

11 Gombrich, E.H. (1967), 'The leaven of criticism in Renaissance art', in Singleton, C.S. (ed.), *Art, Science and History in the Renaissance*, Baltimore.

12 Gombrich, E.H. (1969), 'The evidence of images. I: The variability of vision', in Singleton, C.S. (ed.), *Interpretation: Theory and Practice*, Baltimore. Tinbergen quoted p.48, 'impossible objects' discussed, pp.61 f.

13 Gombrich, E.H. (1972*a*), 'Action and expression in Western art', in Hinde, R.A. (ed.), *Non-Verbal Communication*, Cambridge. The reference is to p.393

14 Gombrich, E.H. (1972*b*), 'The 'What' and the 'How': perspective represent-ation and the phenomenal world', in Rudner, R. and Scheffler, I. (eds), *Logic and Art: Essays in Honor of N. Goodman*, New York.

15 Gombrich, E.H. (1972*c*), 'The mask and the face: the perception of physiognomic likeness in life and in art', in *Art, Perception and Reality*, Baltimore.

16 Gombrich, E.H. (1972*d*), 'The visual image', *Sci. Amer.* September, 82-96

Illusion and art

17 Gombrich, E.H. (1973), 'Huizinga's *Homo Ludens*', *Bijdragen en Mede-delingen betreffende de Geschiedenis der Nederlanden, 66*, 2, 275-296.

18 Gombrich, E.H. (In press), 'The sky is the limit', in Macleod, R.B. and Pick Jr, H.L. (ed.), *Studies in Perception, Essays in Honor of J.J. Gibson*, New York.

19 Gombrich, R. (1966), 'The consecration of a Buddhist image', *Journal of Asian Studies 26*, 1, 23-36.

20 Gombrich, R. (1971), *Precept and Practice: Traditional Buddhism in the Rural Highlands of Ceylon*, Oxford.

21 Goodman, N. (1968), *Languages of Art: An Approach to a Theory of Symbols*, New York.

22 Gregory, R.L. (1966), *Eye and Brain: The Psychology of Seeing*, London and New York.

23 Gregory, R.L. (1970), *The Intelligent Eye*, London and New York.

24 Hochberg, J. (1972), 'The representation of things and people', in *Art, Perception and Reality*, Baltimore.

25 Holt, R.R. (1972), 'On the nature and generality of mental images', in Sheenan, P.W. (ed.), *The Function and Nature of Imagery*, New York and Boston. The reference is to pp. 3-34.

26 Huizinga, J. (1949), *Homo Ludens*, London.

27 Kaden, S.E., Wapner, S. and Werner, H. (1955) 'Studies in physiognomic perception. II: The effect of directional dynamics of pictured objects and of words on the position of the apparent horizon', *J. Psychol. 39*, 61-70.

28 Koenig, O. (1970) *Kultur und Verhaltensforschung*, Munich.

29 Kris, E. and Kurz, O. (1934), *Die Legende vom Künstler, Ein geschichtlicher Versuch*, Vienna.

30 Neisser, U. (1967), *Cognitive Psychology*, New York.

31 Polanyi, M. (1970), 'What is a painting?', *The American Scholar 39*, 4, 655-669.

32 Popper, K.R. (1962), *Conjectures and Refutations: The Growth of Scientific Knowledge*, London.

33 Popper, K.R. (1972), *Objective Knowledge: An Evolutionary Approach*, Oxford. The references are to p. 6.

34 Simmel, M.L. (1972), 'Mime and reason: notes on the creation of the perceptual object', *Journal of Aesthetics and Art Criticism 31*, 2, 193-200.

35 Thorpe, W.H. (1972), 'The comparison of vocal communication in animals and man', in Hinde, R.A. (ed.), *Non-Verbal Communication*, Cambridge.

36 Thouless, R.H. (1972), 'Perceptual constancy or perceptual compromise', *Aust. J. of Psychol. 24*, 2, 133-140.

37 Tinbergen, N. (1953), *Social Behaviour in Animals*, London. The reference is to p. 95.

38 Ward, R.R. (1972), *The Living Clocks*, London.

39 Wickhoff, F. (1895), *Die Wiener Genesis*, Vienna (Eng. tr. as *Roman Art* by E. Strong, London 1900).

40 Wollheim, R. (1959), *F.H. Bradley*, Harmondsworth. The reference is to p.33.

41 Wollheim, R. (1963), 'Art and illusion', *British Journal of Aesthetics 3*, 1.

42 Wollheim, R. (1964), *On Drawing an Object*, Inaugural Lecture delivered at University College London.

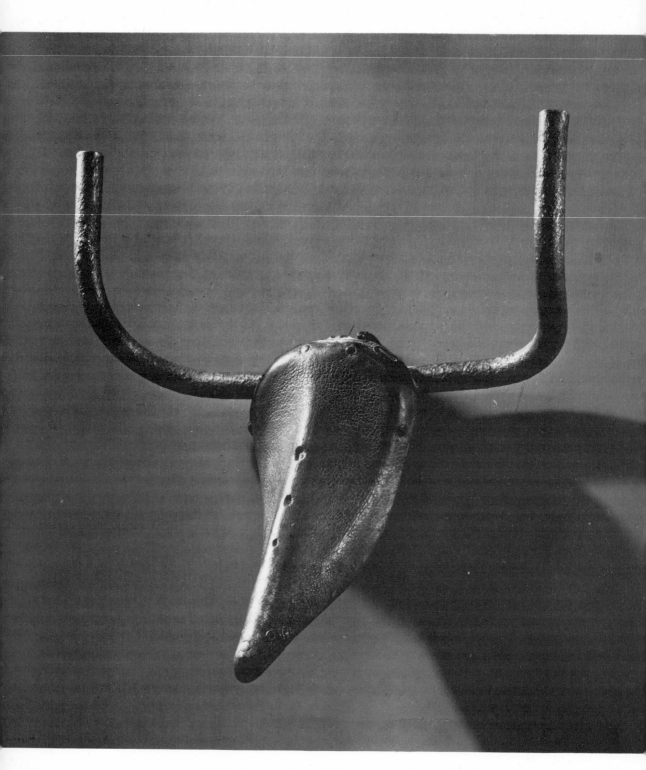

244

6   In Praise of Illusion

Roland Penrose

We have chosen in this book to probe into the nature of illusion and examine its effects to the best of our ability, rather than dismiss it in oriental fashion with the whole of existence as 'Maya', the condition responsible for our presence in this disquieting yet intriguing vale of tears. But as we begin an enquiry into this elusive quality, it is disconcerting to find an initial gap, difficult to measure, between the attitudes towards it of science and the arts. In his statement of the problem from the scientist's point of view, Professor Gregory begins by saying that we 'regard illusions as errors', (see pp. 49-51), whereas a painter such as Delacroix declares in his journal that 'those things which are most real are the illusions I create in my painting'.

From a more detached angle, Erasmus speaks of illusion in his brilliant satire *Praise of Folly*, the title of which I am responsible for plagiarising. I must therefore add hastily that I pretend to rival neither his erudition nor his wit and that I praise illusion without cynicism and with genuine admiration for its qualities. Coming in on the side of the arts, Erasmus claims that 'to destroy illusion is to ruin the whole play', adding: 'What else is the whole of life but a sort of play?' The familiar exclamation of dismay, 'You have destroyed my illusion!', also encourages us to suppose that we not only cherish at least occasionally this equivocal state of mind but may hope to gain some important enlightenment from being its victim.

It seems indisputable that the mood which deliberately seeks the aid and enjoyments of illusion is one that is propitious to a kind of fertility of thought, closely linked to the emotions, and that it belongs to those 'lower reaches of the soul' of which Plato was suspicious. The implications are discussed by Professor Gombrich with admirable clarity. Thanks to the trend of contemporary thought we have today become more willing to consider these lower reaches, the unconscious levels of the psyche, as harbouring imagination, intuition and the complex world of dreams. This concept has influenced deeply not only those scientists who consider that the

Fig. 1 *Picasso, Bull's Head, 1943*

245

involuntary processes of the psyche should be examined, but also those artists of this century who have come to believe that, to quote Gregory, 'perhaps all creative thought, in both science and art, may have its sources in the sources of illusion'. In these sources of sources, deep in the womb of the mind, science and art, it would seem, are bound to meet, if only as twins, separated but with similar and inalienable birthrights. Should this fail to happen a deadly schism is inevitable.

It is not only from experiments, calculations and carefully sifted data that the importance of this inquiry becomes apparent. We have only to watch the growth in the intelligence of a child to see how it develops in sensibility and understanding when nourished judiciously by illusions and make-believe. The fairy tale, the doll, the mask, the game are all used universally to foster its growth. My praise of illusion is given not only because of its ability to create amusements, but also because it can sustain a power which is of inestimable value in our search for knowledge, our lasting enjoyment of life and our search for the fragile key to reality.

Illusion and fashion

It is true that every civilization and every culture discloses its character in its art, and it follows that every style adopts forms of illusion appropriate to its attitude to reality. The various types of illusion that we find throughout the history of art become fashionable or lose their appeal because of social and religious changes that happen continuously. The priority given to the imitation of nature in Greek art, and the criterion of beauty based on the idealization of the human form that it demanded, yielded to the hieratic symbolism of the Byzantine style and the mysticism of Gothic art, in which illusion became closely associated with magic and allegory. Since the Renaissance there have been many variations of this kind, but in general the return to Hellenistic imitation of nature was dominant until near the end of the nineteenth century. It was then that the Impressionists brought representation to its climax in their painstaking attempt to reproduce faithfully their perception of light and colour in the world they could see by limiting observation to a given time and a given place. By coincidence this happened soon after the invention of photography. Both these events were to be important factors in the revolution that began around the turn of the century.

At that time a group of young artists had started to react against the predominant importance given to the imitation of nature. They

Fig. 2 *Picasso, Sculptor and Model, 1933*

also attacked the academic search for beauty – that quality which had come to be thought of as a simile for truth, an absolute. They turned their attention instead to the search for a quality equally elusive – reality. There have been few artists at any time who would wish to claim that their work has no relation to reality. I have already quoted Delacroix, and his belief has been echoed more recently by Picasso who has declared that 'like all Spaniards, I am a realist'.[9] In consequence we enter here into an impulsive marriage of two qualities which are usually deemed to be opposite: reality and illusion. The artist is deliberately using illusion to approach reality, without being able to state in words what exactly is his aim, a circumstance which need not invalidate his achievements. I shall now try to describe some of the ways in which contemporary artists, in developing new styles, have devised new methods and adapted old ways of using illusions as their ally in their pursuit of reality.

Representation and conceptual art

Technology and the accelerated tempo of twentieth-century life have brought abrupt changes in style and in the type of illusion used by painters. The reaction, I have claimed, came as a result of dissatisfaction with what has been called as a generalization 'illusionist' art, meaning all art that had as its aim the imitation of visual experience and, as far as painting was concerned, the representation

247

on a two-dimensional surface of a three-dimensional world. Such types of illusion lost their appeal in face of a desire to produce a new form of art which could have a greater impact and which would contain those irrational elements essential to the arts, surprise and wonder.

There were many divergent tendencies among the innovators. With the abandonment of illusionist painting there were those who wished to work towards an abstract art in which all images of the visible world were to be eliminated and an aesthetic based on geometry was to take their place. Before 1914 the neoplastic school, founded by Mondrian and his friends, developed a style of great purity from which the games of imitation and make-believe had been rigorously excluded. But the same urge for new forms of expression led others in a different direction.

Many artists, discontented with former ideals, shared the conviction that the pursuit of beauty which was directed towards an absolute perfection, either in the form of ideal human proportions or as an abstraction, was a serious error. The idea had already been expressed by William Blake when he wrote 'Exuberance is Beauty'. This was echoed a hundred years later by André Breton when he asserted that 'beauty will be convulsive or will cease to be',[2] and was later reaffirmed by Henry Moore, who considers beauty as a by-product of his work, subservient to the power of its emotional appeal.[6]

'Primitive' art and cognitive participation

In the first decade of this century a group of artists discovered the hitherto despised appeal of African tribal art. Vlaminck, Derain and Matisse showed their interest by collecting masks and fetishes, but its influence on their work was less direct than it came to be in the subversive inventions of Picasso. That enigmatic picture *Les Demoiselles d'Avignon*, painted in the winter of 1906-7, has been called the first cubist painting, and it was in the two figures on the right of the composition that a different approach to our perception of the human form and consequently of objects in general appeared. The new style brought with it a new form of illusion. Picasso for the first time showed his discontent with conventional representations limited to what the eye sees at a given time from a fixed point of view of a given object. He decided to paint not only what he *saw* but also what he *knew*. He presents us here with the female form dismembered and re-assembled in a manner that allows us to see back and front at the same time, a device that was to become a keystone

Plate 16

248

Fig. 3 *Matisse, Head, 1935*

of cubism. It implied not only an acquired knowledge of the object but also the movement of the observer around that object.

It is interesting here to compare the introductory remarks on perception put forward by Blakemore in his chapter in this book and the description of the processes of perception put forward by Gregory. Gregory points out that 'shapes are not signalled or represented as wholes; but rather specific features – orientation of line segments, corners and so on – are selected and signalled as elements, somehow to be put together as received patterns'. It is, I venture to suggest, this capacity of the brain to put together data which made it possible for the cubists to invent a new language in painting in which we are required to infer from signs and angles between planes a reconstruction of the object in its totality.

We discover in this process a new factor in our appreciation of painting, a factor which becomes important if we wish to enjoy contemporary art in general. It involves the cognitive participation of the spectator and goes beyond that first ·essential, 'the willing suspension of disbelief', demanding a more active response. One of the simplest examples can be found in line drawings, which have become outstandingly effective and significant in an illusory sense in the hands of Matisse and Picasso. Here there is no trace of shading to indicate the fullness of face, body or limb or even the far distance, but without undue effort we are convinced of the presence of flesh or distant mountains, although given no more than a tenuous outline by the artist. It would seem, to continue to use Gregory's terms, that the artist with great economy of means is providing us with appropriate and adequate hypotheses. In addition he provides us with the enjoyment of completing the illusion ourselves. It is an example of that phenomenon which occurs continually in art, illusion generating truth.

figs 2,3

Fig. 4 *Braque, Violin and Jug, 1910*

Cubism and collage

To return to cubism, I have said already that it was the intention of Picasso to probe reality, a path which at one stage led him and Braque in their enthusiasm into what has been called their hermetic period. The organization of the whole canvas, from which bright colours had already been banished, became simplified and integrated. The model from which the composition originated was analysed, dissected and reconstructed with facets geometric in shape and graded in tone from light to dark, with the result that they appeared to lie at an angle to each other within a shallow depth. Each of these

249

facets was closely related to its neighbour and united in crystalline monochrome. The homogeneous surface was never allowed to appear broken by sudden disjointed areas of seemingly greater depth. Even so, ambiguities arose from the uncertainty as to whether a simple cubic shape appeared to protrude from the picture plane or retreated behind it – whether it was convex or concave. This gave the painting a flicker, as the spectator changed from acceptance of one solution to the other.

In analysing objects and reconstructing their form in this rigorous way, the artists realized that they were beginning to indulge in an aesthetic exercise which was approaching abstraction rather than reality, even though their compositions always had their origin in definite objects. It was at this moment that cubism took a new turn. In order to reinstate a link with reality, Braque on one occasion *fig. 4* painted at the top of his canvas a realistic nail throwing its shadow across a cubist composition which is otherwise difficult to resolve. Picasso took a different line. He introduced letters which, though *fig. 5* fragmentary, gave sufficient indication of words such as JOURNAL, and both Picasso and Braque began to reinstate elements of reality by sticking on to their canvases fragments of paper representing grained wood, corrugated cardboard or real objects such as visiting cards or pieces of cigarette packets. The process of *collage* introduced a new interplay between the hermetic semi-abstract cubist painting and real objects, and also between the simulated and the real.

There is a still life by Picasso in which illusion at various levels becomes intriguing. The central feature, a goblet, treated in cubist style, is depicted as though seen from more than one point of view,

Fig. 5 *Picasso, Still Life with Chair Caning, 1911*

250

Plate 16 *Picasso, Les Demoiselles d'Avignon, 1907*

Plate 17 *Matisse, L'Escargot 1953*

Plate 18 *Ben Nicholson, Painting, 1937*

Plate 19, above *Miro, Painting, 1927*
Plate 20, right *Miro, Head of a Woman, 1938*

254

but both it and the pipe stem which sticks out above the letter O in the first three letters of the word JOURNAL cast shadows across the seat of a caned chair on which they are placed. The question that arises is: Which of these elements do we consider closest to reality – the glass and pipe presented in cubist style, the word JOURNAL, or the chair caning which appears to be real but in reality turns out to be a facsimile printed on a piece of oil cloth, stuck to the canvas and partially painted over? Describing these ambiguities Alfred Barr writes:

> Here then, in one picture, Picasso juggles reality and abstraction in two media and at four different levels or ratios. If we stop to think which is the most 'real' we find ourselves moving from aesthetic to metaphysical speculation. For here what seems to us most false and what seems most remote from everyday reality is perhaps the most real since it is *least an imitation*. Yet however disparate these two media and several kinds or degrees of realism may appear they are held together, if not entirely harmonized, by various means, physical, optical, psychological. First, in space: laterally they are compressed within the oval; in depth they are virtually in the same plane. The optical or apparent depth is slight; some of the forms seeming to spring in front of the canvas or picture plane, others to recede a little behind it. Apparent space is thus precisely controlled and compressed though traditional laws of pictorial perspective are ignored. The oil cloth with its sharp-focused, facsimile detail and its surface apparently so rough yet actually so smooth, is partly absorbed into both the painted surface and the painted forms by letting both overlap it. Similarly the eye-fooling pipe stem disappears into an abstract cubist passage; and the word JOURNAL which starts out so securely as painted letters on painted paper begins to slip off into space by the time it reaches the U, is partly eclipsed by the pipe stem, and dies obscurely in the shadow of the cubist goblet.[1]

In this intricate game of illusions and counter-illusions we are encouraged to make our choice as to which we accept. We can relish the deliberate visual puns or enjoy the artist's skill in presenting a complicated inter-change between illusion and reality.

Texture, real and simulated

The advent of collage brought with it a violation of the surface of the

Roland Penrose

Fig. 6 *Braque, Musical Forms, Guitar and Clarinet, 1918*

picture, which had been scrupulously respected since the Renaissance. Braque and Picasso introduced shapes into their paintings to which they gave a semblance of real material by simulating the surface of grained wood with paint or by sticking to the canvas pieces of paper that imitated wood. This process was accentuated later by using areas of sand, grit and corrugated and crumpled paper to change radically the monotony of a smooth surface. The eye could then compare the actual roughness of sand, etc., with areas of simulated texture elsewhere. It established a rich variety of surfaces in the composition and added a new contrast between the real and the make-believe.

Surrealism and the impact of psychology

The elements which the cubists introduced into art required a new approach. On the one hand, the illusions employed by them were more intellectual, with a tendency towards the sophisticated joke, but on the other they had established closer affinities to conceptual tribal art and symbolism than to the illusionism of their predecessors, and it was these influences that directly affected the Surrealist movement that followed. André Breton, its founder, had studied psychiatry in his youth and had become deeply influenced by Freud. The importance of the subconscious mind and of dreams was to be

256

of major importance to his theories. He also insisted on the necessity of taking into account the irrational as found in its purest forms in the art of primitive civilizations, children and the insane. Although Gombrich approaches this region of thought with caution, he too agrees, as he says, that his own interpretations 'would not clash with such theories as Freud's account of the dream. During sleep the search that goes on in the "lower reaches of the soul" is not restrained by critical reason and almost any internal or external stimuli can trigger anticipating phantoms'. It would, however, we come to realize, be a mistake to equate the dream with illusion, as is so often done. If the unconscious is to be considered as a region of the mind permanently and mysteriously linked to consciousness, it must, as Jung also has stated, be considered an integral part of the psyche and therefore as belonging to reality rather than illusion. This is where any distinction between illusion and reality must of necessity be blurred.

With little respect for academic categories, the Surrealists plunged eagerly into the realms of the unconscious, believing it was there that the main sources of inspiration were to be found. In an endeavour to achieve results which were more spontaneous and instinctive, they widened the gap between themselves and the illusionists. Although the former type of illusions based on the imitation of natural objects and scenes lost their interest, other basic elements such as make-believe, play and humour, which were recognized as being part of our primordial inheritance, in no way dwindled in importance. Thus new types of illusion came to be introduced and its scope was extended.

Evocation of space in cubism

In evoking depth on a two-dimensional surface, the cubists at first denied themselves those well-tried techniques of linear perspective (see Blakemore, p.40) and atmospheric effects. Their compositions were deliberately shallow in depth, constructed with the same limitations as sculpture when it is compressed into a bas relief. The result was that the painting had the appearance of a compact object existing in its own right. In this respect, although the image was obscured by the analytical process of dissection and systematic reconstruction, a cubist painting became a concept related to the African mask and even to the 'conceptual' image of mediaeval art (see Gombrich, p.228). When in its synthetic period cubism retraced its steps back to a more easily recognized relationship with the objective world, by the introduction of collage and colour, both

Roland Penrose

Fig. 7 *Picasso, Mandolin and Guitar, 1924*

Fig. 8 *Chirico, Melancholy of Departure, 1916-17*

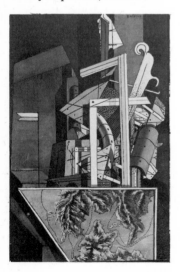

Picasso and Braque re-introduced into their paintings a greater sense of depth and other representational elements. In the *Still-life*, 1924, of Picasso, however, the sky seen through the window is conceptual rather than illusionist. We recognize, from the combination of white patches on a blue ground, that there are clouds, our perception being helped both by knowledge and conventional signs and our pleasure increased by our ability to read the artist's meaning without further explanation. The devices which unite the forms in this still-life and situate them in a three-dimensional plan are too complex for us to examine in detail, but one important point is the apparent continuity of each element. The front edge of the table, for instance, although hidden by the cloth, extends across the picture, and there is an interplay of opacity and transparency, of lighted surfaces and shadow which, without literal representation, completes for us the whole scene of a bottle, fruit and musical instruments placed on a table in front of a window in a thoroughly convincing way. Although the objects are distorted, they are identifiable, and they interlock with their shadows and intervening spaces in such a way that they appear to be solid objects united by clear spatial relationships.

Other methods of evoking space

Painters such as Giorgio de Chirico invented independently other methods of producing a third-dimensional effect. Discarding a systematic use of converging lines, he made arrangements of geometric shapes which act as pointers and lead the eye into the

258

Fig. 9 Klee, Scene with Running Woman, 1925

fig. 10

Plate 17

Fig. 10 Tanguy, Mama, Papa is Wounded! 1927

depths of the picture, whereas Ives Tanguy, in his nebulous dreamlike compositions, found that an object could appear to be floating in air if it were given a small precise shadow detached from it on the ground, thus establishing a simple but convincing distance between the two. Other painters made use of colour. Among them was Matisse, who knew that areas of bright uniform colour placed close to each other do not appear to lie in the same plane. In the great semi-abstract collage, *L'Escargot*, it is impossible to see the whole composition as a flat two-dimensional surface. In places he has employed the simple device of one shape overlapping another, but the main cause of the illusion of depth is the well-known effect of bright colours on a flat surface situating themselves at different distances from the eye, which is used here with great skill. Joan Miró is a master of a similar technique. In his 'dream paintings' of the twenties he achieved a sensation of immeasurable depth, by preparing a background of uneven monochrome which covered the whole canvas and placing small precise forms of brilliant contrasting colour which seem relatively close to the observer. In a more rigidly abstract way, Ben Nicholson obtains an effect of depth by using colour in static geometric compositions.

Transparency and space

As we have seen in the methods used by the cubists, the simulation of transparency is bound to create a sense of depth. Certain artists such as Paul Klee at times introduce linear geometric shapes which

259

Fig. 11 *Bacon, Stu*
for Crouching Nud
1952

Fig. 12 right *Picass*
Construction in Wir
1928-29

Fig. 13 far right *Picass*
Model for monument
sculpture for Civ
Centre, Chicago, 1965

fig. 11

constitute forms that appear to have substance or retreat in transparent perspective. Francis Bacon has used a similar device in paintings where a central figure is framed by the suggestion of a transparent cubic shape, which adds an element of depth around it. These are examples of the inventiveness of contemporary painters in devising new methods of establishing the illusion of a third dimension on a flat surface.

Illusions of space in sculpture

fig. 12

For a sculptor already working in three dimensions, instead of on a flat surface as in painting, the sense of space has a different significance. An inevitable contrast exists in sculpture between solid form and empty space, and the interaction between them can be made significant. In the late twenties both Calder and Picasso began to make transparent sculptures resembling line drawings in space. Calder was more representational in his space drawings of dancers and acrobats made of wire, but Picasso, in a small figure of 1928, produced a work with light iron rods which is more ambiguous. He created, in the void enclosed by the rods, the appearance of a human form surrounded by an invisible skin. Much depends, if we are to appreciate the illusion, on the small round head placed on top which

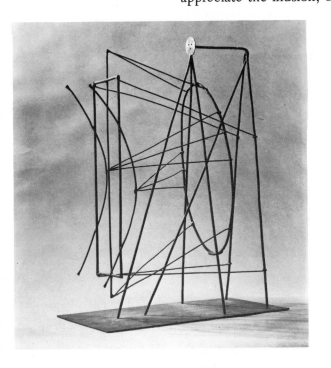

Roland Penrose

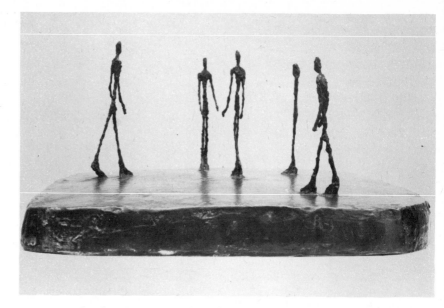

Fig. 14 *Giacometti, City Square, 1948*

Fig. 15 *Giacometti, The Invisible Object, 1934*

gives us a lead. The same idea of giving significance to empty space was further developed by him recently in a monumental sculpture for Chicago. The sculpture represents the head of a woman, constructed with large metal sheets and rods. In it we find an empty space, cut out from the sheets, which form her hair. This has the shape of a head – a head within a head which gains significance from the contrast between solid form and empty space.

Other sculptors use the void in different ways. Giacometti has found more than one way of giving space a mysterious significance. In *City Square* there are figures placed at intervals on a flat plinth. They appear to be walking in various directions; their scale and the spaces between them combined with the suggestion of movement give a convincing illusion of people passing each other in a city square. There is also an earlier work, *The Invisible Object*, where he has produced an uncanny effect of an invisible presence held between the open hands of a large female figure. This space seems by implication to be inevitably more alive than the rest of the space by which the bronze statue is surrounded.

Henry Moore has also deliberately used the antithesis created by areas of solid stone or bronze and the void that is left between them, enclosed by them or even surrounding them. He is able to animate emptiness with the illusion of life in a convincing way. His large reclining figures are often divided into two or three detached parts. The gaps between the solid masses are so conceived that we join them together and see them as a whole. He persuades us that instead

262

of seeing disjointed, meaningless hunks of bronze we are contemplating an arrangement of organic forms, in which the empty spaces supplement and unite the solid shapes, evoking the presence of a reclining female form. And there are many other examples of sculptures in which he has cut holes, hollowed out forms or used the tension of strings covering a hollow area to allow empty space to form an essential partnership with the solid – a marriage of opposites, positive and negative, which carries with it poetic significance.

Tension

The creation of tension between objects or nodal points in both painting and sculpture is common to many works of art in all times. The exchange of glances between faces in which the eyes watch each other is an obvious method of establishing a relationship in space which is both real and mysterious (see Gombrich). Contemporary artists have used this psychological situation in more abstract ways,

Fig. 16 *Henry Moore, Three-piece reclining figure No. 1, 1961-62*

Roland Penrose

Fig 17 *Rowntree, Venetian Arrangement, Study, 1960*

realizing that it forms the basis of what is known as composition in a work of art.

These lines of tension, invisible as they are, hold the composition together and create an area of accentuated animation between them. Although they may exist mainly in the interpretation of images — the direction of a glance, the pointing finger or the movement of figures such as those in *City Square* of Giacometti — there are innumerable examples where abstract forms are so placed that, if one is covered, the tension is broken and the composition robbed of its interest. An example of this is found in Kenneth Rowntree's painting *Venetian Arrangement*. Here the geometric shapes are related to each other in a subtle composition of frozen movement. The slightest shift of position of any shape would break the tension which governs the whole painting. It is founded on a sense of balance which excludes and replaces any reference to symmetry.

fig. 14

fig. 17

Scale

Artists have always been involved in creating illusions to accentuate the importance of some chosen feature at the expense of others around it. These can be achieved by the usual tricks of linear perspective, or by a change of size giving the effect of the giant

264

among dwarfs. If we take two objects similar in shape but one bigger than the other and place them at the same distance, we can make two suppositions. Either one is bigger than the other, or they are the same size and one is further away. This establishes an ambiguity which an artist is able to exploit in various abstract ways, but his main purpose will often be to give the appearance of dominant importance to some chosen feature by contrast or by isolation such as occurs in an isolated figure towering above the horizon with no point of comparison.

fig. 22

Among contemporary artists physical distortions such as those used in Picasso's *Le Train Bleu* played an important role in illusions of scale which give monumental proportions to the human form. Sculptors have used the technique of placing small forms beside tall elongated masses to enhance the contrast between them. There is a drawing by Henry Moore of a crowd of spectators gazing up at a veiled figure which appears to be enormous when compared with the well-known scale of the men standing beside it. Giacometti in his drawings uses a progressive reduction in the proportions of a statuesque figure to give it the sensation of towering height. The enormous feet grow into greatly elongated legs, a shorter body and a head minute in comparison, which therefore seems at a great distance from the spectator. The device of giving a pin-head to a massive sculpture has often been used with the same purpose in view, but when the change from big to small is too rapid our willingness to enter into the illusion can break down. It is here that the skill of the artist lies: in making this change of scale sufficiently subtle for it to be acceptable.

Fig. 18 *Giacometti, Figure, 1950*

Movement observed

Throughout history the problem of the representation of movement in art, inevitably allied to the representation of space, has received special attention. From the time of the paintings in the caves of Lascaux to our own it has found a variety of solutions. Although there are those painters and sculptors who have decided recently to dispense with illusions of movement by making their kinetic works in themselves mobile, even so there are many others who still value the paradox that movement presents to the artist in a medium which is fundamentally static. Art has the unique quality of being able to halt the march of time while still giving us the illusion of movement. It is to this phenomenon that I wish to draw attention, with the following examples.

Fig. 19 *Boccioni, The City Rises, 1910*

Fig. 20 *Duchamp, Nude Descending a Staircase, 1916*

In the early part of the century, prompted by the rivalry of the moving picture, Marcel Duchamp painted *Nude Descending a Staircase* with the express intention of introducing the illusion of movement in a way suggested to him by photography. He repeated the figure of a girl moving downwards as though it were a sequence of exposures. Similar ideas were taken up by the Futurists. Balla painted a dog running beside its mistress, images of every part of it – legs, head, body and tail – being superimposed in successive positions. The success of this simple method is in some ways convincing, but it depends to a large degree on previous knowledge of the technique of the cinema. In the hands of others than Duchamp it began to be no more than a sophisticated joke. On other occasions, however, the idea of using successive images was treated less literally, particularly in the paintings and sculpture of Boccioni. Boccioni's angular forms, repeated like arrows evoking the illusion of movement in a given direction, were coupled with the use of 'dynamic' rhythms.

With the intention of creating a compulsive image of movement, Picasso used another device, closer in some ways to traditional

In praise of illusion

methods and yet provoking hostile criticism at the time. It was based on the time-honoured association between movement and muscular effort, seen clearly in Greek sculptures, such as the *Discobolus*, in which we feel ourselves involved in the bodily exertion of the statue. Picasso accentuated this by the aid of distortions of body and limbs. Let us take as an example a neo-classical sketch made for the drop curtain of a ballet, *Le Train Bleu*, in 1922. We find that the forward thrust of the two figures becomes irresistible because of a combination of calculated distortions acting in concert. The lead is given by a greatly enlarged arm stretched forward and pointing in the direction that the girls are running. This is backed up in every detail by flowing hair and garments, elongated clouds and the empty horizon between beach and sky across which they run. But the most telling feature is the haptic tension between the pointing hand and the much smaller foot almost left behind in the haste of the leading figure. We are presented, in fact, with a powerful make-believe, strengthened by a multiplicity of devices both plastic and psychological, such as the appearance of reluctance in the companion to be carried along at such a pace, which acts as a foil. The illusion becomes so compulsive that it is as though we ourselves were participating in their orgiastic movement.

Fig. 21 *Balla, Dog on a Leash, 1912*

Fig. 22 *Picasso, The Race (Le Train Bleu), 1922*

Roland Penrose   *Movement of the observer*

There is, however, a fundamental difference between the illusion of movement in *Le Train Bleu* and the cubist conception of movement which, as I have said, is the movement of the observer around the object so as to gain knowledge of it from all points of view, resulting in the data being put together in a static composition. It is not the movement itself which appears in the picture, but rather a reference to the consequences of our continuous movement in relation to the world around us.

Picasso found, however, a means of combining the movement of both the observed and the observer in portraits such as that of his daughter Maïa. By representing the face in profile with both eyes visible he succeeded in combining subjective and objective movement in a mysteriously lifelike portrait. The term 'lifelike' is here particularly appropriate since this dual statement implies movement in both observer and observed. In order to see that which is normally hidden – the eye on the far side of the face – either the girl must turn her head or we must move round her. Picasso implies in a single image that both movements occur simultaneously, as indeed can happen in reality. This brings an illusion of animation into the girl's face and creates a contrast with the inanimate stare of the doll.

I should mention here that it seems probable that this invention, which appears highly original, may have stemmed from Picasso's interest in the drawings of children. In an essay on children's drawings,[3] Freeman quotes Goodenough and Harris as saying that 'a child draws what he feels, rather than what he sees or knows to be true', and gives an instance of a girl of four who was given an outline drawing of a pig with a head, an eye and a mouth – as though seen in profile – and thereupon added two additional eyes. This example of what Luquet[3] calls 'intellectual realism' appears to be widespread. In fact it is rare for children of this age not to place two eyes in every head they draw; the angle from which we conceive it to be seen is unimportant to them. The acute interest shown by Picasso in the peculiarities of children's drawings is borne out by Herbert Read's account of their meeting in an exhibition of child art, and Picasso's saying: 'When I was their age I could draw like Raphael, but it took me a lifetime to learn to draw like them.'[7] There are many other features he adopted and used with mature ability that appear to come from the same source. The rapid change of model that a child will make while drawing, from, say, dog to wolf or cat has many parallels in Picasso's methods. To quote Freeman on this:

Fig. 23 *Picasso, Portrait of Maïa, 1938*

268

The child may even change his apparent point of view in the same drawing if examplarity seems to demand it . . . . 'Aerial views' are a common method of portraying scenes. Relationships of visual overlap may be ignored (producing apparent violations of opacity, i.e. the so called 'transparencies' which are such a marked feature of children's drawings). All these devices testify to the child's inventiveness in the service of intellectual realism.[7]

I do not mean to suggest by this that Picasso and other artists such as Jean Dubuffet, Klee and Miró are plagiarizing children's drawings. It springs rather from their own spontaneity and a desire to regain the original perception of a child and restore it to a place of recognition in art. There is a striking parallel in the last quotation from Freeman to the attitude of Braque and Picasso in their creation of cubism – a parallel which characterizes the most significant changes that have taken place in our perception of reality under the influence of the art of this century.

Movement and space

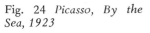

fig. 14

I have already mentioned the illusion of space which Giacometti achieved in *City Square*, but there are numerous examples in the work of Picasso, as in *By the Sea*, where the cause of an illusion of depth must be attributed to distortions of the body. In this painting the extreme elongation of the figure stretching her arm towards the

Fig. 24 *Picasso, By the Sea, 1923*

Fig. 25 *Klee, 17 IRR, 1923*

horizon gives a clear indication of space which recurs in many other works by Picasso and other painters such as Salvador Dali, and can often be found in distortions obtained with the camera. Paul Klee in his more schematic works was often content to rely on the compulsive direction given more economically by a sign — the arrow.

Evocation of emotion: violence

The traditional methods of portraying violence are well known. Scenes of bloodshed, catastrophes and martyrdom have had their greatest impact when a dramatic incident, such as we see in Goya's *Third of May*, is treated with a realism that stirs our emotions by images that seem to transport us literally to the scene of action. But artists of our time have preferred to use less direct forms of realism. There are those who rely on powerful distortions. This can be combined with another means that for its impact uses symbols which have their source in the unconscious and which gain strength from archetypal concepts.

Expressionists such as Grosz and Beckmann arrived at an intense effect of brutality by cariacature and distortion of the human form, and we also find in Picasso, Miró, Ernst and Bacon distortions often used to convey violence. During the decade of war, 1936-1946, Miró produced very powerful images of savage violence, of which *Head of a Woman*, 1938, is perhaps the most extreme. To obtain this effect he has used contrasts of colour, an entirely illogical scale of proportions and arbitrary distortions of the human form. There is nothing of illusionism in his methods; yet we are presented with an image of terror and aggression, a nightmare, childish and grotesque, at which we might wish to laugh were not its primitive strength so overwhelming.

Another painting of the same period, Picasso's *Guernica*, conveys a more universal sense of violence owing to the symbolic elements that he has called to his aid. Much has already been written commenting on this great work from many angles and it is unnecessary for me to enlarge on it here. The content of works of art such as this surpasses the role played by illusion, although illusion is present at different levels in every detail. A fact I wish to emphasize, however, is that the painting conveys the horror of the bombing of the capital of the Basques on market day, not by an illusionist description of the event but by an iconography created by Picasso and drawn from archetypal legends and myths stored in the unconscious. He was deeply concerned in revealing reality through the fiction of painting and

Plate 20

270

Plate 21 *Vasarely, Vonal, 1966*

Plate 22 *Magritte, The Domain of Arnheim, 1949*

chose to bring this about by using simple images with direct appeal. As Herbert Read pointed out:

> His symbols are banal, like the symbols of Homer, Dante, Cervantes. For it is only when the widest commonplace is inspired with the intensest passion that a great work of art, transcending all schools and categories, is born.[5]

It is precisely this desire to use the commonplace which distinguishes the painting of Picasso and many other contemporary artists from those of the past, but it should be noted that Read compares these references to reality to symbols found in literature. Illusion here is being absorbed into the realm of fiction, or rather poetry. This has little in common with illusions regarded as errors. To quote Gregory: 'It is a mistake to equate "fiction" with "false". This being the case, we should not regard fiction in quite the same way that we regard illusion — though the *sources* of fiction, imagination and illusion may be similar or the same.' I would add to fiction that even more potent means of expression — poetry.

Ambiguity and metamorphosis

A more direct use of illusion which belongs also to contemporary art is the use it has made of the enigmatic nature of reality and the uncertainty with which we are able to identify objects. The experience, common to all, of feeling satisfied that a stick lying in our path is insignificant, only to be suddenly disturbed when it moves and is found in reality to be a snake, brings with it a surprise which can make us laugh or cringe. This is symptomatic of the unreliability of perception and the sudden shock, disturbing or pleasurable, that is caused by a change of identity. This reaction has been frequently exploited in the arts. The mask is the oldest, most universal and the most effective means of changing a personality. Contemporary artists have not been slow to add their inventions to this game, and among them it was the Surrealists who gave it special significance. It appealed to them because it could stimulate an assessment of what is real, once the ambiguity and lack of certainty that haunt our judgments were recognized. We are, in fact, obliged by the artist to reconsider fundamentally the hypotheses we have formed previously.

When in the thirties the game of seeing and provoking ambiguity in objects became fashionable, Breton spoke of 'the crisis of the object', a crisis which had begun with visual puns such as we found in

Fig. 26 *Man Ray, Emak Bakia, 1927*

fig 1

Fig. 27 opposite *Picasso, Baboon and Young, 1951*

Picasso's *Still Life with the Chair Caning* and then spread to the identity of objects in general. A very early example of the disconcerting nature of this crisis was Duchamp's now famous contribution to an art exhibition in New York, which was a porcelain urinal signed and entered as a serious work of art. Later Mêret Oppenheim caused alarm by exhibiting a tea cup, saucer and spoon covered with fur, and Max Ernst a stone from the desert in the shape of an eye. Man Ray took the neck of a violin and placed a tress of blonde hair where the strings should be. Dali decorated a dinner-jacket with liqueur glasses full of crême de menthe, with a fly in each. He called it *Aphrodisiac Waistcoat*. These are instances of the wide field which the crisis was covering. The problem of illusion was now producing more than clever *trompe l'oeil* paintings; it was beginning to attack our acceptance of the reality of everything in the objective world. Each invention acted as an insult to preconceived ideas.

The crisis also affected Picasso. During the darkest months of war, he surprised his friends by producing a realistic head of a bull made out of no more than the handle bars and saddle of a bicycle. As he pointed out, the metamorphosis that had taken place was reversible; one day a clever mechanic might find it and say: 'This bull's head will make excellent handle bars and a saddle for my bicycle.' Many more recent sculptures were conceived by him in a similar way. Knowing that illusion and humour are good companions, he continued to create sculptures in which metamorphosis plays a leading role. *Baboon and Young*, 1951, is an excellent example of a sculpture composed of discarded objects and junk which have been brought to life again and given new meaning. The realistic head of the ape, when examined closely, is found to be a toy motor car, but thanks to its dominating position on top of a body which also on examination turns out to be composed of rubbish, it appears as a lifelike portrait of an ape – a circumstance which causes us to marvel at the ambiguity of reality.

During the twenties there were artists, particularly Max Ernst, who developed an interest in that astonishing mimicry which has afforded a means of survival for so many species in nature, and which is dealt with authoritatively in this book by Professor Hinton. This pheno-menon caused the Surrealists to marvel and attracted them by its closeness to the metamorphoses and ambiguities that they were fond of. The hallucinating effect found in mimetism achieved by a natural process became the envy of Ernst, who recognised in it poetic and metaphysical associations as well as a mysterious inventiveness. In his

274

Fig. 28 *Max Ernst, L'Origine de la Pendule, 1926*

Fig. 29 *Dali, The Great Paranoiac, 1936*

Histoire Naturelle of 1926, and in many paintings, he invented birds, beasts, fish, insects and plants that were of indeterminate origin. The same creatures have coverings which are a mixture of leaves, feathers, scales or the grain of wood, but they give the impression that each one belonged to an authentic species. The technique invented by Ernst for these images was also based on illusion. By making rubbings on paper or canvas of textures such as book covers or the grain of wood, he discovered he could give the results new interpretations. The metamorphoses he obtained so successfully owed much to his observations of illusionistic natural phenomena.

A few years later Salvador Dali used his talent and wit to exploit the dual interpretation that can be given to an image. The game had been played before in the seventeenth century by Archimboldo, who enjoyed creating two totally different interpretations of the same composition — a man's head could equally well be a pile of fruit. But

Fig. 30 *Mondrian, Composition with red, yellow and blue, 1921*

Dali was able to invent in his 'paranoiac' paintings dual images of startling effect which established the presence of two contradictory interpretations of a single image, leaving us with the troubling conviction that two conflicting truths can be present in a single statement.

Optical games

I have already mentioned the movement towards an art in which all representation of nature was eliminated, that began early in this century. The abstractionists tackled their problem from various angles. There were those who used geometric shapes with surfaces of uniform colour or, at the other extreme, others like Jackson Pollock who applied paint to a canvas with complete spontaneity so that the gesture and movement of the artist could become imprinted on the canvas. They presented in static abstraction the illusion of physical and emotional activity.

Mondrian, pioneer of geometric abstraction, was intent on freeing art from every vestige of its former purpose, the imitation of nature, and with others he introduced a style which owed all its interest to carefully planned geometric design and flat primary colours. It was the antithesis of illusionist art, but ironically certain simple optical effects, such as lines bending when in reality they are straight, could not be eliminated. Most noticeable is the blurred spot which occurs at the interceptions of the rectangular grid of black lines which Mondrian used to divide up his paintings. This effect, known as the

In praise of illusion

Fig. 32 *Bridget Riley, Fall, 1963*

Hermann grid, is discussed above by Blakemore. Paradoxically it introduced illusion into works which were expressly conceived so as to avoid it in its traditional form.

More recently, however, artists have deliberately used optical effects to create illusions in order to enhance the interest afforded by their work and introduced new subtleties. Vasarely has played ingeniously with geometric shapes using colour and tone to produce three dimensional depth in patterns which are reminiscent of effects enjoyed by the Romans in their mosaics. In exploiting this technique he has added arrangements of form which are ambiguous and reversible in their three-dimensional implications.

Plate 20, fig. 31

Following this lead, Bridget Riley has used her ingenuity to produce an extensive range of works that are well-organised in design and which produce a surprising variety of optical illusions. Using linear patterns, she has been able to produce wave-like effects that appear to have a convincing three-dimensional reality. Similar

Fig. 31 *Vasarely, Gestalt Bleu, 1969*

279

illusions are obtained by her arrangements of black dots of varying sizes, which again create their own perspective. But some of her most mysterious effects come from black lines on white paper, or coloured lines, that work on the optical system in such a way as to create colours which in reality do not exist on the paper. We find in consequence that physiological effects on the eye can be brought into play, to introduce illusions deliberately where they might least be expected, and this undoubtedly gives pleasure.

The work of Escher is also based on the amusement that carefully calculated visual absurdities can produce. Escher, however, employs images to enhance his effects and produces paradoxes of the same *Chap. 2, fig. 20* nature as the 'impossible triangle' figure which is described by Gregory. Other optical illusions were invented by the ingenuity and wit of Duchamp. His *Rotative Demi-sphere* was made to rotate and produce the hypnotic effect of a spiral in motion which becomes overpoweringly three-dimensional. He developed this process by the simple method of setting discs in rotation, which gives the effect of transparent depth. Their virtue depends purely on the enjoyment we receive from our 'willing suspension of disbelief' and our delight in being deceived so convincingly by what we know to be an illusion.

Fig. 33 Duchamp, Rotative Demi-sphere, 1925

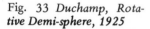

True or false

The ambiguous relationship between illusion and reality, which can be exploited in many ways by the fiction of painting, has been used with disconcerting humour and paradox by Magritte. He speaks of the state of mind he wishes to provoke as the 'moment of lucidity'. Where this occurs he is able to extract from familiar things a disconcerting mystery. His manner of presenting images is without painterly charm. He uses throughout his work a commonplace system of modelling and perspective. But the interest lies in his ability to present images as a dreamlike experience defying logic.

> He evokes extreme or impossible physiological states or events which have an intense effective import — being crowded, being trapped, being immobilized, defying gravity, etc. — with great immediacy but no sensuous correlative, just as in dreams the action is all in one's head. He portrays uncanny happenings with a conspicuous absence of distortion, so that the artist seems to have no attitude towards the phenomenon and the spectator, not distracted by speculation as to what is meant, is left free to concentrate on what is there.[8]

280

Selecting a few example we find that, *The Hunters at the Edge of Night* produces the panic of claustrophobia, *The Listening-room* a suffocation caused by the unwarranted change in scale of the apple, *The Sense of Realities* a denial of the laws of gravity.

Magritte uses illusion with commonplace means to persuade us of a fiction, but he introduces a further degree of illusion which mocks the very idea of the fiction. *The Domain of Arnheim* attacks the veracity of the image. We are presented with a view through a broken window, which has nothing abnormal about it except that the broken pieces of glass lying on the floor carry with them fragments of the mountain itself. The ambiguity becomes intriguing. What are we to consider as the truth of this fiction: the mountain, the transparent window glass, or the fragments which imply that the window was a picture painted on the glass and identical with the view beyond, which after all is no more than a painting?

In another painting he offers us the enigma between the real and the representation of the real in a form which is even more basic. *The Wind and the Song* tells bluntly that the image of the pipe which cannot possibly be mistaken for any other object is a falsehood. 'This is not a pipe', he states. Magritte avoids the subterfuge of the symbol. There is no way out but to admit that the painted image is a truthful statement of reality and that the written statement is false or vice

Plate 22

Fig. 34 *Magritte, The Wind and the Song, 1928-29*

versa. We have in fact in the same image truth and falsehood, and we are given the pleasure of deciding for ourselves which we accept — the truth of illusion or its unreality.

The reality of illusion

In this brief chapter I have hoped to raise a few points of interest in an attempt to analyse the uses and delights that illusion in one form or another offers us through the arts. When we compare the simplest form of illusion, the optical illusion, which brings innocent enjoyment and childish wonder, with the complex emotional involvement of *Guernica*, we realize that we are speaking of many different levels, and that its role in the arts becomes obscured by other considerations in proportion to the complexity of the content of the work of art. This is more noticeable in the twentieth century with the return of symbolic statement and the decline in the importance attached to the imitation of nature.

That illusion must be considered as a basic element in the arts in general seems to be beyond dispute, but it would be wrong to think it is the only aim. If deep emotional understanding is the ultimate measure of their value, we must give illusion its place as a useful element which becomes eclipsed by other qualities as the work of art rises in intensity. It is understandable for us to find delight in the arcadian illusions of Titian's *Bacchus and Ariadne*, just as we enjoy the fantasies of *A Midsummer Night's Dream*. But illusion exists here as a convention rather than a physiological phenomenon, it is a background or a fertile culture which generates an incalculable multitude of ideas, one of its virtues being that since it is in itself irrational, it can encourage that same element which is germane to the arts. It can also be a true reflection rather than reality itself. Illusion can act as a mirror, or it can transform reality into allegory, symbol or metaphor. And should this transformation take place it will become evident that symbol and illusion are no longer identical. A symbol such as the minotaur in the work of Picasso has archetypal significance: it embodies and embraces themes such as the animal in man, his nobility, and the blindness of his bestiality. This clearly takes us beyond the realism of illusion considered as entertainment. Illusion has become more than an illusion of the objective world — it is a revelation, creating a vision of a new world.

I have quoted Gregory as saying that all creative thought has its sources in the sources of illusion, but if we consider the emergence of creative thought in the drawings of children, we find that they are conceptual rather than illusionistic in the earliest stages: We admit that:

A child draws what he feels, rather than what he sees or knows to be true.[3]

Illusion begins to appear with an increase in skill and with imitation of methods used by his elders. It does not, however, begin consciously to play an important role until the age of 7 or 8, when the child begins to copy from others and from nature itself. This suggests that the process of illusion in the arts is sophisticated and intellectual rather than instinctive and may be the product of sensory processes in which perception in its earliest form has initially proved insufficient and conscious sifting of data has had to be employed.

All this seems to point to a difference between the origins of the phenomenon of illusory practices in nature and the presence of illusion in the arts, since there is also a difference in their purpose, the first being for survival and the second for disinterested, though profound, enjoyment. Further research in this area where art and science meet is likely to be our best means of enlightenment.

There is another aspect which I must mention briefly, and this is the link that exists between illusion and play. In his brilliant book on the development of play as a cultural phenomenon, already referred to by Gombrich, Huizinga makes it clear that the use of illusion, whether deliberate or spontaneous, is an integral part of the play element and a major factor in the creation of myth and ritual. He develops the theme that in the process of formation, 'civilization as a whole becomes more and more serious — law and war, commerce, techniques and science lose touch with play; and eventually even ritual, once the field par excellence of its expression, seems to share the process of dissociation. Finally, only poetry remains as the stronghold of living and noble play.'[4]

Huizinga, however, while keeping his faith in poetry as a play element, sees little or no room for play in the plastic arts. Although insofar as ritual is concerned I am bound to agree, there is, in the arts of the twentieth century a strong current of poetry, thanks largely to the Surrealists, who reinstated a fundamental link between poets and painters. I have tried to emphasize the marked increase of the play elements of ambiguity and metamorphosis which are characteristic of the art of our century. If we wish to search for the sources of illusion we must realize that we are entering the same sphere as the sources of play. 'Really to play, a man must play as a child' Huizinga tells us, and he also states that the play element was 'present before human creatures and human speech existed.'[4] It is these factors that have drawn the attention of contemporary artists to the spontaneity and

Roland Penrose

primitive magic contained in the early drawings of children and in tribal art.

The sense in which I have approached the concept of illusion brings it inevitably close to play and perhaps a true analogy exists between the antitheses of play and seriousness and of illusion and reality. But however intent we may be in this pursuit of the sources of illusion, it, like play being a gift of nature, will remain by definition mysterious. On whatever level it is considered – the mere will-o'-the-wisp, the ventriloquist, the ghost in Hamlet, the Sistine Chapel or *Guernica* – whatever we think of the role it plays in our dreams or in practical daily experience, whether it produces laughter or fear, wonder or disgust, we are bound to honour illusion not only for the pleasure it gives but also for the stimulus it provides, the new horizons it can reveal and the answers it can offer us through paradox in our search for reality and truth.

References

1 Barr, A.H. (1946), *Picasso: Fifty years of his Art*, New York.
2 Breton, A. (1928), *Nadja,* Nouvelle Revue Francaise.
3 Freeman, N.H. (1972), 'Process and product of children's drawing', *Perception 1.*
4 Huizinga, J. (1949, 1970), *Homo ludens*, London and New York.
5 Read, H. (1938), 'Picasso: Guernica', *London Bulletin 6.*
6 Read, H. (1944), *Henry Moore*, London.
7 Read, H. (1956), Letter to *The Times,* 26 October.
8 Sylvester, D. (1969), *Magritte*, Arts Council of Great Britain.
9 Conversation with the author, 1968.

Acknowledgments

title page Bridget Riley *Movement in Squares*. Courtesy The Arts Council of Great Britain

8 Leonardo da Vinci. Windsor Inv. No. 12603. Reproduced by Gracious Permission of her Majesty Queen Elizabeth II.

14 René Descartes *Traité de l'Homme* 1686

15 Ramon y Cajal *Histologie du SystèmeNerveux de l'Homme et des Vertébrés* 1911

21 Complex synapse. Reproduced by kind permission of Professor J. Dowling, Harvard University.

22 Real and apparent edges. Photo: Dr John Robson and P. Starling, University of Cambridge.

25 Vasarely *Supernovae* 1959-61. The Tate Gallery London. © by SPADEM, Paris 1973

29 Picasso *Woman in an Armchair* 1918. © by SPADEM, Paris 1973 Cartoon. © Jules Fieffer, 1973 Courtesy THE OBSERVER

30 Spencer Moseley *Little Portuguese Bend* 1966. The Henry Art Gallery, Seattle

41 Manuscript 691, fol. 131v, *Table of Christian Faith*. The Pierpont Morgan Library, New York
Daddi *Annunciation* The Louvre, Paris. Photo: Giraudon, Paris

42 Crivelli *Annunciation*. Reproduced by courtesy of the Trustees, The National Gallery, London

43 Monet *Les Coquelicots*. The Louvre, Paris. Photo: Giraudon, Paris. © by SPADEM, Paris 1973
Jan Brueghel de Velours *Le Paradis Terrestre*, The Louvre, Paris. Photo: Giraudon, Paris

44 Braque *Guitar and Jug* 1927. The Tate Gallery London
Turner *Norham Castle, Sunrise* c. 1840-45. The Tate Gallery London

45 Nolde *Head of a Prophet* 1912. National Gallery of Art, Washington D.C., Rosenwald Collection.

48 René Magritte *Personal Values* 1952. Collection Harry Torczyner, New York. © by ADAGP, Paris 1973

83 Post holes. Muffon, C. 'House plans and pre-history', in *Current Archaeology 21*, p.267

101 Drone fly *Eristalis*. L. Hugh Newman. Photo: Stephen Dalton
Honey bee *Apis*. L. Hugh Newman. Photo: Stephen Dalton

102 *Danaus chrysippus* and *Hypolimnas misippus*. L. Hugh Newman. Photo: Colin Wyatt

127 *Argiope argentata*. Photo: R.H. McConnell. By courtesy of the Royal Society and The Royal Geographical Society

160 Egyptian might-jar. Photo: J.B. Nelson

165 Fig. 3. Courtesy of UNESCO

171 Fig. 5. Courtesy of Dr W. Hudson

173 Courtesy of Dr W. Hudson

187 Courtesy of the University of Aberdeen Anthropological Museum

192 Rembrandt *Portrait of the Painter in Old Age*, detail. Reproduced by courtesy of the Trustees, The National Gallery, London

195 Vienna Genesis, fol 32. National Library Vienna

201 Leonardo da Vinci. Windsor Inv. Nos. 12363, 12521, 12474. Reproduced by Gracious Permission of her Majesty Queen Elizabeth II.

202 Drawing from Louis Corinth, *Das Erlernen der Malerei*.

204 Eye spot on wing of Emperor moth. Heather Angel

205 Buddha statue, central Ceylon. Richard Gombrich.

206 Agnolo Gaddi *Madonna of Humility*. Courtauld Institute Galleries, London, Gambier Parry Collection
Renoir *La Loge* 1874. Courtauld Institute Galleries, London

207 Houdon, bust of Voltaire, 1781. Crown Copyright, Victoria and Albert Museum

209 Ringed Plover. Eric Hosking Still from 'Duck Soup'. MCA London

212 Marcel Marceau. BBC Copyright Photograph

225 Map of Vienna. Austrian National Tourist Office

226-7 Vienna, Votivkirche and environs, Austrian Embassy, London

229 Stuttgart Psalter. Landesbibliothek, Stuttgart. Photo: Warburg Institute, London

230-1 Hobbema *The Avenue, Middelharnis*. Reproduced by courtesy of the Trustees, The National Gallery, London

232 Claude Lorrain *The Tiber above Rome*. Courtesy The Trustees of the British Museum

233 Renoir *La Loge* 1874. detail. Courtauld Institute Galleries, London
Agnolo Gaddi *Madonna of Humility*, detail. Courtauld Institute Galleries, London, Gambier Parry Collection

234 Van der Velde *The Shore at Scheveningen*. Reproduced by courtesy of the Trustees, The National Gallery, London
Van Eyck *The Van der Paele Altarpiece*, detail. Groeningenmuseum, Bruges, Photo: H. Vanhaelewyn

235 Van der Velde the Younger *Two Men of War at Anchor with Three Small Boats*. Courtesy of the Fogg Art Museum, Harvard University. Bequest: Meta and Paul J. Sachs

236-7 Mariette etching. Author's collection.

238 Italian vase and cover, c. 1740. Crown Copyright, Victoria and Albert Museum

240 Winson figure. Elizabeth Winson Alphabet and Image

244 Picasso *Bull's Head* 1943. © by SPADEM, Paris 1973. Photo: John Webb

247 Picasso *Sculptor and Model*, Vollard Suite 1933. © by SPADEM, Paris 1973. Photo: Eileen Tweedy

249 Matisse *Head* 1935. Cahiers

d'Art 1936. © by SPADEM. Paris 1973. Photo: E. Tweedy
Braque *Violin and Jug* 1910. Kunstmueum Basle. © by ADAGP. Paris 1973

250 Picasso *Still Life with Chair Caning* 1911. © by SPADEM, Paris, 1973. Courtesy The Arts Council of Great Britain

251 Picasso *Demoiselles d'Avignon* 1907. Collection The Museum of Modern Art, New York. © by SPADEM, Paris 1973

252 Matisse *L'Escargot* 1953. The Tate Gallery London. © by SPADEM, Paris 1973. Photo: John Webb

253 Nicholson *Painting* 1937. The Tate Gallery London

254 Miró *Painting* 1927. The Tate Gallery London. © by ADAGP, Paris 1973
Miró *Head of a Woman* 1938. Courtesy Mr and Mrs Donald Winston

256 Braque *Musical Forms, Guitar and Clarinet* 1918. Philadelphia Museum of Art, The Louise and Walter Arensberg Collection. © by ADAGP, Paris 1973

258 Picasso *Mandolin and Guitar* 1924. The Solomon R. Guggenheim Museum. © by SPADEM, Paris 1973
Chirico *Melancholy of Departure* 1916-17. Author's collection. Photo: John Webb

259 Klee *Scene with Running Woman* 1925. © by SPADEM, Paris 1973. Photo: Eileen Tweedy
Tanguy *Mama, Pap is Wounded* 1927. Collection The Museum of Modern Art, New York.

260 Bacon *Study for a Crouching Nude* 1952. The Detroit Insti-

tute of Arts, gift of Dr William R. Valentiner

261 Picasso *Construction in Wire* 1928-29. © by SPADEM, Paris 1973. Courtesy The Arts Council of Great Britain. Photo: John Webb.
Picasso, Maquette for the Civic Centre, Chicago 1965. Courtesy The Art Institute of Chicago

262 Giacometti *City Square* 1948. Collection The Museum of Modern Art, New York. © by ADAGP, Paris 1973
Giacometti *The Invisible Object* 1934. Courtesy Galerie Beyeler, Basle. © by ADAGP, Paris 1973

263 Moore *Three-piece Reclining Figure No. 1* 1961-62. Courtesy Henry Moore

264 Rowntree *Venetian Arrangement, Study* 1960. Courtesy Kenneth Rowntree

265 Giacometti *Figure* 1950. Author's collection. Photo: Eileen Tweedy

266 Boccioni *The City Rises* 1910. Collection The Museum of Modern Art, New York, Mrs Simon Guggenheim Fund
Duchamp *Nude Descending a Staircase* 1916. Philadelphia Museum of Art, Louise and Walter Arensberg Collection.

267 Balla *Dog on a Leash* 1912. Courtesy George F. Goodyear and the Buffalo Fine Arts Academy
Picasso *The Race* 1922. © by SPADEM, Paris 1973

268 Picasso *Portrait of Maia* 1938. © by SPADEM, Paris 1973

269 Picasso *By the Sea* 1923. © by SPADEM, Paris 1973

270 Klee *17 IRR* 1923. Kupferstich-kabinett der Oeffentlichen

Kunstmuseum Basle. © by SPADEM, Paris 1973

271 Vasarely *Vonal* 1966. © by SPADEM, Paris 1973

272 Réné Magritte *The Domain of Arnheim* 1949. Courtesy Mr and Mrs Arthur Young and Mr Christopher Young. © by ADAGP, Paris 1973

274 Man Ray *Emak Bakia* 1927. © by ADAGP, Paris 1973. Photo: Eileen Tweedy

275 Picasso *Baboon and Young* 1951. Collection The Museum of Modern Art, New York, Mrs Simon Guggenheim Fund. Courtesy Norman Granz. © by SPADEM, Paris 1973. Photo: The Arts Council of Great Britain

276 Max Ernst *L'Origine de la Pendule* 1926. © by SPADEM Paris 1973
Dali *The Great Paranoiac.* The Edward James Foundation

277 Mondrian *Composition with red, yellow and blue* 1921. Collection Haags Gemeentemuseum, The Hague

278 Vasarely *Gestalt Bleu* 1969. © by SPADEM, Paris 1973

279 Bridget Riley *Fall* 1963. The Tate Gallery London

280 Duchamp *Rotative Demi-sphere* 1925. Courtesy Trianon Press. © by ADAGP, Paris 1973. Photo: Eileen Tweedy

281 Magritte *The Wind and the Song* 1928-29. Courtesy William N. Copley. © by ADAGP, Paris

All other photographs and diagrams are the property of the authors of the respective chapters, the photographs in Chapter 2 being taken by Philip Clark.

Index